An Explanation of
Catholic Morals

An Explanation of
CATHOLIC MORALS

Fr. John H. Stapleton

STABAT MATER PRESS

PUBLISHED BY STABAT MATER PRESS

STABATMATERPRESS.COM

Cover art and interior typesetting by Stabat Mater Press. All artwork not cited is in the public domain.

ISBN (Paperback): 979-8-9997560-8-4

Contents

PREFACE

The contents of this volume appeared originally in *The Catholic Transcript*, of Hartford, Connecticut, in weekly installments, from February, 1901, to February, 1903. During the course of their publication, it became evident that the form of instruction adopted was appreciated by a large number of readers in varied conditions of life—this appreciation being evinced, among other ways, by a frequent and widespread demand for back-numbers of the publishing journal. The management finding itself unable to meet this demand, suggested the bringing out of the entire series in book-form; and thus, with very few corrections, we offer the "Briefs" to all desirous of a better acquaintance with Catholic Morals.

The Author

PART ONE

MORALITY

CHAPTER 1

BELIEVING AND DOING

M orals pertain to right living, to the things we do, in relation to God and His law, as opposed to right thinking, to what we believe, to dogma. Dogma directs our faith or belief, morals shape our lives. By faith we know God, by moral living we serve Him; and this double homage, of our mind and our works, is the worship we owe our Creator and Master and the necessary condition of our salvation.

Faith alone will save no man. It may be convenient for the easy-going to deny this, and take an opposite view of the matter; but convenience is not always a safe counsellor. It may be that the just man liveth by faith; but he lives not by faith alone. Or, if he does, it is faith of a different sort from what we define here as faith, viz., a firm assent of the mind to truths revealed. We have the testimony of Holy Writ, again and again reiterated, that faith, even were it capable of moving mountains, without good works is of no avail. The Catholic Church is convinced that this doctrine is genuine and reliable enough to make it her own; and sensible enough, too. For faith does not make a man impeccable; he may believe rightly, and live badly. His knowledge of what God expects of him will not prevent him from doing just the contrary; sin is as easy to a believer as to an unbeliever. And he who pretends to have found religion, holiness, the Holy Ghost, or whatever else he may call it, and can therefore no longer prevaricate against the law, is, to common-sense people, nothing but a sanctified humbug or a pious idiot.

Nor are good works alone sufficient. Men of emancipated intelligence and becoming breadth of mind, are often heard to proclaim with a greater flourish of verbosity than of reason and argument, that the golden rule is religion enough for them, without the trappings of creeds and dogmas; they respect themselves and respect their neighbors, at least they say they do, and this, according to them, is the fulfilment of the law. We submit that this sort of worship was in vogue a good many centuries before the God-Man came down upon earth; and if it fills the bill now, as it did in those days, it is difficult to see the utility of Christ's coming, of His giving of a law of belief and of His founding of a Church. It is beyond human comprehension that He should have come for naught, labored for naught and died for naught. And such must be the case, if the observance of the natural law is a sufficient worship of the Creator. What reasons Christ may have had for imposing this or that truth upon our belief, is beside the question; it is enough that He did reveal truths, the acceptance of which glorifies Him in the mind of the believer, in order that the mere keeping of the commandments appear forthwith an insufficient mode of worship.

Besides, morals are based on dogma, or they have no basis at all; knowledge of the manner of serving God can only proceed from knowledge of who and what He is; right living is the fruit of right thinking. Not that all who believe rightly are righteous and walk in the path of salvation: losing themselves, these are lost in spite of the truths they know and profess; nor that they who cling to an erroneous belief and a false creed can perform no deed of true moral worth and are doomed; they may be righteous in spite of the errors they profess, thanks alone to the truths in their creeds that are not wholly corrupted. But the natural order of things demands that our works partake of the nature of our convictions, that truth or error in mind beget truth or error correspondingly in deed and that no amount of self-confidence in a man can make a course right when it is wrong, can make a man's actions good when they are materially bad. This is the principle of the tree and its fruit and it is too old-fashioned to be easily denied. True morals spring from true faith and true dogma; a false creed cannot teach correct morality, unless accidentally, as the result of a sprinkling of truth through the mass of false teaching. The only accredited moral instructor is the true Church. Where there is no dogma, there can logically be no morals, save such as human instinct and reason devise; but this is an absurd morality, since there is no recognition of an authority, of a legislator, to make the moral law binding and to give it a sanction. He who says he is a law unto himself chooses thus to veil his proclaiming freedom from all law. His golden rule is a thing too easily twistable to be of any assured benefit to others than himself; his moral sense, that is, his sense of right and wrong, is very likely where his faith is— nowhere.

It goes without saying that the requirements of good morals are a heavy burden for the natural man, that is, for man left, in the midst of seductions and allurements, to the purely human resources of his own unaided wit and strength; so heavy a burden is this, in fact, that according to Catholic doctrine, it cannot be borne without assistance from on high, the which assistance we call grace. This supernatural aid we believe essential to the shaping of a good moral life; for man, being destined, in preference to all the rest of animal creation, to a supernatural end, is thereby raised from the natural to a supernatural order. The requirements of this order are therefore above and beyond his native powers and can only be met with the help of a force above his own. It is labor lost for us to strive to climb the clouds on a ladder of our own make; the ladder must be let down from above. Human air-ships are a futile invention and cannot be made to steer straight or to soar high in the atmosphere of the supernatural. One-half of those who fail in moral matters are those who trust altogether, or too much, in their own strength, and reckon without the power that said "Without Me you can do nothing."

The other half go to the other extreme. They imagine that the Almighty should not only direct and aid them, but also that He should come down and drag them along in spite of themselves; and they complain when He does not, excuse and justify themselves on the ground that He does not, and blame Him for their failure to walk straight in the narrow path. They expect Him to pull them from the clutches of temptation into which they have deliberately walked. The drunkard expects Him to knock the glass out of his hand: the imprudent, the inquisitive and the vicious would have it so that they might play with fire, yea, even put in their hand, and not be scorched or burnt. 'Tis a miracle they want, a miracle at every turn, a suspension of the laws of nature to save them from the effects of their voluntary perverseness. Too lazy to employ the means at their command, they thrust the whole burden on the Maker. God helps those who help themselves. A supernatural state does not dispense us from the obligation of practising natural virtue. You can build a supernatural life only on the foundations of a natural life. To do away with the latter is to build in the air; the structure will not stay up, it will and must come down at the first blast of temptation.

Catholic morals therefore require faith in revealed truths, of which they are but deductions, logical conclusions; they presuppose, in their observance, the grace of God; and call for a certain strenuosity of life without which nothing meritorious can be effected. We must be convinced of the right God has to trace a line of conduct for us; we must be as earnest in enlisting His assistance as if all depended on Him; and then go to work as if it all depended on ourselves.

CHAPTER 2

THE MORAL AGENT

Morals are for man, not for the brute; they are concerned with his thoughts, desires, words and deeds; they suppose a moral agent.

What is a moral agent?

A moral agent is one who, in the conduct of his life, is capable of good and evil, and who, in consequence of this faculty of choosing between right and wrong is responsible to God for the good and evil he does.

Is it enough, in order to qualify as a moral and responsible agent, to be in a position to respect or to violate the Law?

It is not enough; but it is necessary that the agent know what he is doing; know that it is right or wrong; that he will to do it, as such; and that he be free to do it, or not to do it. Whenever any one of these three elements—knowledge, consent and liberty—is wanting in the commission or omission of any act, the deed is not a moral deed; and the agent, under the circumstances, is not a moral agent.

When God created man, He did not make him simply a being that walks and talks, sleeps and eats, laughs and cries; He endowed him with the faculties of intelligence and free will. More than this, He intended that these faculties should be exercised in all the details of life; that the intelligence should direct, and the free will approve, every step taken, every act performed, every deed left undone. Human energy being thus controlled, all that man does is said to be voluntary and bears the peculiar stamp of morality, the quality of being good or evil in the sight of God and worthy of His praise or blame, according as it squares or not with the Rule of Morality laid down by Him for the shaping of human life. Of all else He takes no cognizance, since all else refers to Him not indifferently from the rest of animal creation, and offers no higher homage than that of instinct and necessity.

When a man in his waking hours does something in which his intelligence has no share, does it without being aware of what he is doing, he is said to be in a state of mental aberration, which is only another name for insanity or folly, whether it be momentary or permanent of its nature. A human being, in such a condition, stands on the same plane with the animal, with this difference, that the one is a freak and the other is not. Morals, good or bad, have no meaning for either.

If the will or consent has no part in what is done, we do nothing, another acts through us; 'tis not ours, but the deed of another. An instrument or tool used in the accomplishment of a purpose possesses the same negative merit or demerit, whether it be a thing without a will or an unwilling human being. If we are not free, have no choice in the matter, must consent, we differ in nothing from all brutish and inanimate nature that follows necessarily, fatally, the bent of its instinctive inclinations and obeys the laws of its being. Under these conditions, there can be no morality or responsibility before God; our deeds are alike blameless and valueless in His sight.

Thus, the simple transgression of the Law does not constitute us in guilt; we must transgress deliberately, wilfully. Full inadvertence, perfect forgetfulness, total blindness is called invincible ignorance; this destroys utterly the moral act and makes us involuntary agents. When knowledge is incomplete, the act is less voluntary; except it be the case of ignorance brought on purposely, a wilful blinding of oneself, in the vain hope of escaping the consequences of one's acts. This betrays a stronger willingness to act, a more deliberately set will.

Concupiscence has a kindred effect on our reason. It is a consequence of our fallen nature by which we are prone to evil rather than to good, find it more to our taste and easier to yield to wrong than to resist it. Call it passion, temperament, character, what you will,—it is an inclination to evil. We cannot always control its action. Everyone has felt more or less the tyranny of concupiscence, and no child of Adam but has it branded in his nature and flesh. Passion may rob us of our reason, and run into folly or insanity; in which event we are unconscious agents, and do nothing voluntary. It may so obscure the reason as to make us less ourselves, and consequently less willing. But there is such a thing as, with studied and refined malice and depravity, to purposely and artificially, as it were, excite concupiscence, in order the more intensely and savagely to act. This is only a proof of greater deliberation, and renders the deed all the more voluntary.

A person is therefore more or less responsible according as what he does, or the good or evil of what he does, is more or less clear to him. Ignorance or the passions may affect his clear vision of right and wrong, and under the stress of this deception, wring a reluctant yielding of the will, a consent only half willingly given. Because there is consent, there is guilt but the guilt is measured by the degree of premeditation. God looks upon things solely in their relation to Him. An abomination before men may be something very different in His sight who searches the heart and reins of man and measures evil by the malice of the evil-doer. The only good or evil He sees in our deeds is the good or evil we ourselves see in them before or while we act.

Violence and fear may oppress the will, and thereby prove destructive to the morality of an act and the responsibility of the agent. Certain it is, that we can be forced to act against our will, to perform that which we abhor, and do not consent to do. Such force may be brought to bear upon us as we cannot withstand. Fear may influence us in a like manner. It may paralyze our faculties and rob us of our senses. Evidently, under these conditions, no voluntary act is possible, since the will does not concur and no consent is given. The subject becomes a mere tool in the hands of another.

Can violence and fear do more than this? Can it not only rob us of the power to will, not only force us to act without consent, but also force the will, force us to consent? Never; and the simple reason is that we cannot do two contradictory things at the same time—consent and not consent, for that is what it means to be forced to consent. Violence and fear may weaken the will so that it finally yield. The fault, if fault there be, may be less inexcusable by reason of the pressure under which it labored. But once we have willed, we have willed, and essentially, there is nothing unwilling about what is willingly done.

The will is an inviolable shrine. Men may circumvent, attack, seduce and weaken it. But it cannot be forced. The power of man and devil cannot go so far. Even God respects it to that point.

In all cases of pressure being brought to bear upon the moral agent for an evil purpose, when resistance is possible, resistance alone can save him from the consequences. He must resist to his utmost, to the end, never yield, if he would not incur the responsibility of a free agent. Non-resistance betokens perfect willingness to act. The greater the resistance, the less voluntary the act in the event of consent being finally given; for resistance implies reluctance, and reluctance is the opposition of a will that battles against an oppressing influence. In moral matters, defeat can never be condoned, no matter how great the struggle, if there is a final yielding of the will; but the circumstance of energetic defense stands to a man's credit and will protect him from much of the blame and disgrace due to defeat.

Thus we see that the first quality of the acts of a moral agent is that he think, desire, say and do with knowledge and free consent. Such acts, and only such, can be called good or bad. What makes them good and bad, is another question.

CHAPTER 3

CONSCIENCE

T he will of God, announced to the world at large, is known as the Law of God; manifested to each individual soul, it is called conscience. These are not two different rules of morality, but one and the same rule. The latter is a form or copy of the former. One is the will of God, the other is its echo in our souls.

We might fancy God, at the beginning of all things, speaking His will concerning right and wrong, in the presence of the myriads of souls that lay in the state of possibility. And when, in the course of time, these souls come into being, with unfailing regularity, at every act, conscience, like a spiritual phonograph, gives back His accents and reechoes: "it is lawful," or "it is not lawful." Or, to use another simile, conscience is the compass by which we steer aright our moral lives towards the haven of our souls' destination in eternity. But just as behind the mariner's compass is the great unseen power, called attraction, under whose influence the needle points to the star; so does the will or Law of God control the action of the conscience, and direct it faithfully towards what is good.

We have seen that, in order to prevaricate it is not sufficient to transgress the Law of God: we must know; conscience makes us know. It is only when we go counter to its dictates that we are constituted evil-doers. And at the bar of God's justice, it is on the testimony of conscience that sentence will be passed. Her voice will be that of a witness present at every deed, good or evil, of our lives.

Conscience should always tell the truth, and tell it with certainty. Practically, this is not always the case. We are sometimes certain that a thing is right when it is really wrong. There are therefore two kinds of conscience: a true and a certain conscience, and they are far from being one and the same thing. A true conscience speaks the truth, that is, tells us what is truly right and truly wrong. It is a genuine echo of the voice of God. A certain conscience, whether it speaks the truth or not, speaks with assurance, without a suspicion of error, and its voice carries conviction. When we act in accordance with the first, we are right; we may know it, doubt it or think it probable, but we are right in fact. When we obey the latter, we know, we are sure that we are right, but it is possible that we be in error. A true conscience, therefore, may be certain or uncertain; a certain conscience may be true or erroneous.

A true conscience is not the rule of morality. It must be certain. It is not necessary that it be true, although this is always to be desired, and in the normal state of things should be the case. But true or false, it must be certain. The reason is obvious. God judges us according as we do good or evil. Our merit or demerit is dependent upon our responsibility. We are responsible only for the good or evil we know we do. Knowledge and certainty come from a certain conscience, and yet not from a true conscience which may be doubtful.

Now, suppose we are in error, and think we are doing something good, whereas it is in reality evil. We perceive no malice in the deed, and, in performing it, there is consequently no malice in us, we do not sin. The act is said to be materially evil, but formally good; and for such evil God cannot hold us responsible. Suppose again that we err, and that the evil we think we do is really good. In this instance, first, the law of morality is violated,—a certain, though erroneous conscience: this is sinful. Secondly, a bad motive vitiates an act even if the deed in itself be good. Consequently, we incur guilt and God's wrath by the commission of such a deed, which is materially good, but formally bad.

One may wonder and say: "how can guilt attach to doing good?" Guilt attaches to formal evil, that is, evil that is shown to us by our conscience and committed by us as such. The wrong comes, not from the object of our doing which is good, but from the intention which is bad. It is true that nothing is good that is not thoroughly good, that a thing is bad only when there is something lacking in its goodness, that evil is a defect of goodness; but formal evil alone can be imputed to us and material cannot. The one is a conscious, the other an unconscious, defect. Here an erroneous conscience is obeyed; there the same conscience is disregarded. And that kind of a conscience is the rule of morality; to go against it is to sin.

There are times when we have no certitude. The

conscience may have nothing to say concerning the honesty of a cause to which we are about to commit ourselves. This state of uncertainty and perplexity is called doubt. To doubt is to suspend judgment; a dubious conscience is one that does not function.

In doubt the question may be: "To do; is it right or wrong? May I perform this act, or must I abstain therefrom?" In this case, we inquire whether it be lawful or unlawful to go on, but we are sure that it is lawful not to act. There is but one course to pursue. We must not commit ourselves and must refrain from acting, until such a time, at least, as, by inquiring and considering, we shall have obtained sufficient evidence to convince us that we may allow ourselves this liberty without incurring guilt. If, on the contrary, while still doubting, we persist in committing the act, we sin, because in all affairs of right and wrong we must follow a certain conscience as the standard of morality.

But the question may be: "To do or not to do; which is right and which is wrong?" Here we know not which way to turn, fearing evil in either alternative. We must do one thing or the other. There are reasons and difficulties on both sides. We are unable to resolve the difficulties, lay the doubt, and form a sure conscience, what must we do?

If all action can be momentarily suspended, and we have the means of consulting, we must abstain from action and consult. If the affair is urgent, and this cannot be done; if we must act on the spot and decide for ourselves, then, we can make that dubious conscience prudently certain by applying this principle to our conduct: "Of two evils, choose the lesser." We therefore judge which action involves the least amount of evil. We may embrace the course thus chosen without a fear of doing wrong. If we have inadvertently chosen the greater evil, it is an error of judgment for which we are in nowise responsible before God. But this means must be employed only where all other and surer means fail. The certainty we thereby acquire is a prudent certainty, and is sufficient to guarantee us against offending.

CHAPTER 4

LAXITY AND SCRUPLES

I n every question of conscience there are two opposing factors: Liberty, which is agreeable to our nature, which allows us to do as we list; and Law which binds us unto the observance of what is unpleasant. Liberty and law are mutually antagonistic. A concession in favor of one is an infringement upon the claims of the other.

Conscience, in its normal state, gives to liberty and to law what to each is legitimately due, no more, no less.

Truth lies between extremes. At the two opposite poles of conscientious rectitude are laxity and scruples, one judging all things lawful, the other all things forbidden. One inordinately favors liberty, the other the law. And neither has sufficient grounds on which to form a sound judgment.

They are counterfeit consciences, the one dishonest, the other unreasonable. They do unlawful business; and because the verdict they render is founded on nothing more solid than imaginations, they are in nowise standards of morality, and should not be considered as such.

The first is sometimes known as a "rubber" conscience, on account of its capacity for stretching itself to meet the exigencies of a like or a dislike.

Laxity may be the effect of a simple illusion. Men often do wrong unawares. They excuse themselves with the plea: "I did not know any better." But we are not here examining the acts that can be traced back to self-illusion; rather the state of persons who labor under the disability of seeing wrong anywhere, and who walk through the commandments of God and the Church with apparent unconcern. What must we think of such people in face of the fact that they not only could, but should know better! They are supposed to know their catechism. Are there not Catholic books and publications of various sorts? What about the Sunday instructions and sermons? These are the means and opportunities, and they facilitate the fulfilment of what is in us a bounden duty to nourish our souls before they die of spiritual hunger.

A delicate, effeminate life, spiritual sloth, and criminal neglect are responsible for this kind of laxity.

This state of soul is also the inevitable consequence of long years passed in sin and neglect of prayer. Habit blunts the keen edge of perception. Evil is disquieting to a novice; but it does not look so bad after you have done it a while and get used to it. Crimes thus become ordinary sins, and ordinary sins peccadillos.

Then again there are people who, like the Pharisees of old, strain out a gnat and swallow a camel. They educate themselves up to a strict observance of all things insignificant. They would not forget to say grace before and after meals, but would knife the neighbor's character or soil their minds with all filthiness, without a scruple or a shadow of remorse.

These are they who walk in the broad way that leadeth to destruction. In the first place, their conscience or the thing that does duty for a conscience, is false and they are responsible for it. Then, this sort of a conscience is not habitually certain, and laxity consists precisely in contemning doubts and passing over lurking, lingering suspicions as not worthy of notice. Lastly, it has not the quality of common prudence since the judgment it pronounces is not supported by plausible reasons. Its character is dishonesty.

A scruple is a little sharp stone formerly used as a measure of weight. Pharmacists always have scruples. There is nothing so torturing as to walk with one or several of these pebbles in the shoe. Spiritual scruples serve the same purpose for the conscience. They torture and torment; they make devotion and prayer impossible, and blind the conscience; they weaken the mind, exhaust the bodily forces, and cause a disease that not infrequently comes to a climax in despair or insanity.

A scrupulous conscience is not to be followed as a standard of right and wrong, because it is unreasonable. In its final analysis it is not certain, but doubtful and improbable, and is influenced by the most futile reasons. It is lawful, it is even necessary, to refuse assent to the dictates of such a conscience. To persons thus afflicted the authoritative need of a prudent adviser must serve as a rule until the conscience is cured of its morbid and erratic tendencies.

It is not scruples to walk in the fear of God, and avoid sin and the occasions thereof: that is wisdom; nor to frequent the sacraments and be assiduous in prayer through a deep concern for the welfare of one's soul: that is piety.

It is not scruples to be at a loss to decide whether a thing is wrong or right; that is doubt; nor to suffer keenly after the commission of a grievous sin; that is remorse.

It is not scruples to be greatly anxious and disturbed over past confessions when there is a reasonable cause for it: that is natural.

A scrupulous person is one who, outside these several contingencies, is continually racked with fears, and persists, against all evidence, in seeing sin where there is none, or magnifies it beyond all proportion where it really is.

The first feature—empty and perpetual fears—concerns confessions which are sufficient, according to all the rules of prudence; prayers, which are said with overwrought anxiety, lest a single distraction creep in and mar them; and temptations, which are resisted with inordinate contention of mind, and perplexity lest consent be given.

The other and more desperate feature is pertinacity of judgment. The scrupulous person will ask advice and not believe a word he is told. The more information he gets, the worse he becomes, and he adds to his misery by consulting every adviser in sight. He refuses to be put under obedience and seems to have a morbid affection for his very condition.

There is only one remedy for this evil, and that remedy is absolute and blind obedience to a prudent director. Choose one, consult him as often as you desire, but do not leave him for another. Then submit punctiliously to his direction. His conscience must be yours, for the time being. And if you should err in following him, God will hold him, and not you, responsible.

CHAPTER 5

THE LAW OF GOD AND ITS BREACH

Without going into any superflous details, we shall call the Law of God an act of His will by which He ordains what things we may do or not do, and binds us unto observance under penalty of His divine displeasure.

The law thus defined pertains to reasonable beings alone, and supposes on our part, as we have seen, knowledge and free will. The rest of creation is blindly submissive under the hand of God, and yields a necessary obedience. Man alone can obey or disobey; but in this latter case he renders himself amenable to God's justice who, as his Creator, has an equal right to command him, and be obeyed.

The Maker first exercised this right when He put into His creature's soul a sense of right and wrong, which is nothing more than conscience, or as it is called here, natural law. To this law is subject every human being, pagan, Jew and Christian alike. No creature capable of a human act is exempt.

The provisions of this law consider the nature of our being, that is, the law prescribes what the necessities of our being demand, and it prohibits what is destructive thereof. Our nature requires physically that we eat, drink and sleep. Similarly, in a moral sense, it calls for justice, truthfulness, respect of God, of the neighbor, and of self. All its precepts are summed up in this one: "Do unto others as you would have them do unto you"—the golden rule. Thence flows a series of deducted precepts calculated to protect the moral and inherent rights of our nature.

But we are more concerned here with what is known as the positive Law of God, given by Him to man by word of mouth or revelation.

We believe that God gave a verbal code to Moses who promulgated it in His name before the Jewish people to the whole world. It was subsequently inscribed on two stone tables, and is known as the Decalogue or Ten Commandments of God. Of these ten, the first three pertain to God Himself, the latter seven to the neighbor; so that the whole might be abridged in these two words, "Love God, and love thy neighbor." This law is in reality only a specified form of the natural law, and its enactment was necessitated by the iniquity of men which had in time obscured and partly effaced the letter of the law in their souls.

Latterly God again spoke, but this time in the person of Jesus Christ. The Saviour, after confirming the Decalogue with His authority, gave other laws to men concerning the Church He had founded and the means of applying to themselves the fruits of the Redemption. We give the name of dogma to what He tells us to believe and of morals to what we must do. These precepts of Jesus Christ are contained in the Gospel, and are called the Evangelical Law. It is made known to us by the infallible Church through which God speaks.

Akin to these divine laws is the purely ecclesiastical law or law of the Church. Christ sent forth His Church clothed with His own and His Father's authority. "As the Father sent me, so I send you." She was to endure, perfect herself and fulfil her mission on earth. To enable her to carry out this divine plan she makes laws, laws purely ecclesiastical, but laws that have the same binding force as the divine laws themselves, since they bear the stamp of divine authority. God willed the Church to be; He willed consequently all the necessary means without which she would cease to be. For Catholics, therefore, as far as obligations are concerned, there is no practical difference between God's law and the law of His Church. Jesus Christ is God. The Church is His spouse. To her the Saviour said: "He that heareth you, heareth me, and he that despiseth you despiseth Me."

A breach of the law is a sin. A sin is a deliberate transgression of the Law of God. A sin may be committed in thought, in desire, in word, or in deed, and by omission as well as by commission.

It is well to bear in mind that a thought, as well as a deed, is an act, may be a human and a moral act, and consequently may be a sin. Human laws may be violated only in deed; but God, who is a searcher of hearts, takes note of the workings of the will whence springs all malice. To desire to break His commandments is to offend Him as effectually as to break them in deed; to relish in one's mind forbidden fruits, to meditate and deliberate on evil purposes, is only a degree removed from actual commission of wrong. Evil is perpetrated in the will, either by a longing to prevaricate or by affection for that which is prohibited. If the evil materializes exteriorly, it does not constitute one in sin anew, but only completes the malice already existing. Men judge their fellows by their works; God judges us by our thoughts, by the inner workings of the soul, and takes notice of our exterior doings only in so far as they are related to the will. Therefore it is that an offense against Him, to be an offense, need not necessarily be perpetrated in word or in deed; it is sufficient that the will place itself in Opposition to the Will of God, and adhere to what the Law forbids.

Sin is not the same as vice. One is an act, the other is a state or inclination to act. One is transitory, the other is permanent. One can exist without the other. A drunkard is not always drunk, nor is a man a drunkard for having once or twice overindulged.

In only one case is vice less evil than sin, and that is when the inclination remains an unwilling inclination and does not pass to acts. A man who reforms after a protracted spree still retains an inclination, a desire for strong drink. He is nowise criminal so long as he resists that tendency.

But practically vice is worse than sin, for it supposes frequent wilful acts of sin of which it is the natural consequence, and leads to many grievous offenses.

A vice is without sin when one struggles successfully against it after the habit has been retracted. It may never be radically destroyed. There may be unconscious, involuntary lapses under the constant pressure of a strong inclination, as in the vice of parsing, and it remains innocent as long as it is not wilfully yielded to and indulged. But to yield to the ratification of an evil desire or propensity, without restraint, is to doom oneself to the most prolific of evils and to lie under the curse of God.

PART TWO

SIN

CHAPTER 6

SIN

I f the Almighty had never imposed upon His creatures a Law, there would be no sin; we would be free to do as we please. But the presence of God's Law restrains our liberty, and it is by using, or rather abusing, our freedom, that we come to violate the Law. It is for this reason that Law is said to be opposed to Liberty. Liberty is a word of many meanings. Men swear by it and men juggle with it. It is the slogan in both camps of the world's warfare. It is in itself man's noblest inheritance, and yet there is no name under the sun in which more crimes are committed.

By liberty as opposed to God's law we do not understand the power to do evil as well as good. That liberty is the glory of man, but the exercise of it, in the alternative of evil, is damnable, and debases the creature in the same proportions as the free choice of good ennobles him. That liberty the law leaves untouched. We never lose it; or rather, we may lose it partially when under physical restraint, but totally, only when deprived of our senses. The law respects it. It respects it in the highest degree when in an individual it curtails or destroys it for the protection of society.

Liberty may also be the equal right to do good and evil. There are those who arrogate to themselves such liberty. No man ever possessed it, the law annihilated it forever. And although we have used the word in this sense, the fact is that no man has the right to do evil or ever will have, so long as God is God. These people talk much and loudly about freedom—the magic word!—assert with much pomp and verbosity the rights of man, proclaim his independence, and are given to much like inane vaunting and braggadocio.

We may be free in many things, but where God is concerned and He commands, we are free only to obey. His will is supreme, and when it is asserted, we purely and simply have no choice to do as we list. This privilege is called license, not liberty. We have certain rights as men, but we have duties, too, as creatures, and it ill-becomes us to prate about our rights, or the duties of others towards us, while we ignore the obligations we are under towards others and our first duty which is to God. Our boasted independence consists precisely in this: that we owe to Him not only the origin of our nature, but even the very breath we draw, and which preserves our being, for "in Him we live, move and have our being."

The first prerogative of God towards us is authority or the right to command. Our first obligation as well as our highest honor as creatures is to obey. And until we understand this sort of liberty, we live in a world of enigmas and know not the first letter of the alphabet of creation. We are not free to sin.

Liberty rightly understood, true liberty of the children of God, is the right of choice within the law, the right to embrace what is good and to avoid what is evil. This policy no man can take from us; and far from infringing upon this right, the law aids it to a fuller development. A person reading by candlelight would not complain that his vision was obscured if an arc light were substituted for the candle. A traveler who takes notice of the signposts along his way telling the direction and distance, and pointing out pitfalls and dangers, would not consider his rights contested or his liberty restricted by these things. And the law, as it becomes more clearly known to us, defines exactly the sphere of our action and shows plainly where dangers lurk and evil is to be apprehended. And we gladly avail ourselves of this information that enables us to walk straight and secure. The law becomes a godsend to our liberty, and obedience to it, our salvation.

He who goes beyond the bounds of true moral liberty, breaks the law of God and sins. He thereby refuses to God the obedience which to Him is due. Disobedience involves contempt of authority and of him who commands. Sin is therefore an offense against God, and that offense is proportionate to the dignity of the person offended.

The sinner, by his act of disobedience, not only sets at naught the will of his Maker, but by the same act, in a greater or lesser degree, turns away from his appointed destiny; and in this he is imitated by nothing else in creation. Every other created thing obeys. The heavens follow their designated course. Beasts and birds and fish are intent upon one thing, and that is to work out the divine plan. Man alone sows disorder and confusion therein. He shows irreverence for God's presence and contempt for His friendship; ingratitude for His goodness and supreme indifference for the penalty that follows his sin as surely as the shadow follows its object. So that, taken all in all, such a creature might fitly be said to be one part criminal and two parts fool. Folly and sin are synonymous in Holy Writ. "The fool saith in his heart there is no God."

Sin is essentially an offense. But there is a difference of degree between a slight and an outrage. There are direct offenses against God, such as the refusal to believe in Him or unbelief; to hope in Him, or despair, etc. Indirect offenses attain Him through the neighbor or ourselves.

All duties to neighbor or self are not equally imperious and to fail in them all is not equally evil. Then again, not all sins are committed through pure malice, that is, with complete knowledge and full consent. Ignorance and weakness are factors to be considered in our guilt, and detract from the malice of our sins. Hence two kinds of sin, mortal and venial. These mark the extremes of offense. One severs all relation of friendship, the other chills the existing friendship. By one, we incur God's infinite hatred, by the other, His displeasure. The penalty for one is eternal; the other can be atoned for by suffering.

It is not possible in all cases to tell exactly what is mortal and what venial in our offenses. There is a clean-cut distinction between the two, but the line of demarcation is not always discernible. There are, however, certain characteristics which enable us in the majority of cases to distinguish one from the other.

First, the matter must be grievous in fact or in intention; that is, there must be a serious breach of the law of God or the law of conscience. Then, we must know perfectly well what we are doing and give our full consent. It must therefore be a grave offense in all the plenitude of its malice. Of course, to act without sufficient reason, with a well-founded doubt as to the malice of the act, would be to violate the law of conscience and would constitute a mortal sin. There is no moral sin without the fulfilment of these conditions. All other offenses are venial.

We cannot, of course, read the soul of anybody. If, however, we suppose knowledge and consent, there are certain sins that are always mortal. Such are blasphemy, luxury, heresy, etc. When these sins are deliberate, they are always mortal offenses. Others are usually mortal, such as a sin against justice. To steal is a sin against justice. It is frequently a mortal sin, but it may happen that the amount taken be slight, in which case the offense ceases to be mortal.

Likewise, certain sins are usually venial, but in certain circumstances a venial sin may take on such malice as to be constituted mortal.

Our conscience, under God, is the best judge of our malevolence and consequently of our guilt.

Chapter 7

How to Count Sins

The number of sins a person may commit is well-nigh incalculable, which is only one way of saying that the malice of man has invented innumerable means of offending the Almighty—a compliment to our ingenuity and the refinement of our natural perversity. It is not always pleasant to know, and few people try very hard to learn, of what kind and how many are their daily offenses. This knowledge reveals too nakedly our wickedness which we prefer to ignore. Catholics, however, who believe in the necessity of confession of sins, take a different view of the matter. The requirements of a good confession are such as can be met only by those who know in what things they have sinned and how often.

There are many different kinds of sin. It is possible by a single act to commit more than one sin. And a given sin may be repeated any number of times.

To get the exact number of our misdeeds we must begin by counting as many sins at least as there are kinds of sin. We might say there is an offense for every time a commandment or precept is violated, for sin is a transgression of the law. But this would be insufficient inasmuch as the law may command or forbid more than one thing.

Let the first commandment serve as an example. It is broken by sins against faith, or unbelief, against hope, or despair, against charity, against religion, etc. All these offenses are specifically different, that is, are different kinds of sin; yet but one precept is transgressed. Since therefore each commandment prescribes the practice of certain virtues, the first rule is that there is a sin for every virtue violated.

But this is far from exhausting our capacity for evil. Our virtue may impose different obligations, so that against it alone we may offend in many different ways. Among the virtues prescribed by the first commandment is that of religion, which concerns the exterior homage due to God. I may worship false gods, thus offending against the virtue of religion, and commit a sin of idolatry. If I offer false homage to the true God, I also violate the virtue of religion, but commit a sin specifically different, a sin of superstition. Thus these different offenses are against but one of several virtues enjoined by one commandment. The virtue of charity is also prolific of obligations; the virtue of chastity even more so. One act against the latter may contain a fourfold malice.

It would be out of place here to adduce more examples: a detailed treatment of the virtues and commandments will make things clearer. For the moment it is necessary and sufficient to know that a commandment may prescribe many virtues, a virtue may impose many obligations, and there is a specifically different sin for each obligation violated.

But we can go much farther than this in wrongdoing, and must count one sin every time the act is committed.

"Yes, but how are we to know when there is one act or more than one act! An act may be of long or short duration. How many sins do I commit if the act lasts, say, two hours? And how can I tell where one act ends and the other begins?"

In an action which endures an hour or two hours, there may be one and there may be a dozen acts. When the matter a sinner is working on is a certain, specified evil, the extent to which he prevaricates numerically depends upon the action of the will. A fellow who enters upon the task of slaying his neighbor can kill but once in fact; but he can commit the sin of murder in his soul once or a dozen times. It depends on the will. Sin is a deliberate transgression, that is, first of all an act of the will. If he resolves once to kill and never retracts till the deed of blood is done, he sins but once. If he disavows his resolution and afterwards resolves anew, he repeats the sin of murder in his soul as often as he goes through this process of will action. This sincere retraction of a deed is called moral interruption and it has the mysterious power of multiplying sins.

Not every interruption is a moral one. To put the matter aside for a certain while in the hope of a better opportunity, for the procuring of necessary facilities or for any other reason, with the unshaken purpose of pursuing the course entered upon, is to suspend action; but this action is wholly exterior, and does not affect the will. The act of the will perseveres, never loses its force, so there is no moral, but only a physical, interruption. There is no renewal of consent for it has never been withdrawn. The one moral act goes on, and but one sin is committed.

Thus, of two wretches on the same errand of crime, one may sin but once, while the other is guilty of the same sin a number of times. But the several sins last no longer than the one. Which is the more guilty? That is a question for God to decide; He does the judging, we do the counting.

This possible multiplication of sin where a single act is apparent emphasizes the fact that evil and good proceed from the will. It is by the will primarily and essentially that we serve or offend God, and, absolutely speaking, no exterior deed is necessary for the accomplishment of this end.

The exterior deed of sin always supposes a natural preparation of sin— thought, desires, resolution,—which precede or accompany the deed, and without which there would be no sin. It is sinful only inasmuch as it is related to the will, and is the fruit thereof. The interior act constitutes the sin in its being; the exterior act constitutes it in its completeness.

All of which leads up to the conclusion, of a nature perhaps to surprise some, that to resolve to sin and to commit the sin in deed are not two different sins, but one complete sin, in all the fulness of its malice. True, the exterior act may give rise to scandal, and from it may devolve upon us obligations of justice, the reparation of injury done; true, with the exterior complement the sin may be more grievous. But there cannot be several sins if there be one single uninterrupted act of the will.

An evil thing is proposed to your mind; you enjoy the thought of doing it, knowing it to be wrong; you desire to do it and resolve to do it; you take the natural means of doing it; you succeed and consummate the evil—a long drawn out and well prepared deed, 'tis true, but only one sin. The injustices, the scandal, the sins you might commit incidentally, which do not pertain naturally to the deed, all these are another matter, and are other kinds of sins; but the act itself stands alone, complete and one.

But these interior acts of sin, whether or not they have reference to external completion, must be sinful. The first stage is the suggestion of the imagination or simple seeing of the evil in the mind, which is not sinful; the next is the moving of the sensibility or the purely animal pleasure experienced, in which there is no evil, either; for we have no sure mastery over these faculties. From the imagination and sensibility the temptation passes before the will for consent. If consent is denied, there is no deadly malice or guilt, no matter how long the previous effects may have been endured. No thought is a sin unless it be fully consented to.

Chapter 8

Capital Sins

Y ou can never cure a disease till you get at the seat or root of the evil. It will not do to attack the several manifestations that appear on the surface, the aches and pains and attendant disorders. You must attack the affected organ, cut out the root of the evil growth, and kill the obnoxious germ. There is no other permanent remedy; until this is done, all relief is but temporary.

And if we desire to remove the distemper of sin, similarly it is necessary to seek out the root of all sin. We can lay our finger on it at once; it is inordinate self-love.

Ask yourself why you broke this or that commandment. It is because it forbade you a satisfaction that you coveted, a satisfaction that your self-love imperiously demanded; or it is because it prescribed an act that cost an effort, and you loved yourself too much to make that effort. Examine every failing, little or great, and you will trace them back to the same source. If we thought more of God and less of ourselves we would never sin. The sinner lives for himself first, and for God afterwards.

Strange that such a sacred thing as love, the source of all good, may thus, by abuse, become the fountainhead of all evil! Perhaps, if it were not so sacred and prolific of good, its excess would not be so unholy. But the higher you stand when you tumble, the greater the fall; so the better a thing is in itself, the more abominable is its abuse. Love directed aright, towards God first, is the fulfilment of the Law; love misdirected is the very destruction of all law.

Yet it is not wrong to love oneself; that is the first law of nature. One, and one only being, the Maker, are we bound to love more than ourselves. The neighbor is to be loved as ourselves. And if our just interests conflict with his, if our rights and his are opposed to each other, there is no legitimate means but we may employ to obtain or secure what is rightly ours. The evil of self-love lies in its abuse and excess, in that it goes beyond the limits set by God and nature, that it puts unjustly our interests before God's and the neighbor's, and that to self it sacrifices them and all that pertains to them. Self, the "ego," is the idol before which all must bow.

SELF-LOVE, on an evil day, in the garden of Eden, wedded sin, Satan himself officiating under the disguise of a serpent; and she gave birth to seven daughters like unto herself, who in turn became fruitful mothers of iniquity. Haughty Pride, first-born and queen among her sisters, is inordinate love of one's worth and excellence, talents and beauty; sordid Avarice or Covetousness is excessive love of riches; loathsome Lust is the third, and loves carnal pleasures without regard for the law; fiery Anger, a counterpart of pride, is love rejected but seeking blindly to remedy the loss; bestial Gluttony worships the stomach; green-eyed Envy is hate for wealth and happiness denied; finally Sloth loves bodily ease and comfort to excess. The infamous brood! These parents of all iniquity are called the seven capital sins. They assume the leadership of evil in the world and are the seven arms of Satan.

As it becomes their dignity, these vices never walk alone or go unattended, and that is the desperate feature of their malice. Each has a cortege of passions, a whole train of inferior minions, that accompany or follow. Once entrance gained and a free hand given, there is no telling the result. Once seated and secure, the passion seeks to satisfy itself; that is its business. Certain means are required to this end, and these means can be procured only by sinning. Obstacles often stand in the way and new sins furnish steps to vault over, or implements to batter them down. Intricate and difficult conditions frequently arise as the result of self-indulgence, out of which there is no exit but by fresh sins. Hence the long train of crimes led by one capital sin towards the goal of its satisfaction, and hence the havoc wrought by its untrammeled working in a human soul.

This may seem exaggerated to some; others it may mislead as to the true nature of the capital sins, unless it be dearly put forth in what their malice consists. Capital sins are not, in the first place, in themselves, sins; they are vices, passions, inclinations or tendencies to sin, and we know that a vice is not necessarily sinful. Our first parents bequeathed to us as an inheritance these germs of misery and sin. We are all in a greater or lesser degree prone to excess and to desire unlawful pleasures. Yet, for all that, we do not of necessity sin. We sin when we yield to these tendencies and do what they suggest. The simple proneness to evil, devoid of all wilful yielding is therefore not wrong. Why? Because we cannot help it; that is a good and sufficient reason.

These passions may lie dormant in our nature without soliciting to evil; they may, at any moment, awake to action with or without provocation. The sight of an enemy or the thought of a wrong may stir up anger; pride may be aroused by flattery, applause or even compliments; the demon of lust may make its presence known and felt for a good reason, for a slight reason, or for no reason at all; gluttony shows its head at the sight of food or drink, etc.

He who deliberately and without reason arouses a passion, and thus exposes himself imprudently to an assault of concupiscence, is grievously guilty; for it is to trifle with a powerful and dangerous enemy and it betokens indifference to the soul's salvation.

Suggestions, seductions, allurements follow upon the awakening of these passions. When the array of these forces comes in contact with the will, the struggle is on; it is called temptation. Warfare is the natural state of man on earth. Without it, the world here below would be a paradise, but life would be without merit.

In this unprovoked and righteous battle with sin, the only evil to be apprehended is the danger of yielding. But far from being sinful, the greater the danger, the more meritorious the struggle. It matters not what we experience while fighting the enemy. Imagination and sensation that solicit to yielding, anxiety of mind and discouragement, to all this there is no wrong attached, but merit.

Right or wrong depends on the outcome. Every struggle ends in victory or defeat for one party and in temptation there is sin only in defeat. A single act of the will decides. It matters not how long the struggle lasts; if the will does not capitulate, there is no sin.

This resistance demands plenty of energy, a soul inured to like combats and an ample provision of weapons of defense—faith, hatred of sin, love of God. Prayer is essential. Flight is the safest means, but is not always possible. Humility and self-denial are an excellent, even necessary, preparation for assured victory.

No man need expect to make himself proof against temptation. It is not a sign of weakness; or if so, it is a weakness common to all men. There is weakness only in defeat, and cowardice as well. The gallant and strong are they who fight manfully. Manful resistance means victory, and victory makes one stronger and invincible, while defeat at every repetition places victory farther and farther beyond our reach.

Success requires more than strength, it requires wisdom, the wisdom to single out the particular passion that predominates in us, to study its artifices and by remote preparation to make ourselves secure against its assaults. The leader thus exposed and its power for evil reduced to a minimum, it will be comparatively easy to hold in check all other dependent passions.

CHAPTER 9

PRIDE

Excellence is a quality that raises a man above the common level and distinguishes him among his fellow-beings. The term is relative. The quality may exist in any degree or measure. 'Tis only the few that excel eminently; but anyone may be said to excel who is, ever so little, superior to others, be they few or many. Three kinds of advantages go to make up one's excellence. Nature's gifts are talent, knowledge, health, strength, and beauty; fortune endows us with honor, wealth, authority; and virtue, piety, honesty are the blessings of grace. To the possession of one or several of these advantages excellence is attached.

All good is made to be loved. All gifts directly or indirectly from God are good, and if excellence is the fruit of these gifts, it is lawful, reasonable, human to love it and them. But measure is to be observed in all things. Virtue is righteously equidistant, while vice goes to extremes. It is not, therefore, attachment and affection for this excellence, but inordinate, unreasonable love that is damnable, and constitutes the vice of pride.

God alone is excellent and all greatness is from Him alone. And those who are born great, who acquire greatness, or who have greatness thrust upon them, alike owe their superiority to Him. Nor are these advantages and this preeminence due to our merits and deserts. Everything that comes to us from God is purely gratuitous on His part, and undeserved on ours. Since our very existence is the effect of a free act of His will, why should not, for a greater reason, all that is accidental to that existence be dependent on His free choice? Finally, nothing of all this is ours or ever can become ours. Our qualities are a pure loan confided to our care for a good and useful purpose, and will be reclaimed with interest.

Since the malice of our pride consists in the measure of affection we bestow upon our excellence, if we love it to the extent of adjudging it not a gift of God, but the fruit of our own better selves; or if we look upon it as the result of our worth, that is, due to our merits, we are guilty of nothing short of downright heresy, because we hold two doctrines contrary to faith. "What hast thou, that thou hast not received?" If a gift is due to us, it is no longer a gift. This extreme of pride is happily rare. It is directly opposed to God. It is the sin of Lucifer.

A lesser degree of pride is, while admitting ourselves beholden to God for whatever we possess and confessing His bounties to be undeserved, to consider the latter as becoming ours by right of possession, with liberty to make the most of them for our own personal ends. This is a false and sinful appreciation of God's gifts, but it respects His and all subordinate authority. If it never, in practice, fails in this submission, there is sin, because the plan of God, by which all things must be referred to Him, is thwarted; but its malice is not considered grievous. Pride, however, only too often fails in this, its tendency being to satisfy itself, which it cannot do within the bounds of authority. Therefore it is that from being a venial, this species of pride becomes a mortal offense, because it leads almost infallibly to disobedience and rebellion. There is a pride, improperly so called, which is in accordance with all the rules of order, reason and honor. It is a sense of responsibility and dignity which every man owes to himself, and which is compatible with the most sincere humility. It is a regard, an esteem for oneself, too great to allow one to stoop to anything base or mean. It is submissive to authority, acknowledges shortcomings, respects others and expects to be respected in return. It can preside with dignity, and obey with docility. Far from being a vice, it is a virtue and is only too rare in this world. It is nobility of soul which betrays itself in self-respect.

Here is the origin, progress and development of the vice. We first consider the good that is in us, and there is good in all of us, more or less. This consideration becomes first exaggerated; then one-sided by reason of our overlooking and ignoring imperfections and shortcomings. Out of these reflections arises an apprehension of excellence or superiority greater than we really possess. From the mind this estimate passes to the heart which embraces it fondly, rejoices and exults. The conjoint acceptation of this false appreciation by the mind and heart is the first complete stage of pride—an overwrought esteem of self. The next move is to become self-sufficient, presumptuous. A spirit of enterprise asserts itself, wholly out of keeping with the means at hand. It is sometimes foolish, sometimes insane, reason being blinded by error.

The vice then seeks to satisfy itself, craves for the esteem of others, admiration, flattery, applause, and glory. This is vanity, different from conceit only in this, that the former is based on something that is, or has been done, while the latter is based on nothing.

Vanity manifested in word is called boasting; in deed that is true, vain-glory; in deed without foundation of truth, hypocrisy.

But this is not substantial enough for ambition, another form of pride. It covets exterior marks of appreciation, rank, honor, dignity, authority. It seeks to rise, by hook or crook, for the sole reason of showing off and displaying self. Still growing apace, pride becomes indignant, irritated, angry if this due appreciation is not shown to its excellence; it despises others either for antipathy or inferiority. It believes its own judgment infallible and, if in the wrong, will never acknowledge a mistake or yield. Finally the proud man becomes so full of self that obedience is beneath him, and he no longer respects authority of man or of God. Here we have the sin of pride in all the plenitude of its malice.

Pride is often called an honorable vice, because its aspirations are lofty, because it supposes strength, and tends directly to elevate man, rather than to debase and degrade him, like the other vices. Yet pride is compatible with every meanness. It lodges in the heart of the pauper as well as in that of the prince. There is nothing contemptible that it will not do to satisfy itself; and although its prime malice is to oppose God it has every quality to make it as hideous as Satan himself. It goeth before a fall, but it does not cease to exist after the fall; and no matter how deep down in the mire of iniquity you search, you will find pride nethermost. Other vices excite one's pity; pride makes us shudder.

CHAPTER 10

COVETOUSNESS

"What is a miser?" asked the teacher of her pupils, and the bright boy spoke up and answered: one who has a greed for gold. But he and all the class were embarrassed as to how this greed for gold should be qualified. The boy at the foot of the class came to the rescue, and shouted out: misery.

Less wise answers are made every day in our schools. Misery is indeed the lot, if not the vice, of the miser. 'Tis true that this is one of the few vices that arrive at permanent advantages, the others offering satisfaction that lasts but for a moment, and leaves nothing but bitterness behind. Yet, the more the miser possesses the more insatiable his greed becomes, and the less his enjoyment, by reason of the redoubled efforts he makes to have and to hold.

But the miser is not the only one infected with the sin of avarice. His is not an ordinary, but an extreme case. He is the incarnation of the evil. He believes in, hopes in, and loves gold above all things; he prays and sacrifices to it. Gold is his god, and gold will be his reward, a miserable one.

This degree of the vice is rare; or, at least, is rarely suffered to manifest itself to this extent; and although scarcely a man can be found to confess to this failing, because it is universally regarded as most loathsome and repulsive, still few there are who are not more or less slaves to cupidity. Pride is the sin of the angels; lust is the sin of the brute, and avarice is the sin of man. Scripture calls it the universal evil. We are more prone to inveigh against it, and accuse others of the vice than to admit it in ourselves.

Sometimes, it is "the pot calling the kettle black;" more often it is a clear case of "sour grapes." Disdain for the dollars "that speak," "the mighty dollars," in abundance and in super-abundance, is rarely genuine.

There are, concerning the passion of covetousness, two notions as common as they are false. It is thought that this vice is peculiar to the rich, and is not to be met with among the poor. Now, avarice does not necessarily suppose the possession of wealth, and does not consist in the possession, but in the inordinate desire, or greed for, or the lust of, riches. It may be, and is, difficult for one to possess much wealth without setting one's heart on it. But it is also true that this greed may possess one who has little or nothing. It may be found in unrestrained excess under the rags of the pauper and beggar. They who aspire to, or desire, riches with avidity are covetous whether they have much, little, or nothing. Christ promised His kingdom to the poor in spirit, not to the poor in fact. Spiritual poverty can associate with abundant wealth, just as the most depraved cupidity may exist in poverty.

Another prejudice, favorable to ourselves, is that only misers are covetous, because they love money for itself and deprive themselves of the necessaries of life to pile it up. But it is not necessary that the diagnosis reveal these alarming symptoms to be sure of having a real case of cupidity. They are covetous who strive after wealth with passion. Various motives may arouse this passion, and although they may increase the malice, they do not alter the nature, of the vice. Some covet wealth for the sake of possessing it; others, to procure pleasures or to satisfy different passions. Avarice it continues to be, whatever the motive. Not even prodigality, the lavish spending of riches, is a token of the absence of cupidity. Rapacity may stand behind extravagance to keep the supply inexhausted.

It is covetousness to place one's greatest happiness in the possession of wealth, or to consider its loss or privation the greatest of misfortunes; in other words, to over-rejoice in having and to over-grieve in not having.

It is covetousness to be so disposed as to acquire riches unjustly rather than suffer poverty.

It is covetousness to hold, or give begrudgingly, when charity presses her demands.

There is, in these cases, a degree of malice that is ordinarily mortal, because the law of God and of nature is not respected.

It is the nature of this vice to cause unhappiness which increases until it becomes positive wretchedness in the miser. Anxiety of mind is followed by hardening of the heart; then injustice in desire and in fact; blinding of the conscience, ending in a general stultification of man before the god Mammon.

All desires of riches and comfort are not, therefore, avarice. One may aspire to, and seek wealth without avidity. This ambition is a laudable one, for it does not exaggerate the value of the world's goods, would not resort to injustice, and has not the characteristic tenacity of covetousness. There is order in this desire for plenty. It is the great mover of activity in life; it is good because it is natural, and honorable because of its motives.

CHAPTER 11

LUST

Pride resides principally in the mind, and thence sways over the entire man; avarice proceeds from the heart and affections; lust has its seat in the flesh. By pride man prevaricating imitates the angel of whose nature he partakes; avarice is proper to man as being a composite of angelic and animal natures; lust is characteristic of the brute pure and simple. This trinity of concupiscence is in direct opposition to the Trinity of God—to the Father, whose authority pride would destroy; to the Son, whose voluntary stripping of the divinity and the poverty of whose life avarice scorns and contemns to the Holy Ghost, to whom lust is opposed as the flesh is opposed to the spirit. This is the mighty trio that takes possession of the whole being of man, controls his superior and inferior appetites, and wars on the whole being on God. And lust is the most ignoble of the three.

Strictly speaking, it is not here question of the commandments. They prescribe or forbid acts of sin—thoughts, words or deeds; lust is a passion, a vice or inclination, a concupiscence. It is not an act. It does not become a sin while it remains in this state of pure inclination. It is inbred in our nature as children of Adam. Lust is an appetite like any other appetite, conformable to our human nature, and can be satisfied lawfully within the order established by God and nature. But it is vitiated by the corruption of fallen flesh. This vitiated appetite craves for unlawful and forbidden satisfactions and pleasures, such as are not in keeping with the plans of the Creator. Thus the vitiated appetite becomes inordinate. At one and the same time, it becomes inordinate and sinful, the passion being gratified unduly by a positive act of sin.

This depraved inclination, as everyone knows, may be in us, without being of us, that is, without any guilt being imputed to us. This occurs in the event of a violent assault of passion, in which our will has no part, and which consequently does not materialize, exteriorly or interiorly, in a human act forbidden by the laws of morality. Nor is there a transgression, even when gratified, if reason and faith control the inclination and direct it along the lines laid down by the divine and natural laws. Outside of this, all manners, shapes and forms of lust are grievous sins, for the law admits no levity of matter. No further investigation, at the present time, into the essence of this vice is necessary.

There is an abominable theory familiar to, and held by the dissolute, who, not content with spreading the contagion of their souls, aim at poisoning the very wells of morality. They reason somewhat after this fashion: Human nature is everywhere the same. He knows others who best knows himself. A mere glance at themselves reveals the fact that they are chained fast to earth by their vile appetites, and that to break these chains is a task too heavy for them to undertake. The fact is overlooked that these bonds are of their own creation, and that every end is beyond reach of him who refuses to take the means to that end. Incapable, too, of conceiving a sphere of morality superior to that in which they move, and without further investigation of facts to make their induction good, they conclude that all men are like themselves; that open profession of morality is unadulterated hypocrisy, that a pure man is a living lie. A more wholesale impeachment of human veracity and a more brutal indignity offered to human nature could scarcely be imagined. Reason never argued thus; the heart has reasons which the reason cannot comprehend. Truth to be loved needs only to be seen. Adversely, it is the case with falsehood.

It is habitual with this passion to hide its hideousness under the disguise of love, and thus this most sacred and hallowed name is prostituted to signify that which is most vile and loathsome. Depravity? No. Goodness of heart, generosity of affections, the very quintessence of good nature! But God is love, and love that does not see the image of the Creator in its object is not love, but the brutal instinct.

There are some who do not go so far as to identify vice with virtue, but content themselves with esteeming that, since passion is so strong, virtue so difficult and God so merciful to His frail creatures, to yield a trifle is less a sin than a confession of native weakness. This "weakness" runs a whole gamut of euphemisms; imperfections, foibles, frailties, mistakes, miseries, accidents, indiscretions—anything to gloss it over, anything but what it is. At this rate, you could efface the whole Decalogue and at one fell stroke destroy all laws, human and divine. What is yielding to any passion but weakness? Very few sins are sins of pure malice. If one is weak through one's own fault, and chooses to remain so rather than take the necessary means of acquiring strength, that one is responsible in full for the weakness. The weak and naughty in this matter are plain, ordinary sinners of a very sable dye.

Theirs is not the view that God took of things when He purged the earth with water and destroyed the five cities with fire. From Genesis to the Apocalypse you will not find a weakness against which He inveighs so strongly, and chastises so severely. He forbids and condemns every deliberate yielding, every voluntary step taken over the threshold of moral cleanness in thought, word, desire or action.

The gravity and malice of sin is not to be measured by the fancies, opinions, theories or attitude of men. The first and only rule is the will of God which is sufficiently clear to anyone who scans the sacred pages whereon it is manifested. And the reason of His uncompromising hostility to voluptuousness can be found in the intrinsic malice of the evil. In man, as God created him, the soul is superior to the body, and of its nature should rule and govern. Lust inverts this order, and the flesh lords it over the spirit. The image of God is defiled, dragged in the mire of filth and corruption, and robbed of its spiritual nature, as far as the thing is possible. It becomes corporal, carnal, animal. And thus the superior soul with its sublime faculties of intelligence and will is made to obey under the tyranny of emancipated flesh, and like the brute seeks only for things carnal.

It is impossible to say to what this vice will not lead, or to enumerate the crimes that follow in its wake. The first and most natural consequence is to create a distaste and aversion for prayer, piety, devotion, religion and God; and this is God's most terrible curse on the vice, for it puts beyond reach of the unfortunate sinner the only remedy that could save him.

But if God's justice is so rigorous toward the wanton, His mercy is never so great as toward those who need it most, who desire it and ask it. The most touching episodes in the Gospels are those in which Christ opened wide the arms of His charity to sinful but repentant creatures, and lifted them out of their iniquity. That same charity and power to shrive, uplift and strengthen resides to-day, in all its plenitude, in the Church which is the continuation of Christ. Where there is a will there is a way. The will is the sinner's; the way is in prayer and the sacraments.

CHAPTER 12

ANGER

Never say, when you are angry, that you are mad; it makes you appear much worse than you really are, for only dogs get mad. The rabies in a human being is a most unnatural and ignoble thing. Yet common parlance likens anger to it.

It is safe to say that no one has yet been born that never yielded, more or less, to the sway of this passion. Everybody gets angry. The child sulks, the little girl calls names and makes faces, the boy fights and throws stones; the maiden waxes huffy, spiteful, and won't speak, and the irascible male fumes, rages, and says and does things that become him not in the least. Even pious folks have their tiffs and tilts. All flesh is frail, and anger has an easy time of it; not because this passion is so powerful, but because it is insidious and passes for a harmless little thing in its ordinary disguise. And yet all wrath does not manifest itself thus exteriorly. Still waters are deepest. An imperturbable countenance may mask a very inferno of wrath and hatred.

To hear us talk, there is no fault in all this, the greater part of the time. It is a soothing tonic to our conscience after a fit of rage, to lay all the blame on a defect of character or a naturally bad temper. If fault there is, it is anybody's but our own. We recall the fact that patience is a virtue that has its limits, and mention things that we solemnly aver would try the enduring powers of the beatified on their thrones in heaven. Some, at a loss otherwise to account for it, protest that a particular devil got hold of them and made resistance impossible.

But it was not a devil at all. It was a little volcano, or better, a little powder magazine hidden away somewhere in the heart. The imp Pride had its head out looking for a caress, when it received a rebuff instead. Hastily disappearing within, it spat fire right and left, and the explosion followed, proportionate in energy and destructive power to the quantity of pent-up self-love that served as a charge. Once the mine is fired, in the confusion and disorder that follow, vengeance stalks forth in quest of the miscreant that did the wrong.

Anger is the result of hurt pride, of injured self-love. It is a violent and inordinate commotion of the soul that seeks to wreak vengeance for an injury done. The causes that arouse anger vary infinitely in reasonableness, and there are all degrees of intensity.

The malice of anger consists wholly in the measure of our deliberate yielding to its promptings. Sin, here as elsewhere, supposes an act of the will, A crazy man is not responsible for his deeds; nor is anyone, for more than what he does knowingly.

The first movement or emotion of irascibility is usually exempt of all fault; by this is meant the play of the passion on the sensitive part of our nature, the sharp, sudden fit that is not foreseen and is not within our control, the first effects of the rising wrath, such as the rush of blood, the trouble and disorder of the affections, surexcitation and solicitation to revenge. A person used to repelling these assaults may be taken unawares and carried away to a certain extent in the first storm of passion, in this there is nothing sinful. But the same faultlessness could not be ascribed to him who exercises no restraining power over his failing, and by yielding habitually fosters it and must shoulder the responsibility of every excess. We incur the burden of God's wrath when, through our fault, negligence or a positive act of the will, we suffer this passion to steal away our reason, blind us to the value of our actions, and make us deaf to all considerations. No motive can justify such ignoble weakness that would lower us to the level of the madman. He dishonors his Maker who throws the reins to his animal instincts and allows them to gallop ahead with him, in a mad career of vengeance and destruction.

Many do not go to this extent of fury, but give vent to their spleen in a more cool and calculating manner. Their temper, for being less fiery, is more bitter. They are choleric rather than bellicose. They do not fly to acts but to desires and well-laid plans of revenge. If the desire or deed lead to a violation of justice or charity, to scandal or any notable evil consequence, the sin is clearly mortal; the more so, if this inward brooding be of long duration, as it betrays a more deep-seated malice.

Are there any motives capable of justifying these outbursts of passion? None at all, if our ire has these two features of unreasonableness and vindictiveness. This is evil. No motive, however good, can justify an evil end.

If any cause were plausible, it would be a grave injury, malicious and unjust. But not even this is sufficient, for we are forbidden to return evil for evil. It may cause us grief and pain, but should not incite us to anger, hatred and revenge. What poor excuses would therefore be accidental or slight injuries, just penalties for our wrongdoings and imaginary grievances! The less excusable is our wrath, the more serious is our delinquency. Our guilt is double-dyed when the deed and the cause of the deed are both alike unreasonable.

Yet there is a kind of anger that is righteous. We speak of the wrath of God, and in God there can be no sin. Christ himself was angry at the sight of the vendors in the temple. Holy Writ says: Be ye angry and sin not. But this passion, which is the fruit of zeal, has three features which make it impossible to confound it with the other. It is always kept within the bounds of a wise moderation and under the empire of reason; it knows not the spirit of revenge; and it has behind it the best of motives, namely, zeal for the glory of God. It is aroused at the sight of excesses, injustices, scandals, frauds; it seeks to destroy sin, and to correct the sinner. It is often not only a privilege, but a duty. It supposes, naturally, judgment, prudence, and discretion, and excludes all selfish motives.

Zeal in an inferior and more common degree is called indignation, and is directed against all things unworthy, low and deserving of contempt. It respects persons, but loathes whatever of sin or vice that is in, or comes from, unworthy beings. It is a virtue, and is the effect of a high sense of respectability.

Impatience is not anger, but a feeling somewhat akin to it, provoked by untoward events and inevitable happenings, such as the weather, accidents, etc. It is void of all spirit of revenge. Peevishness is chronic impatience, due to a disordered nervous system and requires the services of a competent physician, being a physical, not moral, distemper.

Anger is a weakness and betrays many other weaknesses; that is why sensible people never allow this passion to sway them. It is the last argument of a lost cause: "You are angry, therefore you are wrong." The great misery of it is that hot-tempered people consider their mouths to be safety-valves, while the truth is that the wagging tongue generates bile faster than the open mouth can give exit to it. St. Liguori presented an irate scold with a bottle, the contents to be taken by the mouthful and held for fifteen minutes, each time her lord and master returned home in his cups. She used it with surprising results and went back for more. The saint told her to go to the well and draw inexhaustibly until cured.

For all others, the remedy is to be found in a meditation of these words of the "Our Father:" "forgive us our trespasses, as we forgive those who trespass against us." The Almighty will take us at our word.

CHAPTER 13

GLUTTONY

S elf-preservation is nature's first law, and the first and essential means of preserving one's existence is the taking of food and drink sufficient to nourish the body, sustain its strength and repair the forces thereof weakened by labor, fatigue or illness. God, as well as nature, obliges us to care for our bodily health, in order that the spirit within may work out on earth the end of its being.

Being purely animal, this necessity is not the noblest and most elevating characteristic of our nature. Nor is it, in its imperious and unrelenting requirements, far removed from a species of tyranny. A kind Providence, however, by lending taste, savor and delectability to our aliments, makes us find pleasure in what otherwise would be repugnant and insufferably monotonous.

An appetite is a good and excellent thing. To eat and drink with relish and satisfaction is a sign of good health, one of the precious boons of nature. And the tendency to satisfy this appetite, far from being sinful, is wholly in keeping with the divine plan, and is necessary for a fulsome benefiting of the nourishment we take.

On the other hand, the digestive organism of the body is such a delicate and finely adjusted piece of mechanism that any excess is liable to clog its workings and put it out of order. It is made for sufficiency alone. Nature never intended man to be a glutton; and she seldom fails to retaliate and avenge excesses by pain, disease and death.

This fact coupled with the grossness of the vice of gluttony makes it happily rare, at least in its most repulsive form; for, be it said, it is here question of the excessive use of ordinary food and drink, and not of intoxicants to which latter form of gluttony we shall pay our respects later.

The rich are more liable than the poor to sin by gluttony; but gluttony is fatal to longevity, and they who enjoy best life, desire to live longest. 'Tis true, physicians claim that a large portion of diseases are due to over-eating and over-drinking; but it must be admitted that this is through ignorance rather than malice. So that this passion can hardly be said to be commonly yielded to, at least to the extent of grievous offending.

Naturally, the degree of excess in eating and drinking is to be measured according to age, temperament, condition of life, etc. The term gluttony is relative. What would be a sin for one person might be permitted as lawful to another. One man might starve on what would constitute a sufficiency for more than one. Then again, not only the quantity, but the quality, time and manner, enter for something in determining just where excess begins. It is difficult therefore, and it is impossible, to lay down a general rule that will fit all cases.

It is evident, however, that he is mortally guilty who is so far buried in the flesh as to make eating and drinking the sole end of life, who makes a god of his stomach. Nor is it necessary to mention certain unmentionable excesses such as were practiced by the degenerate Romans towards the fall of the Empire. It would likewise be a grievous sin of gluttony to put the satisfaction of one's appetite before the law of the Church and violate wantonly the precepts of fasting and abstinence.

And are there no sins of gluttony besides these? Yes, and three rules may be laid down, the application of which to each particular case will reveal the malice of the individual. Overwrought attachment to satisfactions of the palate, betrayed by constant thinking of viands and pleasures of the table, and by avidity in taking nourishment, betokens a dangerous, if not a positively sinful, degree of sensuality. Then, to continue eating or drinking after the appetite is appeased, is in itself an excess, and mortal sin may be committed even without going to the last extreme. Lastly, it is easy to yield inordinately to this passion by attaching undue importance to the quality of our victuals, seeking after delicacies that do not become our rank, and catering to an over-refined palate. The evil of all this consists in that we seem to eat and drink, if we do not in fact eat and drink, to satisfy our sensuality first, and to nourish our bodies afterwards; and this is contrary to the law of nature.

We seemed to insist from the beginning that this is not a very dangerous or common practice. Yet there must be a hidden and especial malice in it. Else why is fasting and abstinence—two correctives of gluttony—so much in honor and so universally recommended and commanded in the Church? Counting three weeks in Advent, seven in Lent and three Ember days four times a year, we have, without mentioning fifty-two Fridays, thirteen weeks or one-fourth of the year by order devoted to a practical warfare on gluttony. No other vice receives the honor of such systematic and uncompromising resistance. The enemy must be worthy.

As a matter of fact, there lies under all this a great moral principle of Christian philosophy. This philosophy sought out and found the cause and seat of all evil to be in the flesh. The forces of sin reside in the flesh while the powers of right-eousness—faith, reason and will— are in the spirit. The real issue of life is between these forces contending for supremacy. The spirit should rule; that is the order of our being. But the flesh revolts, and by ensnaring the will endeavors to dominate over the spirit.

Now it stands to reason that the only way for the supe-rior part to succeed is to weaken the inferior part. Just as prayer and the grace of the sacraments fortify the soul, so do food and drink nourish the animal; and if the latter is cared for to the detriment of the soul, it waxes strong and formidable and becomes a menace.

The only resource for the soul is then to cut off the supply that benefits the flesh, and strengthen herself thereby. She acts like a wise engineer who keeps the explosive and dangerous force of his locomotive within the limit by reducing the quantity of food he throws into its stomach. Thus the passions being weakened become docile, and are easily held under sway by the power that is destined to govern, and sin is thus rendered morally impossible.

It is gluttony that furnishes the passion of the flesh with fuel by feeding the animal too well; and herein lies the great danger and malice of this vice. The evil of a slight excess may not be great in itself; but that evil is great in its consequences. Little over-indulgences imperceptibly, but none the less surely, strengthen the flesh against the spirit, and when the temptation comes the spirit will be overcome. The ruse of the saints was to starve the enemy.

CHAPTER 14

DRINK

Intemperance is the immoderate use of anything, good or bad; here the word is used to imply an excessive use of alcoholic beverages, which excess, when it reaches the dignity of a habit or vice, makes a man a drunkard. A drunkard who indulges in "highballs" and other beverages of fancy price and name, is euphemistically styled a "tippler;" his brother, a poor devil who swallows vile concoctions or red "pizen" is called a plain, ordinary "soak." Whatever name we give to such gluttons, the evil in both is the same; 'tis the evil of gluttony.

This vice differs from gluttony proper in that its object is strong drink, while the latter is an abuse of food and nourishment necessary, in regulated quantity, for the sustenance of the body. But alcohol is not necessary to sustain life as an habitual beverage; it may stimulate, but it does not sustain at all. It has its legitimate uses, like strychnine and other poison and drugs; but being a poison, it must be detrimental to living tissues, when taken frequently, and cannot have been intended by the Creator as a life-giving nourishment. Its habitual use is therefore not a necessity. Its abuse has therefore a more far-fetched malice.

But its use is not sinful, any more than the use of any drug, for alcohol, or liquor, is a creature of God and is made for good purposes. Its use is not evil, whether it does little good, or no good at all. The fact of its being unnecessary does not make it a forbidden fruit. The habit of stimulants, like the habit of tobacco, while it has no title to be called a good habit, cannot be qualified as an intrinsically bad habit; it may be tolerated as long as it is kept within the bounds of sane reason and does not give rise to evil consequences in self or others. Apart, therefore, from the danger of abuse—a real and fatal danger for many, especially for the young—and from the evil effects that may follow even a moderate use, the habit is like another; a temperate man is not, to any appreciable degree, less righteous than a moderate smoker. The man who can use and not abuse is just as moral as his brother who does not use lest he abuse. He must, however, be said to be less virtuous than another who abstains rather than run the risk of being even a remote occasion of sin unto the weak.

The intrinsic malice therefore of this habit consists in the disorder of excess, which is called intoxication. Intoxication may exist in different degrees and stages; it is the state of a man who loses, to any extent, control over his reasoning faculties through the effects of alcohol. There is evil and sin the moment the brain is affected; when reason totters and falls from its throne in the soul, then the crime is consummated. When a man says and does and thinks what in his sober senses he would not say, do, or think, that man is drunk, and there is mortal sin on his soul. It is not an easy matter to define just when intoxication properly begins and sobriety ends; every man must do that for himself. But he should consider himself well on the road to guilt when, being aware that the fumes of liquor were fast beclouding his mind, he took another glass that was certain to still further obscure his reason and paralyze his will.

Much has been said and written about the grossness of this vice, its baneful effects and consequences, to which it were useless here to refer. Suffice it to say there is nothing that besots a man more completely and lowers him more ignobly to the level of the brute. He falls below, for the most stupid of brutes, the ass, knows when it has enough; and the drunkard does not. It requires small wit indeed to understand that there is no sin in the catalogue of crime that a person in this state is not capable of committing. He will do things the very brute would blush to do; and then he will say it was one of the devil's jokes. The effects on individuals, families and generations, born and unborn, cannot be exaggerated; and the drunkard is a tempter of God and the curse of society.

Temperance is a moderate use of strong drink; teetotalism is absolute abstention therefrom. A man may be temperate without being a teetotaler; all teetotalers are temperate, at least as far as alcohol is concerned, although they are sometimes, some of them, accused of using temperance as a cloak for much intemperance of speech. If this be true—and there are cranks in all causes—then temperance is itself the greatest sufferer. Exaggeration is a mistake; it repels right-thinking men and never served any purpose. We believe it has done the cause of teetotalism a world of harm. But it is poor logic that will identify with so holy a cause the rabid rantings of a few irresponsible fools.

The cause of total abstinence is a holy and righteous cause. It takes its stand against one of the greatest evils, moral and social, of the day. It seeks to redeem the fallen, and to save the young and inexperienced. Its means are organization and the mighty weapon of good example. It attracts those who need it and those who do not need it; the former, to save them; the latter, to help save others. And there is no banner under which Catholic youth could more honorably be enrolled than the banner of total abstinence. The man who condemns or decries such a cause either does not know what he is attacking or his mouthings are not worth the attention of those who esteem honesty and hate hypocrisy. It is not necessary to be able to practice virtue in order to esteem its worth. And it does not make a fellow appear any better even to himself to condemn a cause that condemns his faults.

Saloon-keepers are engaged in an enterprise which in itself is lawful; the same can be said of those who buy and sell poisons and dynamite and fire-arms. The nature of his merchandise differentiates his business from all other kinds of business, and his responsibilities are of the heaviest. It may, and often does, happen that this business is criminal; and in this matter the civil law may be silent, but the moral law is not. For many a one such a place is an occasion of sin, often a near occasion. It is not comforting to kneel in prayer to God with the thought in one's mind that one is helping many to damnation, and that the curses of drunkards' wives and mothers and children are being piled upon one's head. How far the average liquor seller is guilty, God only knows; but a man with a deep concern for his soul's salvation, it seems would not like to take the risk.

CHAPTER 15

ENVY

When envy catches a victim she places an evil eye in his mind, gives him a cud to chew, and then sends him gadding.

If the mind's eye feeds upon one's own excellence for one's own satisfaction, that is pride; if it feeds upon the neighbor's good for one's own displeasure and unhappiness, that is envy. It is not alone this displeasure that makes envy, but the reason of this displeasure, that is, what the evil eye discerns in the neighbor's excellence, namely, a detriment, an obstacle to one's own success. It is not necessary that another's prosperity really work injury to our own; it is sufficient that the evil eye, through its discolored vision, perceive a prejudice therein. "Ah!" says envy, "he is happy, prosperous, esteemed! My chances are spoiled. I am overshadowed. I am nothing, he is everything. I am nothing because he is everything."

Remember that competition, emulation, rivalry are not necessarily envy. I dread to see my rival succeed. I am pained if he does succeed. But the cause of this annoyance and vexation is less his superiority than my inferiority. I regret my failure more than his success. There is no evil eye. 'Tis the sting of defeat that causes me pain. If I regret this or that man's elevation because I fear he will abuse his power; if I become indignant at the success of an unworthy person; I am not envious, because this superiority of another does not appear to me to be a prejudice to my standing. Whatever sin there is, there is no sin of envy.

We may safely assume that a person who would be saddened by the success of another, would not fail to rejoice at that other's misfortune. This is a grievous offense against charity, but it is not, properly speaking, envy, for envy is always sad; it is rather an effect of envy, a natural product thereof and a form of hatred.

This unnatural view of things which we qualify as the evil eye, is not a sin until it reaches the dignity of a sober judgment, for only then does it become a human act. Envy like pride, anger, and the other vicious inclinations, may and often does crop out in our nature, momentarily, without our incurring guilt, if it is checked before it receives the acquiescence of the will, it is void of wrong, and only serves to remind us that we have a rich fund of malice in our nature capable of an abundant yield of iniquity.

After being born in the mind, envy passes to the feelings where it matures and furnishes that supply of misery which characterizes the vice. Another is happy at our expense; the sensation is a painful one, yet it has a diabolical fascination, and we fondle and caress it. We brood over our affliction to the embittering and souring of our souls. We swallow and regurgitate over and over again our dissatisfaction, and are aptly said to chew the cud of bitterness.

Out of such soil as this naturally springs a rank growth of uncharity and injustice in thought and desire. The mind and heart of envy are untrammeled by all bonds of moral law. It may think all evil of a rival and wish him all evil. He becomes an enemy, and finally he is hated. Envy points directly to hatred.

Lastly, envy is "a gadding passion, it walketh the street and does not keep home." It were better to say that it "talketh." There is nothing like language to relieve one's feelings; it is quieting and soothing, and envy has strong feelings. Hence, evil insinuations, detraction, slander, etc. Justice becomes an empty word and the seamless robe of charity is torn to shreds. As an agent of destruction envy easily holds the palm, for it commands the two strong passions of pride and anger, and they do its bidding.

People scarcely ever acknowledge themselves envious. It is such a base, unreasonable and unnatural vice. If we cannot rejoice with the neighbor, why be pained at his felicity? And what an insanity it is to imagine that in this wide world one cannot be happy without prejudicing the happiness of another! What a severe shock it would be to the discontented, the morosely sour, the cynic, and other human owls, to be told that they are victims of this green-eyed monster. They would confess to calumny, and hatred; to envy, never!

Envy can only exist where there is abundant pride. It is a form of pride, a shape which it frequently assumes, because under this disguise it can penetrate everywhere without being as much as noticed. And it is so seldom detected that wherever it gains entrance it can hope to remain indefinitely.

Jealousy and envy are often confounded; yet they differ in that the latter looks on what is another's, while the former concerns itself with what is in one's own possession. I envy what is not mine; I am jealous of what is my own. Jealousy has a saddening influence upon us, by reason of a fear, more or less well grounded, that what we have will be taken from us. We foresee an injustice and resent it.

Kept within the limits of sane reason, jealousy is not wrong, for it is founded on the right we have to what is ours. It is in our nature to cling to what belongs to us, to regret being deprived of it, and to guard ourselves against injustice.

But when this fear is without cause, visionary, unreasonable, jealousy partakes of the nature and malice of envy. It is even more malignant a passion, and leads to greater disorders and crimes, for while envy is based on nothing at all, there is here a true foundation in the right of possession, and a motive in right to repel injustice.

Chapter 16

Sloth

Not the least, if the last, of capital sins is sloth, and it is very properly placed; for who ever saw the sluggard or victim of this passion anywhere but after all others, last!

Sloth, of course, is a horror of difficulty, an aversion for labor, pain and effort, which must be traced to a great love of one's comfort and ease. Either the lazy fellow does nothing at all—and this is sloth; or he abstains from doing what he should do while otherwise busily occupied—and this too, is sloth; or he does it poorly, negligently, half-heartedly—and this again is sloth. Nature imposes upon us the law of labor. He who shirks in whole or in part is slothful.

Here, in the moral realm, we refer properly to the difficulty we find in the service of God, in fulfiling our obligations as Christians and Catholics, in avoiding evil and doing good; in a word, to the discharge of our spiritual duties. But then all human obligations have a spiritual side, by the fact of their being obligations. Thus, labor is not, like attendance at mass, a spiritual necessity; but to provide for those who are dependent upon us is a moral obligation and to shirk it would be a sin of sloth.

Not that it is necessary, if we would avoid sin, to hate repose naturally and experience no difficulty or repugnance in working out our soul's salvation. Sloth is inbred in our nature. There is no one but would rather avoid than meet difficulties. The service of God is laborious and painful. The kingdom of God suffers violence. It has always been true since the time of our ancestor Adam, that vice is easy, and virtue difficult; that the flesh is weak, and repugnance to effort, natural because of the burden of the flesh. So that, in this general case, sloth is an obstacle to overcome rather than a fault of the will. We may abhor exertion, feel the laziest of mortals; if we effect our purpose in spite of all that, we can do no sin.

Sometimes sloth takes on an acute form known as aridity or barrenness in all things that pertain to God. The most virtuous souls are not always exempt from this. It is a dislike, a distaste that amounts almost to a disgust for prayer especially, a repugnance that threatens to overwhelm the soul. That is simply an absence of sensible fervor, a state of affliction and probation that is as pleasing to God as it is painful to us. After all where would the merit be in the service of God, if there were no difficulty?

The type of the spiritually indolent is that fixture known as the half-baked Catholic—some people call him "a poor stick"—who is too lazy to meet his obligations with his Maker. He says no prayers, because he can't; he lies abed Sunday mornings and lets the others go to mass—he is too tired and needs rest; the effort necessary to prepare for and to go to confession is quite beyond him. In fine, religion is altogether too exacting, requires too much of a man.

And, as if to remove all doubt as to the purely spiritual character of this inactivity, our friend can be seen, without a complaint, struggling every day to earn the dollar. He will not grumble about rising at five to go fishing or cycling. He will, after his hard day's work, sit till twelve at the theatre or dance till two in the morning. He will spend his energy in any direction save in that which leads to God.

Others expect virtue to be as easy as it is beautiful. Religion should conduce to one's comfort. They like incense, but not the smell of brimstone. They would remain forever content on Tabor, but the dark frown of Calvary is insupportable. Beautiful churches, artistic music, eloquent preaching on interesting topics, that is their idea of religion; that is what they intend religion—their religion—shall be, and they proceed to cut out whatever jars their finer feelings. This is fashionable, but it is not Christian: to do anything for God—if it is easy; and if it is hard,—well, God does not expect so much of us.

You will see at a glance that this sort of a thing is fatal to the sense of God in the soul; it has for its first, direct and immediate effect to weaken little by little the faith until it finally kills it altogether. Sloth is a microbe. It creeps into the soul, sucks in its substance and causes a spiritual consumption. This is neither an acute nor a violent malady, but it consumes the patient, dries him up, wears him out, till life goes out like a lamp without oil.

PART THREE

BELIEF

CHAPTER 17

WHAT WE BELIEVE

Our first duty to God, and the first obligation imposed upon us by the First Commandment is Faith, or belief in God—we must know Him.

Belief is solely a manner of knowing. It is one way of apprehending, or getting possession of, a truth. There are other ways of acquiring knowledge; by the senses, for instance, seeing, hearing, etc., and by our intelligence or reason. When truth comes to us through the senses, it is called experience; if the reason presents it, it is called science; if we use the faculty of the soul known as faith, it is belief.

You will observe that belief, experience and science have one and the same object, namely, truth. These differ only in the manner of apprehending truth. Belief relies on the testimony of others; experience, on the testimony of the senses; science, on that of the reason. What I believe, I get from others; what I experience or understand, I owe to my individual self. I neither believe nor understand that Hartford exists—I see it. I neither understand nor see that Rome exists —I believe it. I neither see nor believe that two parallel lines will never meet—I reason it out, I understand it.

Now it is beside the question here to object that belief, or what we believe, may or may not be true. Neither is all that we see, nor all that our reason produces, true. Human experience and human reason, like all things human, may err. Here we simply remark that truth is the object of our belief, as it is the object of our experience and of understanding. We shall later see that if human belief may err, faith or divine belief cannot mislead us, cannot be false.

Neither is it in order here to contend that belief, of its very nature, is something uncertain, that it is synonymous of opinion; or if it supposes a judgment, that judgment is "formidolose," liable at any moment to be changed or contradicted. The testimony of the senses and of reason does not always carry certain conviction. We may or may not be satisfied with the evidence of human belief. As for the divine, or faith, it is certain, or it is not at all; and who would not be satisfied with the guarantee offered by the Word of God!

And the truths we believe are those revealed by God, received by us through a double agency, the written and the oral word, known as Scripture and Tradition. Scripture is contained in the two Testaments; Tradition is found in the bosom, the life of the Church of Christ, in the constant and universal teachings of that Church.

The Scripture being a dead letter cannot explain or interpret itself. Yet, since it is applied to the ever-varying lives of men, it needs an explanation and an interpretation; it is practically of no value without it. And in order that the truth thus presented be accepted by men, it is necessary, of prime necessity, that it have the guarantee of infallibility. This infallibility the Church of Christ possesses, else His mission were a failure.

This infallibility is to control the vagaries of Tradition, for Tradition, of its very nature, tends to exaggeration, as we find in the legends of ancient peoples. Exaggerated, they destroy themselves, but in the bosom of God's Church these truths forever retain their character unchanged and unchangeable.

If you accept the truth, the whole truth, and nothing but the truth as revealed by God and delivered to man by the infallible Church from the Bible and Tradition, you have what is called ecclesiastical, Catholic or true faith. There is no other true faith. It is even an open question whether there is any faith at all outside of this; for outside the Church there is no reasonable foundation for faith, and our faith must be reasonable.

However, granting that such a thing can be, the faith of him who takes and leaves off the divine Word is called divine faith. He is supposed to ignore invincibly a portion of revealed truth, but he accepts what he knows. If he knew something and refused to embrace it, he would have no faith at all. The same is true of one who having once believed, believes no longer. He impeaches the veracity of God, and therefore cannot further rely on His Word.

Lastly, it matters not at all what kind of truths we receive from God. Truth is truth always and ever. We may not be able to comprehend what is revealed to us, and little the wonder. Our intelligence is not infinite, and God's is. Many things that men tell us we believe without understanding; God deserves our trust more than men. Our incapacity for understanding all that faith teaches us proves one thing: that there are limits to our powers, which may be surprising to some, but is nevertheless true.

CHAPTER 18

WHY WE BELIEVE

B elief, we have said, is the acceptance of a truth from another. We do not always accept what others present to us as truth, for the good reason that we may have serious doubts as to whether they speak the truth or not. It is for us to decide the question of our informant's intellectual and moral trustworthiness. If we do believe him, it is because we consider his veracity to be beyond question.

The foundation of our belief is therefore the veracity of him whose word we take. They tell me that Lincoln was assassinated. Personally, I know nothing about it. But I do know that they who speak of it could know, did know, and could not lead us all astray on this point. I accept their evidence; I believe on their word.

It is on the testimony of God's word that we believe in matters that pertain to faith. The idea we have of God is that He is infinitely perfect, that He is all-wise and all-good. He cannot, therefore, under pain of destroying His very existence, be deceived or deceive us. When, therefore, He speaks, He speaks the truth and nothing but the truth. It would be a very stultification of our reason to refuse to believe Him, once we admit His existence.

Now, it is not necessary for us to inquire into the things He reveals, or to endeavor to discover the why, whence and wherefore. It is truth, we are certain of it; what more do we need! It may be a satisfaction to see and understand these truths, just as it is to solve a problem two or three different ways. But it is not essential, for the result is always the same —truth.

But suppose, with my senses and my reason, I come to a result at variance with the first, suppose the testimony of God's word and that of my personal observations conflict, what then? There is an error somewhere. Either God errs or my faculties play me false. Which should have the prefer- ence of my assent? The question is answered as soon as it is put. I can conceive an erring man, but I cannot conceive a false God. Nothing human is infallible; God alone is proof against all error. This would not be my first offense against truth.

"Yes, all this is evident. I shall and do believe everything that God deigns to reveal, because He says it, whether or not I see or understand it. But the difficulty with me is how to know that God did speak, what He said, what He meant. My difficulty is practical, not theoretical."

And by the same token you have shifted the question from "Why we believe" to "Whence we believe;" you no longer seek the authority of your faith, but its genesis. You believe what God says, because He says it; you believe He did say it because—the Church says it. You are no longer dealing with the truth itself, but with the messenger that brings the truth to be believed. The message of the Church is: these are God's words. As for what these words stand for, you are not to trust her, but Him. The foundation of divine belief is one thing; the motives of credibility are another.

We should not confound these two things, if we would have a clear notion of what faith is, and discover the numerous counterfeits that are being palmed off nowadays on a world that desires a convenient, rather than a genuine article.

The received manner of belief is first to examine the truths proposed as coming from God, measure them with the rule of individual reason, of expediency, feeling, fancy, and thus to decide upon their merits. If this proposition suits, it is accepted. If that other is found wanting, it is forthwith rejected. And then it is in order to set out and prove them to be or not to be the word of God, according to their suitability or non-suitability.

One would naturally imagine, as reason and common sense certainly suggest, that one's first duty would be to convince oneself that God did communicate these truths; and if so, then to accept them without further dally or comment. There is nothing to be done, once God reveals, but to receive His revelation.

Outside the Church, this procedure is not always followed, because of the rationalistic tendencies of latter-day Protestantism. It is a glaring fact that many do not accept all that God says because He says, but because it meets the requirements of their condition, feelings or fancy. They lay down the principle that a truth, to be a truth, must be understood by the human intelligence. This is paramount to asserting that God cannot know more than men—blasphemy on the face of it. Thus the divine rock-bed of faith is torn away, and a human basis substituted. Faith itself is destroyed in the process.

It is, therefore, important, before examining whence comes our faith, to remember why we believe, and not to forget it. This much gained, and for all time, we can go farther; without it, all advance is impossible.

CHAPTER 19

WHENCE OUR BELIEF: REASON

My faith is the most reasonable thing in the world, and it must needs be such. The Almighty gave me intelligence to direct my life. When He speaks He reveals Himself to me as to an intelligent being: and He expects that I receive His word intelligently. Were I to abdicate my reason in the acceptance of His truths, I would do my Maker as great an injury as myself. All the rest of creation offers Him an homage of pure life, of instinct or feeling; man alone can, and must, offer a higher, nobler and more acceptable homage—that of reason.

My faith is reasonable, and this is the account my reason gives of my faith: I can accept as true, without in the least comprehending, and far from dishonoring my reason, with a positive and becoming dignity,— I can accept!—but I must accept—whatever is confided to me by an infallible authority, an authority that can neither deceive nor be deceived. There is nothing supernatural about this statement.

That which is perfect cannot be subject to error, for error

is evil and perfection excludes evil. If God exists He is perfect. Allow one imperfection to enter into your notion of God, and you destroy that notion. When, therefore, God speaks He is an infallible authority. This is the philosophy of common sense.

Now I know that God has spoken. The existence of that historical personage known as Jesus of Nazareth is more firmly established than that of Alexander or Caesar. Four books relate a part of His sayings and doings; and I have infinitely less reason to question their authenticity than I have to doubt the authenticity of Virgil or Shakespeare. No book ever written has been subjected to such a searching, probing test of malevolent criticism, at all times but especially of late years in Germany and France. Great men, scholars, geniuses have devoted their lives to the impossible task of explaining the Gospels away, with the evident result that the position of the latter remains a thousandfold stronger. Unless I reject all human testimony, and reason forbids, I must accept them as genuine, at least in substance.

These four books relate how Jesus healed miraculously the sick, raised the dead to life, led the life of the purest, most honest and sagest of men, claimed to be God, and proved it by rising from the dead Himself. That this man is divine, reason can admit without being unreasonable, and must admit to be reasonable; and revelation has nothing to do with the matter.

A glaring statement among all others, one that is reiterated and insisted upon, is that all men should share in the fruit of His life; ana for this purpose He founded a college of apostles which He called His Church, to teach all that He said and did, to all men, for all time. The success of His life and mission depends upon the continuance of His work.

Why did He act thus? I do not know. Are there reasons for this economy of salvation? There certainly are, else it would not have been established. But we are not seeking after reasons; we are gathering facts upon which to build an argument, and these facts we take from the authentic life of Christ.

Now we give the Almighty credit for wisdom in all His plans, the wisdom of providing His agencies with the means to reach the end they are destined to attain. To commission a church to teach all men without authority, is to condemn it to utter nothingness from the very beginning. To expect men to accept the truths He revealed, and such truths! without a guarantee against error in the infallibility of the teacher, is to be ignorant of human nature. And since at no time must it cease to teach, it must be indefectible. Being true, it must be one; the work of God, it must be holy; being provided for all creatures, it must be Catholic or universal; and being the same as Christ founded upon His Apostles, it must be apostolic. If it is not all these things together, it is not the teacher sent by God to Instruct and direct men.

No one who seeks with intelligence, single-mindedness and a pure heart, will fail to find these attributes and marks of the true Church of Christ. Whether, after finding them, one will make an act of faith, is another question. But that he can give his assent with the full approval of his reason is abso-lutely certain. Once he does so, he has no further use for his reason. He enters the Church, an edifice illumined by the superior light of revelation and faith. He can leave reason, like a lantern, at the door.

Therein he will learn many other truths that he never could have found out with reason alone, truths superior, but not contrary, to reason. These truths he can never repudiate without sinning against reason, first, because reason brought him to this pass where he must believe without the immediate help of reason.

One of the first things we shall hear from the Church speaking on her own authority is that these writings, the four relations of Christ's life, are inspired. However a person could discover and prove this truth to himself is a mystery that will never be solved. We cannot assume it; it must be proven. Unless it be proven, the faith based on this assumption is not reasonable; and proven it can never be, unless we take it from an authority whose infallibility is proven. That is why we say that it is doubtful if non-Catholic faith is faith at all, because faith must be reasonable; and faith that is based on an assumption is to say the least doubtfully reasonable.

CHAPTER 20

WHENCE OUR BELIEF: GRACE AND WILL

To believe is to assent to a truth on the authority of God's word. We must find that the truth proposed is really guaranteed by the authority of God. In this process of mental research, the mind must be satisfied, and the truth found to be in consonance with the dictates of right reason, or at least, not contrary thereto.

But the fact that we can securely give our assent to this truth does not make us believe. Something more than reason enters into an act of faith.

Faith is not something natural, purely human, beginning and ending in the brain, and a product thereof. This is human belief, not divine, and is consequently not faith.

We believe that faith is, of itself, as far beyond the native powers of a human being as the sense of feeling is beyond the power of a stone, or intelligence, the faculty of comprehension, is beyond the power of an animal. In other words, it is supernatural, above the natural forces, and requires the power of God to give it existence. "No man can come to me, unless the Father who has sent Me, draw him."

Some have faith, others have it not. Where did you get your faith? You were not born with it, as you were with the natural, though dormant faculties of speech, reason, and free will. You received it through Baptism. You are a product of nature; therefore nature should limit your existence. But faith aspires to, and obtains, an end that is not natural but supernatural. It consequently must itself be supernatural, and cannot be acquired without divine assistance.

Unless God revealed, you could not know the truths of religion. Unless He established a court of final appeal in His Church, you could not be sure what He did reveal or what He meant to say. Because of the peculiar character of these truths and the nature the certitude we possess, many would not believe all, if God's grace were not there to help them, even though one could and would believe, there no divine belief or faith proper until the soul lives the faculty from Him who alone can give it.

The reason why many do not believe is not because God's grace is wanting nor because their minds cannot be satisfied, not because they cannot, but because they will not.

Faith is a gift of God, but not that alone; it is a conviction, but not that alone. It is a firm assent of the will. We are free to believe or not to believe.

"As one may be convinced and not act according to his conviction, so may one be convinced and not believe according to his conviction. The arguments of religion do not compel anyone to believe, just as the arguments for good conduct do not compel anyone to obey. Obedience is the consequence of willing to obey, and faith is the consequence of willing to believe."

I am not obliged to receive as true any religious dogma, as I am forced to accept the proposition that two and two are four. I believe because I choose to believe. My faith is a submission of the will. The authority of God is not binding on me physically, for men have refused and still do refuse to submit to His authority and the authority He communicated to His Church. And I know that I, too, can refuse and perhaps more than once have been tempted to refuse, my assent to truths that interfered too painfully with my interests and passions.

Besides, faith is meritorious, and in order to merit one must do something difficult and be free to act. The difficulty is to believe what we cannot understand, through pride of intelligence, and to bring that stiff domineering faculty to recognize a superior. The difficulty is to bend the will to the acceptance of truths, and consequent obligations that gall our self-love and the flesh'. The believer must have humility and self-denial. The grace of God follows these virtues into a soul, and then your act of faith is complete.

Herein we discover the great wisdom of God who sets the price of faith, and of salvation that depends on it, not on the mind, but on the will; not on the intelligence alone, but on the heart. To no man is grace denied. Every man has the will to grasp what is good. But though to all He gives a will, all have not the same degree of intelligence; He does not endow them equally in this respect. How then could He make intelligence the first principle of salvation and of faith? God searches the heart, not the mind. A modicum of wit is guaranteed to all to know that they can safely believe. Be one ever so unlettered and ignorant, and dull, faith and heaven are to him as accessible as to the sage, savant and the genius. For all, the way is the same.

CHAPTER 21

How We Believe

Faith is the edifice of a Christian life. It is, of itself, a mere shell, so to speak, for unless good works sustain and adorn it, it will crumble, and the Almighty in His day will reduce it to ashes; faith without works is of no avail. The corner stone of this edifice is the authority of the word of God, while His gratuitous grace, our intelligence and will furnish the material for building. Now, there are three features of that spiritual construction that deserve a moment's consideration.

First, the edifice is solid; our faith must be firm. No hesitation, no wavering, no deliberate doubting, no suspicion, no take-and-leave. What we believe comes from God, and we have the infallible authority of the Church for it, and of that we must be certain. That certainly must not for a moment falter, and the moment it does falter, there is no telling but that the whole edifice so laboriously raised will tumble down upon the guilty shoulders of the imprudent doubter.

And of reasons for hesitating and disbelieving there is

absolutely none, once we have made the venture of faith and believe sincerely and reasonably. No human power can in reason impugn revealed truths for they are impervious to human intelligence. One book may not at the same time be three books; but can one divine nature be at one and the same time three divine persons? Until we learn what divinity and personality are we can affirm nothing on the authority of pure reason. If we cannot assert, how can we deny? And if we know nothing about it, how can we do either? The question is not how is it, but if it is. While it stands thus, and thus ever it must stand, no objection or doubt born of human mind can influence our belief. Nothing but pride of mind and corruption of heart can disturb it.

If you have a difficulty, well, it is a difficulty, and nothing more. A difficulty does not destroy a thesis that is solidly founded. Once a truth is clearly established, not all the difficulties in the world can make it an untruth. A difficulty as to the truth revealed argues an imperfect intelligence; it is idle to complain that we are finite. A difficulty regarding the infallible Church should not make her less infallible in our mind, it simply demands a clearing away-Theological difficulties should not surprise a novice in theological matters; they are only misunderstandings that militate less against the Church than against the erroneous notions we have of her. To allow such difficulties to undermine faith is like overthrowing a solid wall with a soap-bubble. Common sense demands that nothing but clearly demonstrated falsity should make us change firm convictions, and such demonstration can never be made against our faith.

Not from difficulties, properly speaking, but from our

incapacity for understanding what we accept as true, results a certain obscurity, which is another feature of faith. Believing is not seeing. Such strange things we do believe! Who can unravel the mysteries of religion? Moral certitude is sufficient to direct one's life, to make our acts human and moral and is all we can expect in this world where nothing is perfect. But because the consequences of faith are so far-reaching, we would believe nothing short of absolute, metaphysical certitude.

But this is impossible. Hence the mist, the vague dimness that surrounds faith, baffling every effort to penetrate it; and within, a sense of rarefied perception that disquiets and torments unless humility born of common sense be there to soothe and set us at rest. Moral truths are not geometric theorems and multiplication tables, and it is not necessary that they should be.

Of course, if, as in science so in faith, reason were everything, our position would hardly be tenable, for then there should be no vagueness but clear vision. But the will enters for something in our act of faith. If everything we believe were as luminous as "two and two are four," a special act of the will would be utterly uncalled for. We must be able, free to dissent, and this is the reason of the obscurity of our faith.

It goes without saying that such belief is meritorious. Christ Himself said that to be saved it is necessary to believe, and no man is saved but through his own merit. Faith is, therefore, gratuitous on His part and meritorious on ours. It is in reality a good work that proceeds from the will, under the dictates of right reason, with the assistance of divine grace.

CHAPTER 22

FAITH AND ERROR

Intolerance is a harsh term. It is stern, rigid, brutal, almost. It makes no compromise, combats a outrance and exacts blind and absolute obedience. Among individuals tolerance should prevail, man, should be liberal with man, the Law of Charity demands it. In regard to principles, there must and shall eternally be antagonism between truth and error, justice demands it. It is a case of self-preservation; one destroys the other. Political truth can never tolerate treason preached or practised; neither can religious truth tolerate unbelief and heresy preached or practised.

Now our faith is based on truth, the Church is the custodian of faith, and the Church, on the platform of religious truth, is absolutely uncompromising and intolerant, just as the State is in regard to treason. She cannot admit error, she cannot approve error; to do so would be suicidal. She cannot lend the approval of her presence, nay even of her silence, to error. She stands aloof from heresy, must always see in it an enemy, condemns it and cannot help condemning it, for she stands for truth, pure and unalloyed truth, which error pollutes and outrages.

Call this what you will, but it is the attitude of honesty first, and of necessity afterwards. "He who is liberal with what belongs to him is generous, he who undertakes to be generous with what does not belong to him is dishonest." Our faith is not founded on an act or agreement of men, but on the revelation of God. No human agency can change or modify it. Neither Church nor Pope can be liberal with the faith of which they are the custodians. Their sole duty is to guard and protect it as a precious deposit for the salvation of men.

This is the stand all governments take when there is question of political truth. And whatever lack of generosity or broadmindedness there be, however contrary to the spirit of this free age it may seem, it is nevertheless the attitude of God Himself who hates error, for it is evil, who pursues it with His wrath through time and through eternity. How can a custodian of divine truth act otherwise? Even in human affairs, can one admit that two and three are seven?

We sometimes hear it said that this intolerance takes from Catholics the right to think. This is true in the same sense that penitentiaries, or the dread of them, deprive citizens of the right to act. Everybody, outside of sleeping hours and with his thinking machine in good order, thinks. Perhaps if there were a little more of it, there would be more solid convictions and more practical faith. Holy Writ has it somewhere that the whole world is given over to vice and sin because there is no one who thinks.

But you have not and never had the right to think as you

please, inside or outside the Church. This means the right to form false judgments, to draw conclusions contrary to fact. This is not a right, it is a defect, a disease. Thus to act is not the normal function of the brain. It is no more the nature of the mind to generate falsehoods than it is the nature of a sewing machine to cut hair. Both were made for different things. He therefore who disobeys the law that governs his mind prostitutes that faculty to error.

But suppose, being a Catholic, I cannot see things in that true light, what then? In such a case, either you persist, in the matter of your faith, in being guided by the smoky lamp of your reason alone, or you will be guided by the authority of God's appointed Church. In the first alternative, your place is not in the Church, for you exclude yourself by not living up to the conditions of her membership. You cannot deny but that she has the right to determine those conditions.

If you choose the latter, then correct yourself. It is human to err, but it is stupidity to persist in error and refuse to be enlightened. If you cannot see for yourself, common sense demands that you get another to see for you. You are not supposed to know the alpha and omega of theological science, but you are bound to possess a satisfactory knowledge in order that your faith be reasonable.

Has no one a right to differ from the Church? Yes, those who err unconsciously, who can do so conscientiously, that is, those who have no suspicion of their being in error. These the heavenly Father will look after and bring safe to Himself, for their error is material and not formal. He loves them but He hates their errors. So does the Church abominate the false doctrines that prevail in the world outside her fold, yet at the same time she has naught but compassion and pity and prayers for those deluded ones who spread and receive those errors. To her the individual is sacred, but the heresy is damnable.

Thus we may mingle with our fellow citizens in business and in pleasure, socially and politically, but religiously—never. Our charity we can offer in its fullest measure, but charity that lends itself to error, loses its sacred character and becomes the handmaid of evil, for error is evil.

CHAPTER 23

THE CONSISTENT BELIEVER

The intolerance of the Church towards error, the natural position of One who is the custodian of truth, her only reasonable attitude, makes her forbid her children to read, or listen to, heretical controversy, or to endeavor to discover religious truth by examining both sides of the question. This places the Catholic in a position whereby he must stand aloof from all manner of doctrinal teaching other than that delivered by his Church through her accredited ministers. And whatever outsiders may think of the correctness of his belief and religious principles, they cannot have two opinions as to the logic and consistency of this stand he takes. They may hurl at him all the choice epithets they choose for being a slave to superstition and erroneous creeds; but they must give him credit for being consistent in his belief; and consistency in religious matters is too rare a commodity these days to be made light of.

The reason of this stand of his is that, for him, there can be no two sides to a question which for him is settled; for him, there is no seeking after the truth: he possesses it in its fulness, as far as God and religion are concerned. His Church gives him all there is to be had; all else is counterfeit. And if he believes, as he should and does believe, that revealed truth comes, and can come, only by way of external authority, and not by way of private judgment and investigation, he must refuse to be liberal in the sense of reading all sorts of Protestant controversial literature and listening to all kinds of heretical sermons. If he does not this, he is false to his principles; he contradicts himself by accepting and not accepting an infallible Church; he knocks his religious props from under himself and stands— nowhere. The attitude of the Catholic, therefore, is logical and necessary. Holding to Catholic principles how can he do otherwise? How can he consistently seek after truth when he is convinced that he holds it? Who else can teach him religious truth when he believes that an infallible Church gives him God's word and interprets it in the true and only sense?

A Protestant may not assume this attitude or impose it upon those under his charge. If he does so, he is out of harmony with his principles and denies the basic rule of his belief. A Protestant believes in no infallible authority; he is an authority unto himself, which authority he does not claim to be infallible, if he is sober and sane. He is after truth; and whatever he finds, and wherever he finds it, he subjects it to his own private judgment. He is free to accept or reject, as he pleases. He is not, cannot be, absolutely certain that what he holds is true; he thinks it is. He may discover to-day that yesterday's truths are not truths at all. We are not here examining the soundness of this doctrine; but it does follow therefrom, sound or unsound, that he may consistently go where he likes to hear religious doctrine exposed and explained, he may listen to whomever has religious information to impart. He not only may do it, but he is consistent only when he does. It is his duty to seek after truth, to read and listen to controversial books and sermons.

If therefore a non-Catholic sincerely believes in private judgment, how can he consistently act like a Catholic who stands on a platform diametrically opposed to his, against which platform it is the very essence of his religion to protest? How can he refuse to hear Catholic preaching and teaching, any more than Baptist, Methodist and Episcopalian doctrines? He has no right to do so, unless he knows all the Catholic Church teaches, which case may be safely put down as one in ten million. He may become a Catholic, or lose all the faith he has. That is one of the risks he has to take, being a Protestant.

If he is faithful to his own principles and understands the Catholic point of view, he must not be surprised if his Catholic friends do not imitate his so-called liberality; they have motives which he has not. If he is honest, he will not urge or even expect them to attend the services of his particular belief. And a Catholic who thinks that because a Protestant friend can accompany him to Catholic services, he too should return the compliment and accompany his friend to Protestant worship, has a faith that needs immediate toning up to the standard of Catholicity; he is in ignorance of the first principles of his religion and belief.

A Catholic philosopher resumes this whole matter briefly, and clearly in two syllogisms, as follows:

I.

Major. He who believes in an infallible teacher of revelation cannot consistently listen to any fallible teacher with a view of getting more correct information than his infallible teacher gives him. To do so would be absurd, for it would be to believe and at the same time not believe in the infallible teacher.

Minor. The Catholic believes in an infallible teacher of revelation.

Conclusion. Therefore, the Catholic cannot listen to any fallible teacher with a view of getting more correct information about revealed truth than his Church gives him. To do so would be to stultify himself.

II.

Major. He who believes in a fallible teacher—private judgment or fallible church—is free, nay bound, to listen to any teacher who comes along professing to have information to impart, for at no time can he be certain that the findings of his own fallible judgment or church are correct. Each newcomer may be able to give him further light that may cause him to change his mind.

Minor. The Protestant believes in such fallible teacher —his private judgment or "church."

Conclusion. Therefore, the Protestant is free to hear, and in perfect harmony with his principles, to accept the teaching of any one who approaches him for the purpose of instructing him. He is free to hear with a clear conscience, and let his children hear, Catholic teaching, for the Church claiming infallibility is at its worst as good as his private judgment is at best, namely, fallible.

Religious variations are so numerous nowadays that most people care little what another thinks or believes. All they ask is that they may be able to know at any time where he stands; and they insist, as right reason imperiously demands, that, in all things, he remain true to his principles, whatever they be. Honest men respect sincerity and consistency everywhere; they have nothing but contempt for those who stand, now on one foot, now on the other, who have one code for theory and another for practice, who shift their grounds as often as convenience suggests. The Catholic should bear this well in mind. There can be no compromise with principles of truth; to sacrifice them for the sake of convenience is as despicable before man as it is offensive to God.

Chapter 24

Unbelief

An atheist in principle is one who denies the existence of God and consequently of all revealed truth. How, in practice, a man endowed with reason and a conscience can do this, is one of the unexplained mysteries of life. Christian philosophers refuse to admit that an atheist can exist in the flesh. They claim that his denial is fathered by his desire and wish, that at most he only doubts, and while professing atheism, he is simply an agnostic.

An agnostic does not know whether God exists or not—and cares less. He does not affirm, neither does he deny. All arguments for and against are either insufficient or equally plausible, and they fail to lodge conviction in his mind of minds. Elevated upon this pedestal of wisdom, he pretends to dismiss all further consideration of the First Cause. But he does no such thing, for he lives as though God did not exist. Why not live as though He did exist! From a rational point of view, he is a bigger fool than his atheistic brother, for if certainty is impossible, prudence suggests that the surer course be taken. On one hand, there is all to gain; on the other, all to lose. The choice he makes smacks of convenience rather than of logic or common sense.

No one may be accused of genuine, or as we call it—formal—heresy, unless he persistently refuses to believe all the truths by God revealed. Heresy supposes error, culpable error, stubborn and pertinacious error. A person may hold error in good faith, and be disposed as to relinquish it on being convinced of the truth. To all exterior appearances, he may differ in nothing from a formal heretic, and he passes for a heretic. In fact, and before God, he belongs to the Church, to the soul of the Church; he will be saved if in spite of his unconscious error he lives well. He is known as a material heretic.

An infidel is an unbaptized person, whose faith, even if he does believe in God, is not supernatural, but purely natural. He is an infidel whether he is found in darkest Africa or in the midst of this Christian commonwealth, and in this latter place there are more infidels than most people imagine. A decadent Protestantism rejects the necessity of baptism, thereby ceasing to be Christian, and in its trail infidelity thrives and spreads, disguised, 'tis true, but nevertheless genuine infidelity. It is baptism that makes faith possible, for faith is a gift of God.

An apostate is one who, having once believed, ceases to believe. All heretics and infidels are not apostates, although they may be in themselves or in their ancestors. One may apostatize to heresy by rejecting the Church, or to infidelity by rejecting all revelation; a Protestant may thus become an apostate from faith as well as a Catholic. This going back on the Almighty—for that is what apostasy is,—is, of all misfortunes the worst that can befall man. There may be excuses, mitigating circumstances, for our greatest sins, but here it is useless to seek for any. God gives faith. It is lost only through our own fault. God abandons them that abandon Him. Apostasy is the most patent case of spiritual suicide, and the apostate carries branded on his forehead the mark of reprobation. A miracle may save him, but nothing short of a miracle can do it, and who has a right to expect it? God is good, but God is also just.

It is not necessary to pose as an apostate before the public. One may be a renegade at heart without betraying himself, by refusing his inner assent to a dogma of faith, by wilfully doubting and allowing such doubts to grow upon him and form convictions.

People sometimes say things that would brand them as apostates if they meant what they said. This or that one, in the midst of an orgy of sin, or after long practical irreligion, in order to strangle remorse that arises at an inopportune moment, may seem to form a judgment of apostasy. This is treading on exceedingly thin glass. But it is not always properly defection from faith. Apostasy kills faith as surely as a knife plunged into the heart kills life.

A schismatic does not directly err in matters of faith, but rejects the discipline of the Church and refuses to submit to her authority. He believes all that is taught, but puts himself without the pale of the Church by his insubordination. Schism is a grievous sin, but does not necessarily destroy faith.

The source of all this unbelief is, of course, in the proud mind and sensual heart of man. It takes form exteriorly in an interminable series of "isms" that have the merit of appealing to the weaknesses of man. They all mean the same thing in the end, and are only forms of paganism. Rationalism and Materialism are the most frequently used terms. One stands on reason alone, the other, on matter, and both have declared war to the knife on the Supernatural. They tell us that these are new brooms destined to sweep clean the universe, new lamps intended to dissipate the clouds of ignorance and superstition and to purify with their light the atmosphere of the world. But, truth to tell, these brooms have been stirring up dust from the gutters of passion and sin, and these lamps have been offending men's nostrils by their smoky stench ever since man knew himself. And they shall continue to do service in the same cause as long as human nature remains what it is. But Christ did not bring His faith on earth to be destroyed by the lilliputian efforts of man.

CHAPTER 25

HOW FAITH MAY BE LOST

It is part of our belief that no man can lose his faith without mortal sin. The conscious rejection of all or any religious truth once embraced and forming a part of Christian belief, or the deliberate questioning of a single article thereof, is a sin, a sin against God's light and God's grace. It is a deliberate turning away from God. The moral culpability of such an act is great in the extreme, while its consequences cannot be weighed or measured by any human norm or rule.

No faith was ever wrecked in a day; it takes time to come to such a pass; it is by easy stages of infidelity, by a slow process of half-denials, a constant fostering of habits of ignorance, that one undermines, little by little, one's spiritual constitution. Taking advantage of this state of debility, the microbe of unbelief creeps in, eats its way to the soul and finally sucks out the very vitals of faith. Nor is this growth of evil an unconscious one; and there lies the malice and guilt.

Ignorant pride, neglect of prayer and religious worship, disorders, etc., these are evils the culprit knows of and wills. He cannot help feeling the ravages being wrought in his soul; he cannot help knowing that these are deadly perils to his treasure of faith. He complacently allows them to run their course; and he wakes up one fine morning to find his faith gone, lost, dead—and a chasm yawning between him and his God that only a miracle can bridge over.

We mentioned ignorance: this it is that attacks the underpinning of faith, its rational basis, by which it is made intelligent and reasonable, without which there can be no faith.

Ignorance is, of course, a relative term; there are different degrees and different kinds. An ignorant man is not an unlettered or uncultured one, but one who does not know what his religion means, what he believes or is supposed to believe, and has no reason to give for his belief. He may know a great many other things, may be chock full of worldly learning, but if he ignores these matters that pertain to the soul, we shall label him an ignoramus for the elementary truths of human knowledge are, always have been, and always shall be, the solution of the problems of the why, the whence and the whither of life here below. Great learning frequently goes hand in hand with dense ignorance. The Sunday-school child knows better than the atheist philosopher the answer to these important questions. There is more wisdom in the first page of the Catechism than in all the learned books of sceptics and infidels.

Knowledge, of course, a thorough knowledge of all theological science will not make faith, any more than wheels will make a cart. But a certain knowledge is essential, and its absence is fatal to faith. There are the simple ignorant who have forgotten their Catechism and leave the church before the instruction, for fear they might learn something; who never read anything pertaining to religion, who would be ashamed to be detected with a religious book or paper in their hands. Then, there are the learned ignorant, such as our public schools turn out in great numbers each year; who, either are above mere religious knowledge-seeking and disdain all that smacks of church and faith; or, knowing little or nothing at all, imagine they possess a world of theological lore and know all that is knowable. These latter are the more to be pitied, their ignorance doubling back upon itself, as it were. When a man does not realize his own ignorance, his case is well nigh hopeless.

If learning cannot give faith, neither can it alone preserve it. Learned men, pillars of the Church have fallen away. Pride, you will say. Yes, of course, pride is the cause of all evil. But we have all our share of it. If it works less havoc in some than in others, that is because pride is or is not kept within bounds. It is necessarily fatal to faith only when it is not controlled by prayer and the helps of practical religion. God alone can preserve our faith. He will do it only at our solicitation.

If, therefore, some have not succeeded in keeping the demon of pride under restraint, it is because they refused to consider their faith a pure gift of God that cannot be safely guarded without God's grace; or they forgot that God's grace is assured to no man who does not pray. The man who thinks he is all-sufficient unto himself in matters of religion, as in all other matters, is in danger of being brought to a sense of his own nothingness in a manner not calculated to be agreeable. No man who practised humble prayer ever lost his faith, or ever can; for to him grace is assured.

And since faith is nothing if not practical, since it is a habit, it follows that irreligion, neglect to practise what we believe will destroy that habit. People who neglect their duty often complain that they have no taste for religion, cannot get interested, find no consolation therein. This justifies further neglect. They make a pretence to seek the cause. The cause is lack of faith; the fires of God's grace are burning low in their souls. They will soon go out unless they are furnished with fuel in the shape of good, solid, practical religion. That is their only salvation. Ignorance, supplemented by lack of prayer and practice, goes a long way in the destruction of faith in any soul, for two essentials are deficient.

Disorder, too, is responsible for the loss of much faith. Luther and Henry might have retained their faith in spite of their pride, but they were lewd, and avaricious; and there is small indulgence for such within the Church. Not but that we are all human, and sinners are the objects of the Church's greatest solicitude; but within her pale no man, be he king or genius, can sit down and feast his passions and expect her to wink at it and call it by another name than its own. The law of God and of the Church is a thorn in the flesh of the vicious man. The authority of the Church is a sword of Damocles held perpetually over his head—until it is removed. Many a one denies God in a moment of sin in order to take the sting of remorse out of it. One gets tired of the importunities of religion that tell us not to sin, to confess if we do sin.

When you meet a pervert who, with a glib tongue, protests that his conscience drove him from the Church, that his enslaved intelligence needed deliverance, search him and you will find a skeleton in his closet; and if you do not find it, it is there just the same. A renegade priest some years ago, held forth before a gaping audience, at great length, on the reasons of his leaving the Church. A farmer sitting on the last bench listened patiently to his profound argumentation. When the lecturer was in the middle of his twelfthly, the other arose and shouted to him across the hall: "Cut it short, and say you wanted a wife." The heart has reasons which the reason does not understand.

Not always, but frequently, ignorance, neglect and vice come to this. The young, the weak and the proud have to guard themselves against these dangers, hey work slowly, imperceptibly, but surely. Two things increase the peril and tend to precipitate matters; reading and companionship. The ignorant are often anxious to know the other side, when they do not know their own. The consequence is that they will not understand fully the question; and if they do, will not be able to resolve the difficulty. They are handicapped by their ignorance and can only make a mess out of it. The result is that they are caught by sophistries like a fly in a web.

The company of those who believe differently, or not at all, is also pernicious to unenlightened and weak faith. The example in itself is potent for evil. The Catholic is usually not a persona grata as a Catholic but for some quality he possesses. Consequently, he must hide his religion under the bushel for fear of offending. Then a sneer, a gibe, a taunt are unpleasant things, and will be avoided even at the price of what at other times would look like being ashamed of one's faith. If ignorant, he will be silent; if he has not prayed, he will be weak; if vicious, he will be predisposed to fall.

If we would guard the precious deposit of faith secure against any possible emergency, we must enlighten it, we must strengthen it, we must live up to it.

PART FOUR

RELIGION

CHAPTER 26

HOPE

The First Commandment bids us hope as well as believe in God. Our trust and confidence in His mercy to give us eternal life and the means to obtain it,—this is our hope, founded on our belief that God is what He reveals Himself to us, able and willing to do by us as we would have Him do. Hope is the flower of our faith; faith is the substance of the things we hope for.

To desire and to hope are not one and the same thing. We may long for what is impossible of obtaining, while hope always supposes this possibility, better, a probability, nay, even a moral certitude. This expectation remains hope until it comes to the fruition of the things hoped for.

The desire of general happiness is anchored in the human heart, deep down in the very essence of our being. We all desire to be happy, We may be free in many things; in this we are not free. We must have happiness, greater than the present, happiness of one kind or another, real or apparent. We may have different notions of this happiness; we desire it according to our notions. Life itself is one, long, painful, unsatisfied desire.

When that desire is centered in God and the soul's salvation, it incontinently becomes hope, for then we have real beatitude before us, and all may obtain it. It can be true hope only when founded on faith.

Not only is hope easy, natural, necessary, but it is essential to life. It is the mainspring of all activity. It keeps all things moving, and without it life would not be worth living. If men did not think they could get what they are striving after, they would sit down, fold their arms, let the world move, but they wouldn't.

Especially is Christian hope absolutely necessary for the leading of a Christian life, and no man would take upon himself that burden, if he did not confidently expect a crown of glory beyond, sufficient to repay him for all the things endured here below for conscience's sake. Hope is a star that beckons us on to renewed effort, a vision of the goal that animates and invigorates us; it is also a soothing balm to the wounds we receive in the struggle.

To be without this hope is the lowest level to which man may descend. St. Paul uses the term "men without hope" as the most stinging reproach he could inflict upon the dissolute pagans.

To have abandoned hope is a terrible misfortune—despair. This must not be confounded with an involuntary perturbation, a mere instinctive dread, a phantasmagoric illusion that involves no part of the will. It is not even an excessive fear that goes by the name of pusillanimity. It is a cool judgment like that of Cain: "My sin is too great that I should expect forgiveness."

He who despairs, loses sight of God's mercy and sees only His stern, rigorous justice. After hatred of God, this is perhaps the greatest injury man can do to his Master, who is Love. There has always been more of mercy than of justice in His dealings with men. We might say of Him that He is all mercy in this world, to be all justice in the next. Therefore while there is life, there is hope.

The next abomination is to hope, but to place our supreme happiness in that which should not be the object of our hope. Men live for pleasures, riches, and honors, as though these things were worthy of our highest aspirations, as though they could satisfy the unappeasable appetite of man for happiness. Greater folly than this can no man be guilty of. He takes the dross for the pure gold, the phantom for the reality. Few men theoretically belong to this class; practically it has the vast majority.

The presumptuous are those who hope to obtain the prize and do nothing to deserve it. He who would hope to fly without wings, to walk without feet, to live without air or food would be less a fool than he who hopes to save his soul without fulfiling the conditions laid down by Him who made us. There is no wages without service, no reward without merit, no crown without a cross.

This fellow's mistake is to bank too much on God's mercy, leaving His justice out of the bargain altogether. Yet God is one as well as the other, and both equally. The offense to God consists in making Him a being without any backbone, so to speak, a soft, incapable judge, whose pity degenerates into weakness. And certainly it is a serious offense.

No, hope should be sensible and reasonable. It must keep the middle between two extremes. The measure of our hope should reasonably be the measure of our efforts, for he who wishes the end wishes the means. Of course God will make due allowances for our frailties, but that is His business, not ours; and we have no right to say just how far that mercy will go. Even though we lead the lives of saints, we shall stand in need of much mercy. Prudence tells us to do all things as though it all depended upon us alone; then God will make up for the deficiencies.

CHAPTER 27

LOVE OF GOD

Once upon a time, there lived people who pretended that nothing had existence outside the mind, that objects were merely fictions of the brain; thus, when they gave a name to those objects, it was like sticking a label in the air where they seemed to be. The world is not without folks who have similar ideas concerning charity, to whom it is a name without substance. Scarcely a Christian but will pretend that he has the virtue of charity, and of course one must take his word for it, and leave his actions and conduct out of all consideration. With him, to love God is to say you do, whether you really do or not. This is charity of the "sounding brass and tinkling cymbal" assortment.

To be honest about it, charity or love of God is nothing more or less, practically, than freedom from, and avoidance of, mortal sin. "If any one say, 'I love God' and hates his brother, (or otherwise sins) he is a liar." Strong language, but straight to the point! The state of grace is the first, fundamental, and essential condition to the existence of charity. Charity and mortal sin are two things irreducibly opposed, uncompromisingly antagonistic, eternally inimical. There is no charity where there is sin; there is no sin where there is charity. That is why charity is called the fulfilment of the law.

On the other hand, it sometimes happens that humble folks of the world, striving against temptation and sin to serve the Master, imagine they can hardly succeed. True, they rarely offend and to no great extent of malice, but they envy the lot of others more advantageously situated, they think, nearer by talent and state to perfection, basking in the sunshine of God's love. Talent, position, much exterior activity, much supposed goodness, are, in their eyes, titles to the kingdom, and infallible signs of charity. And then they foolishly deplore their own state as far removed from that perfection, because forsooth their minds are uncultured, their faith simple, and their time taken up with the drudgery of life.

They forget that not this gift or that work or anything else is necessary. One thing alone is necessary, and that is practical love of God. Nothing counts without it. And the sage over his books, the wonder-worker at his task, the apostle in his wanderings and labors, the very martyr on the rack is no more sure of having charity than the most humble man, woman or child in the lowest walks of life who loves God too much to offend Him. It is not necessary to have the tongues of men and angels, or faith that will move mountains, or the fortitude of martyrs; charity expressed in our lives and deeds rates higher than these.

A thing is good in the eyes of its maker if it accomplishes

that for which it was made. A watch that does not tell time, a knife that does not cut, and a soul that does not love God are three utterly useless things. And why? Because they are no good for what they were made. The watch exists solely to tell the hour, the blade to cut and the soul to love and serve its Maker. Failing in this, there is no more reason for their being. Their utility ceasing, they themselves cease to exist to a certain extent, for a thing is really no longer what it was, when it fails to execute that for which it came into being.

Charity, in a word, amounts to this, that we love God, but to the extent of not offending Him. Anything that falls short of such affection is something other than charity, no matter how many tags and labels it may wear. If I beheld a brute strike down an aged parent, I would not for a moment think that affection was behind that blow; and I could not conceive how there could be a spark of filial love in that son's heart until he had atoned for his crime. Now love is not one thing when directed towards God, and another where man is concerned.

The great hypocrisy of life consists in this that people make an outward showing of loving God, because they know full well that it is their first duty; yet, for all that, they do not a whit mend their ways, and to sin costs them nothing. They varnish it over with an appearance of honesty and decency, and fair-minded men take them for what they appear to be, and should be, and they pass for such. These watches are pretty to look upon, beautiful, magnificent, but they are stopped, the interior is out of order, the main-spring is broken, the hands that run across the face lie. These blades are bright and handsome, but they are dull, blunt, full of nicks, good enough for coarse and vulgar work, but useless for the fine, delicate work for which they were made.

The master mechanic and artist of our souls who wants trustworthy timepieces and keen blades, will not be deceived by these gaudy trinkets, and will reject them. Others may esteem you for this or that quality, admire this or that qualification you possess, be taken with their superficial gloss and accidental usefulness. The quality required by Him who made you is that your soul be filled with charity, and proven by absence of sin.

CHAPTER 28

LOVE OF NEIGHBOR

The precept, written in our hearts, as well as in the law, to love God, commands us, at the same time, to love the neighbor. When you go to confession, you are told to be sorry for your sins and to make a firm purpose of amendment. These appear to be two different injunctions; yet in fact and reality, they are one and the same thing, for it is impossible to abhor and detest sin, having at the same moment the intention of committing it. One therefore includes the other; one is not sincere and true without the other; therefore one cannot be without the other. So it is with love of God and of the neighbor; these two parts of one precept are coupled together because they complete each other, and they amount practically to the same thing.

The neighbor we are to love is not alone those for whom we naturally have affection, such as parents, friends, benefactors, etc., whom it is easy to love. But our neighbor is all mankind, those far and those near, those who have blessed us and those who have wronged us, the enemy as well as the friend; all who have within them, as we have, the image and likeness of God. No human being can we put outside the pale of neighborly love.

As for the love we bear others, it is of course one in substance, but it may be different in degree and various in quality. It may be more or less tender, intense, emphatic. Some we love more, others, less; yet for all that, we love them. It is impossible for us to have towards any other being the same feelings we entertain for a parent. The love a good Christian bears towards a stranger is not the love he bears towards a good friend. The love therefore that charity demands admits a variety of shades without losing its character of love.

When it comes to loving certain ones of our neighbors, the idea is not of the most welcome. What! Must I love, really love, that low rascal, that cantankerous fellow, that repugnant, repulsive being? Or this other who has wronged me so maliciously? Or that proud, overbearing creature who looks down on me and despises me?

We have said that love has its degrees, its ebb and flow tide, and still remains love. The low water mark is this: that we refuse not to pray for such neighbors, that we speak not ill of them, that we refuse not to salute them, or to do them a good turn, or to return a favor. A breach in one of these common civilities, due to every man from his fellow-man, may constitute a degree of hatred directly opposed to the charity strictly required of us.

It is not however necessary to go on doing these things all during life and at all moments of life. These duties are exterior, and are required as often as a contrary bearing would betoken a lack of charity in the heart. Just as we are not called upon to embrace and hug an uninviting person as a neighbor, neither are we obliged to continue our civilities when we find that they are offensive and calculated to cause trouble. But naturally there must be charity in the heart.

We should not confound uncharity with a sort of natural repugnance and antipathy, instinctive to some natures, betraying a weakness of character, if you will, but hardly what one could call a clearly defined fault. There are people who can forgive more easily than forget and who succeed only after a long while in overcoming strong feelings. In consequence of this state of mind, and in order to maintain peace and concord, they prefer the absence to the presence of the objects of their antipathy. Of course, to nourish this feeling is sinful to a degree; but while striving against it, to remove prudently all occasions of opening afresh the wound, if we act honestly, this does not seem to have any uncharitable malice.

Now all this is not charity unless the idea of God enter therein. There is no charity outside the idea of God. Philanthropy, humanity is one thing, charity is another. The one is sentiment, the other is love—two very different things. The one supposes natural motives, the other, supernatural. Philanthropy looks at the exterior form and discovers a likeness to self. Charity looks at the soul and therein discovers an image of God, by which we are not only common children of Adam, but also children of God and sharers of a common celestial inheritance. Neither a cup of water nor a fortune given in any other name than that of God is charity.

There are certain positive works of charity, such as almsgiving and brotherly correction, etc., that may be obligatory upon us to a degree of Serious responsibility. We must use prudence and intelligence in discerning these obligations, but once they clearly stand forth they are as binding on us as obligations of justice. We are our brothers' keepers, especially of those whom misfortune oppresses and whose lot is cast under a less lucky star.

CHAPTER 29

PRAYER

No word so common and familiar among Christians as prayer. Religion itself is nothing more than a vast, mighty, universal, never ceasing prayer. Our churches are monuments of prayer and houses of prayer. Our worship, our devotions, our ceremonies are expressions of prayer. Our sacred music is a prayer. The incense, rising in white clouds before the altar, is symbolical of prayer. And the one accent that is dinned into our ears from altar and pulpit is prayer.

Prayer is the life of the Christian as work is the life of the man; without one and the other we would starve spiritually and physically. If we live well, it is because we pray; if we lead sinful lives, it is because we neglect to pray. Where prayer is, there is virtue; where prayer is unknown, there is sin. The atmosphere of piety, sanctity, and honesty is the atmosphere of prayer.

Strange that the nature and necessity of prayer are so often misunderstood! Yet the definition in our Catechism is clear and precise. There are four kinds of prayer; adoration, thanksgiving, petition for pardon, and for our needs, spiritual and bodily.

One need be neither a Catholic nor a Christian to see how becoming it is in us to offer to God our homage of adoration and thanksgiving; it is necessary only to believe in a God who made us and who is infinitely perfect. Why, the very heathens made gods to adore, and erected temples to thank them, so deep was their sense of the devotion they owed the Deity. They put the early Christians to death because the latter refused to adore their gods. Everywhere you go, under the sun, you will find the creature offering to the Creator a homage of worship.

He, therefore, who makes so little of God as to forget to adore and thank Him becomes inferior to the very pagans who, sunk in the darkness of corruption and superstition as they were, did not, however, forget their first and natural duty to the Maker. Neglect of this obligation in a man betrays an absence, a loss of religious instinct, and an irreligious man is a pure animal, if he is a refined one. His refinement and superiority come from his intelligence, and these qualities, far from attenuating his guilt, only serve to aggravate it.

The brute eats and drinks; when he is full and tired he throws himself down to rest. When refreshed, he gets up, shakes himself and goes off again in quest of food and amusement. In what does a man without prayer differ from such a being?

But prayer, strictly speaking, means a demand, a petition, an asking. We ask for our needs and our principal needs are pardon and succor. This is prayer as it is generally understood. It is necessary to salvation. Without it no man can be saved. Our assurance of heaven should be in exact proportion to our asking. "Ask and you shall receive." Ask nothing, and you obtain nothing; and that which you do not obtain is just what you must have to save your soul.

Here is the explanation of it in a nutshell. The doctrine of the Church is that when God created man, He raised him from a natural to a supernatural state, and assigned to him a supernatural end. Supernatural means what is above the natural, beyond our natural powers of obtaining. Our destiny therefore cannot be fulfilled without the help of a superior power. We are utterly incapable by ourselves of realizing the end to which we are called. The condition absolutely required is the grace of God and through that alone can we expect to come to our appointed end.

Here is a stone. That that stone should have feeling is not natural, but supernatural. God, to give sensation to that stone, must break through the natural order of things, because to feel is beyond the native powers of a stone. It is not natural for an animal to reason, it is impossible. God must work a miracle to make it understand. Well, the stone is just as capable of feeling, and the animal of reasoning, as is man capable of saving his soul by himself.

To persevere in the state of grace and the friendship of God, to recover it when lost by sin, are supernatural works. Only by the grace of God can this be effected. Will God do this without being asked? Say rather will God save us in spite of ourselves, or unknown to ourselves. He who does not ask gives no token of a desire to obtain.

Chapter 30

Petitions

For all spiritual needs, therefore, prayer is the one thing necessary. I am in the state of sin. I desire to be forgiven. To obtain pardon is a supernatural act. Alone I can no more do it than fly. I pray then for the grace of a good confession—I prudently think myself in the state of grace. Were I for a moment left to my depraved nature, to the mercy of my passions, I should fall into the lowest depths of iniquity. The holiest, saintliest of men are just as capable of the greatest abominations as the blackest sinner that ever lived. If he does not fall, and the other does, it is because he prays and the other does not.

Some people have certain spiritual maladies, that become second nature to them, called dominant passions. For one, it is cursing and swearing; for another vanity and conceit. One is afflicted with sloth, another with uncleanness of one kind or another. To discover the failing is the first duty, to pray against it is the next. You attack it with prayer as you attack a disease with remedies. And if we only used prayer with half the care, perseverance and confidence that we use medicines, our spiritual distemper would be short-lived.

A person who passes a considerable time without prayer is usually in a bad state of soul. There is probably no one, who, upon reflection, will fail to discover that his best days were those which his prayers sanctified, and his worst, those which had to get along without any. And when a man starts out badly, the first thing he takes care to do is to neglect his prayers. For praying is an antidote and a reminder; it makes him feel uneasy while in sin, and would make him break with his evil ways if he continued to pray. And since he does not wish to stop, he takes no chances, and gives up his prayers. When he wants to stop, he falls back on his prayers.

This brings us to the bodily favors we should ask for. You are sick. You desire to get well, but you do not see the sense of praying for it; for you say, "Either I shall get well or I shall not." For an ordinary statement that is as plain and convincing as one has a right to expect; it will stand against all argument. But the conclusion is not of a piece with the premises. In that case why do you call in the physician, why do you take nasty pills and swallow whole quarts of vile concoctions that have the double merit of bringing distress to your palate and your purse? You take these precautions because your most elementary common sense tells you that such precautions as medicaments, etc., enter for something of a condition in the decree of God which reads that you shall die or not die. Your return to health or your shuffling off of the mortal coil is subject to conditions of prudence, and according as they are fulfiled or not fulfiled the decree of God will go into effect one way or the other.

And why does not your sane common sense suggest to you that prayer enters as just such a condition in the decrees of God, that your recovery is just as conditional on the using of prayer as to the taking of pills?

There are people who have no faith in drugs, either because they have never used any or because having once used them, failed to get immediate relief. Appreciation of the efficacy of prayer is frequently based on similar experience.

To enumerate all the cures effected by prayer would be as bootless as to rehearse all the miracles of therapeutics and surgery. The doctor says: "Here, take this, it will do you good. I know its virtue." The Church says likewise: "Try prayer, I know its virtue." Your faith in it has all to do with its successful working.

As in bodily sickness, so it is in all the other afflictions that flesh is heir to. Prayer is a panacea; it cures all ills. But it should be taken with two tonics, as it were, before and after. Before: faith and confidence in the power of God to cure us through prayer. After: resignation to the will of God, by which we accept what it may please Him to do in our case; for health is not the greatest boon of life, nor are sickness and death the greatest evils. Sin alone is bad; the grace of God alone is good. All other things God uses as means in view of this supreme good and against this supreme evil. Faith prepares the system and puts it in order for the reception of the remedy. Resignation helps it work out its good effects, and brings out all its virtue.

Thus prayer is necessary to us all, whether we be Christians or pagans, whether just or sinners, whether sick or well. It brings us near to God, and God near to us, and thus is a foretaste and an image of our union with Him hereafter.

CHAPTER 31

RELIGION

As far back as the light of history extends, it shows man, of every race and of every clime, occupied in giving expression, in one way or another, to his religious impressions, sentiments, and convictions. He knew God; he was influenced by this knowledge unto devotion; and sought to exteriorize this devotion for the double purpose of proving its truth and sincerity, and of still further nourishing, strengthening, safeguarding it by means of an external worship and sensible things. Accordingly, he built temples, erected altars, offered sacrifices, burnt incense; he sang and wept, feasted and fasted; he knelt, stood and prostrated himself—all things in harmony with his hopes and fears. This is worship or cult. We call it religion, distinct from interior worship or devotion, but supposing the latter essentially. It is commanded by the first precept of God.

He who contents himself with a simple acknowledgment of the Divinity in the heart, and confines his piety to the realm of the soul, does not fulfil the first commandment. The

obligation to worship God was imposed, not upon angels—
pure spirits, but upon men—creatures composed of a body as
well as a soul. The homage that He had a right to expect was
therefore not a purely spiritual one, but one in which the
body had a part as well as the soul. A man is not a man
without a body. Neither can God be satisfied with man's
homage unless his physical being cooperate with his spiritual, unless his piety be translated into acts and become religion, in the sense in which we use the word.

There is no limit to the different forms religion may take
on as manifestations of intense fervor and strong belief.
Sounds, attitudes, practices, etc., are so many vehicles of
expression, and may be multiplied indefinitely. They become
letters and words and figures of a language which, while
being conventional in a way, is also natural and imitative, and
speaks more clearly and eloquently and poetically than any
other human language. This is what makes the Catholic religion so beautiful as to compel the admiration of believers and
unbelievers alike.

Of course, there is nothing to prevent an individual from
making religion a mask of hypocrisy. If in using these practices, he does not mean what they imply, he lies as plainly as
if he used words without regard for their signification. These
practices, too, may become absurd, ridiculous and even
abominable. When this occurs, it is easily explained by the
fact that the mind and heart of man are never proof against
imbecility and depravity. There are as many fools and cranks
in the world as there are villains and degenerates.

The Church of God regulates divine worship for us with
the wisdom and experience of centuries. Her sacrifice is the

first great act of worship. Then there are her ceremonies, rites, and observances; the use of holy water, blessed candles, ashes, incense, vestments; her chants, and fasts and feasts, the symbolism of her sacraments. This is the language in which, as a Church, and in union with her children, she speaks to God her adoration, praise and thanksgiving. This is her religion, and we practice it by availing ourselves of these things and by respecting them as pertaining to God.

We are sometimes branded as idolaters, that is, as people who adore another or others than God. We offer our homage of adoration to God who is in heaven, and to that same God whom we believe to be on our altars. Looking through Protestant spectacles, we certainly are idolaters, for we adore what they consider as simple bread. In this light we plead guilty; but is it simple bread? That is the question. The homage we offer to everything and everybody else is relative, that is, it refers to God, and therefore is not idolatry.

As to whether or not we are superstitious in our practices, that depends on what is the proper homage to offer God and in what does excess consist. It is not a little astonishing to see the no-creed, dogma-hating, private-judgment sycophants sitting in judgment against us and telling us what is and what is not correct in our religious practices. We thought that sort of a thing—dogmatism—was excluded from Protestant ethics; that every one should be allowed to choose his own mode of worship, that the right and proper way is the way one thinks right and proper. If the private-interpreter claims this freedom for himself, why not allow it to us! We thought they objected to this kind of interference in us some few hundred years ago; is it too much if we object most strenuously to it in them in these days! It is strange how easily some people forget first principles, and what a rare article on the market is consistency.

The persons, places and things that pertain to the exterior worship of God we are bound to respect, not for themselves, but by reason of the usage for which they are chosen and set aside, thereby becoming consecrated, religious. We should respect them in a spiritual way as we respect in a human way all that belongs to those whom we hold dear. Irreverence or disrespect is a profanation, a sacrilege.

Chapter 32

Devotions

There is in the Church an abundance and a rich variety of what we call devotions—practices that express our respect, affection and veneration for the chosen friends of God. These devotions we should be careful not to confound with a thing very differently known as devotion—to God Himself. This latter is the soul, the very essence of religion; the former are sometimes irreverently spoken of as "frills."

Objectively speaking, these devotions find their justification in the dogma of the Communion of Saints, according to which we believe that the blessed in heaven are able and disposed to help the unfortunate here below. Subjectively they are based on human nature itself. In our self-conscious weakness and unworthiness, we choose instinctively to approach the throne of God through His tried and faithful friends rather than to hazard ourselves alone and helpless in His presence.

Devotion, as all know, is only another name for charity towards God, piety, holiness, that is, a condition of soul resulting from, and at the same time, conducive to, fidelity to God's law and the dictates of one's conscience. It consists in a proper understanding of our relations to God—creatures of the Creator, paupers, sinners and children in the presence of a Benefactor, Judge and Father; and in sympathies and sentiments aroused in us by, and corresponding with, these convictions. In other words, one is devoted to a friend when one knows him well, is true as steel to him, and basks in the sunshine of a love that requites that fidelity. Towards God, this is devotion.

Devotions differ in pertaining, not directly, but indirectly through the creature to God. No one but sees at once that devotion, in a certain degree is binding upon all men; a positive want of it is nothing short of impiety. But devotions have not the dignity of entering into the essence of God-worship. They are not constituent parts of that flower that grows in God's garden of the soul—charity; they are rather the scent and fragrance that linger around its petals and betoken its genuine quality. They are of counsel, so to speak, as opposed to the precept of charity and devotion. They are outside all commandment, and are taken up with a view of doing something more than escaping perdition "quasi per ignem."

For human nature is rarely satisfied with what is rigorously sufficient. It does not relish living perpetually on the ragged edge of a scant, uncertain meagerness. People want enough and plenty, abundance and variety. If there are many avenues that lead to God's throne, they want to use them. If there are many outlets for their intense fervor and abundant generosity, they will have them. Devotions answer these purposes.

Impossible to enumerate all the different practices that are in vogue in the Church and go under the name of devotions. Legion is the number of saints that have their following of devotees. Some are universal, are praised and invoked the world over; others have a local niche and are all unknown beyond the confines of a province or nation. Some are invoked in all needs and distresses; St. Blase, on the other hand is credited with a special power for curing throats, St. Anthony, for finding lost things, etc. Honor is paid them on account of their proximity to God. To invoke them is as much an honor to them as an advantage to us.

If certain individuals do not like this kind of a thing, they are under no sort of an obligation to practise it. If they can get to heaven without the assistance of the saints, then let them do so, by all means; only let them be sure to get there. No one finds devotions repugnant but those who are ignorant of their real character and meaning. If they are fortunate enough to make this discovery, they then, like nearly all converts, become enthusiastic devotees, finding in their devotions new beauties, and new advantages every day.

And it is a poor Catholic that leaves devotions entirely alone, and a rare one. He may not feel inclined to enlist the favor of this or that particular saint, but he usually has a rosary hidden away somewhere in his vest pocket and a scapular around his neck, or in his pocket, as a last extreme. If he scorns even this, then the chances are that he is

Catholic only in name, for the tree of faith is such a fertile one that it rarely fails to yield fruit and flowers of exquisite fragrance.

Oh! of course the lives of all the saints are not history in the strictest sense of the word. But what has that to do with the Communion of Saints? If simplicity and naivete have woven around some names an unlikely tale, a fable or a myth, it requires some effort to see how that could affect their standing with God, or their disposition to help us in our needs.

Devotions are not based on historical facts, although in certain facts, events or happenings, real or alleged, they may have been furnished with occasions for coming into existence. The authenticity of these facts is not guaranteed by the doctrinal authority of the Church, but she may, and does, approve the devotions that spring therefrom. Independently of the truth of private and individual revelations, visions and miracles, which she investigates as to their probability, she makes sure that there is nothing contrary to the deposit of faith and to morals, and then she gives these devotions the stamp of her approval as a security to the faithful who wish to practise them. A Catholic or non-Catholic may think what he likes concerning the apparitions of the Virgin at Lourdes; if he is dense enough, he may refuse to believe that miracles have been performed there. But he cannot deny that the homage offered to Our Lady at Lourdes, and known as devotion to Our Lady of Lourdes, is in keeping with religious worship as practised by the Church and in consonance with reason enlightened by faith, and so with all other devotions.

A vase of flowers, a lamp, a burning candle before the

statue of a saint is a prayer whose silence is more eloquent than all the sounds that ever came from the lips of man. It is love that puts it there, love that tells it to dispense its sweet perfume or shed its mellow rays, and love that speaks by this touching symbolism to God through a favorite saint.

PART FIVE

SOME DARK FORCES

CHAPTER 33

IDOLATRY AND SUPERSTITION

The first and greatest sinner against religion is the idolater, who offers God-worship to others than God. There are certain attributes that belong to God alone, certain titles that He alone has a right to bear, certain marks of veneration that are due to Him alone. To ascribe these to any being under God is an abomination, and is called idolatry.

The idols of paganism have long since been thrown, their temples destroyed; the folly itself has fallen into disuse, and its extravagances serve only in history "to point a moral or adorn a tale." Yet, in truth, idolatry is not so dead as all that, if one would take the pains to peruse a few pages of the current erotic literature wherein people see heaven in a pair of blue eyes, catch inspired words from ruby lips and adore a well trimmed chin-whisker. I would sooner, with the old-time Egyptians, adore a well-behaved cat or a toothsome cucumber than with certain modern feather-heads and gum-drop hearts, sing hymns to a shapely foot or dimpled cheek and offer incense to "divinities," godlike forms, etc. The way hearts and souls are thrown around from one to another is suggestive of the national game; while the love they bear one another is always infinite, supreme, without parallel on earth or in heaven.

No, perhaps they do not mean what they say; but that helps matters very little, for the fault lies precisely in saying what they do say; the language used is idolatrous. And a queer thing about it is that they do mean more than half of what they say. When degenerate love runs riot, it dethrones the Almighty, makes gods of clay and besots itself before them.

What is superstition and what is a superstitious practice? It is something against the virtue of religion; it sins, not by default as unbelief, but by excess. Now, to be able to say what is excessive, one must know what is right and just, one must have a measure. To attempt to qualify anything as excessive without the aid of a rule or measure is simply guesswork.

The Yankee passes for a mighty clever guesser, outpointing with ease his transatlantic cousin. Over there the sovereign guesses officially that devotion to the Mother of God is a superstitious practice. This reminds one of the overgrown farmer boy, who, when invited by his teacher to locate the center of a circle drawn on the blackboard, stood off and eyed the figure critically for a moment with a wise squint; and then said, pointing his finger to the middle or thereabouts: "I should jedge it to be about thar'." He was candid enough to offer only an opinion. But how the royal guesser could be sure enough to swear it, and that officially, is what staggers plain people.

Now right reason is a rule by which to judge what is and what is not superstitious. But individual reason or private judgment and right reason are not synonyms in the English or in any other language that is human. When reasoning men disagree, right reason, as far as the debated question is concerned, is properly said to be off on a vacation, a thing uncommonly frequent in human affairs. In order, therefore that men should not be perpetually at war concerning matters that pertain to men's salvation, God established a competent authority which even simple folks with humble minds and pure hearts can find. In default of any adverse claimant the Catholic Church must be adjudged that authority. The worship, therefore, that the Church approves as worthy of God is not, cannot be, superstition. And what is patently against reason, or, in case of doubt, what she reproves and condemns in religion is superstitious.

Leaving out of the question for the moment those species of superstition that rise to the dignity of science, to the accidental fame and wealth of humbugs and frauds, the evil embraces a host of practices that are usually the result of a too prevalent psychological malady known as softening of the brain. These poor unfortunates imagine that the Almighty who holds the universe in the hollow of His hand, deals with His creatures in a manner that would make a full-grown man pass as a fool if he did the same. Dreams, luck-pieces, certain combinations of numbers or figures, ordinary or extraordinary events and happenings—these are the means whereby God is made to reveal to men secrets and mysteries as absurd as the means, themselves. Surely God must have descended from His throne of wisdom.

Strange though it appear, too little religion—and not too much—leads to these unholy follies. There is a religious instinct in man. True religion satisfies it fully. Quack religion, pious tomfoolery, and doctrinal ineptitude foisted upon a God-hungry people end by driving some from one folly to another in a pitiful attempt to get away from the deceptions of man and near to God. Others are led on by a sinful curiosity that outweighs their common-sense as well as their respect for God. These are the guilty ones.

It has been said that there is more superstition—that is belief and dabbling in these inane practices—to-day in one of our large cities than the Dark Ages ever was afflicted with. If true, it is one sign of the world's spiritual unrest, the decay of unbelief; and irreligion thus assists at its own disintegration. The Church swept the pagan world clean of superstition once; she may soon be called upon to do the work over again.

CHAPTER 34

OCCULTISM

Spiritism as a theory, a science, a practice, a religion, or —I might add—a profitable business venture, is considered an evil thing by the Church, and by her is condemned as superstition, that is, as a false and unworthy homage to God, belittling His majesty and opposed to the Dispensation of Christ, according to which alone God can be worthily honored. This evil has many names; it includes all dabbling in the supernatural against the sanction of Church authority, and runs a whole gamut of "isms" from fake trance-mediums to downright diabolical possession.

The craft found favor with the pagans and flourished many years before the Christian era. Wondrous things were wrought by the so-called pythonic spirit; evidently outside the natural order, still more evidently not by the agency of God, and of a certainty through the secret workings of the "Old Boy" himself. It was called Necromancy, or the Black Art. It had attractions for the Jews and they yielded to some extent to the temptation of consulting the Python. For this reason Moses condemned the evil as an abomination. These are his words, taken from Deuteronomy:

"Neither let there be found among you any one that consulteth soothsayers, or observeth dreams and omens; neither let there be any wizard, nor charmer, nor any one that consulteth pythonic spirits or fortune tellers, or that seeketh the truth from the dead. For the Lord abhorreth all these things; and for these abominations He will destroy them."

The Black Art had its votaries during the Middle Ages and kept the Church busy warning the faithful against its dangers and its evils. Even so great a name as that of Albert the Great has been associated with the dark doings of the wizard, because, no doubt, of the marvelous fruits of his genius and deep learning, which the ignorant believed impossible to mere human agency. As witchcraft, it nourished during the sixteenth and seventeenth centuries. The excesses to which it gave rise caused severe laws to be enacted against it and stringent measures were taken to suppress it. Many were put to death, sometimes after the most cruel tortures. As is usually the case, the innocent suffered with the guilty. The history of the early New England settlers makes good reading on the subject.

Some people claim that the spiritism of to-day is only a revival of old-time witchery and necromancy, that it is as prevalent now as it was then, perhaps more prevalent. "Only," as Father Lambert remarks, "the witch of to-day instead of going to the stake as formerly, goes about as Madam So-and-So, and is duly advertised in our enlightened press as the great and renowned seeress or clairvoyant, late from the court of the Akoorid of Swat, more recently from the Sublime Porte, where she was in consultation with the Sultan of Turkey, and more recently still from the principal courts of Europe. As her stay in the city will be brief, those who wish to know the past or future or wish to communicate with deceased friends, are advised to call on her soon. Witchcraft is as prevalent as it ever was, and the witches are as real. They may not have cats on their shoulders or pointed caps, or broomsticks for quick transit, but they differ from the witches of the past only in being liberally paid, instead of liberally punished."

The Church does not deny the possibility of intercourse between the living and the souls of the dead; she goes farther and admits the fact that such intercourse has taken place, pointing, as well she may, to the Scriptures themselves wherein such facts are recorded. The lives of her saints are not without proof that this world may communicate with the unknown. And this belief forms the groundwork, furnishes the basic principles, of Spiritism.

Nevertheless, the Church condemns all attempts at establishing such communication between the living and the dead, or even claiming, though falsely, such intercourse. If this is done in the name of religion, she considers it an insult to God, Who thereby is trifled with and tempted to a miraculous manifestation of Himself outside the ordinary channels of revelation. As an instrument of mere human curiosity, it is criminal, since it seeks to subject Him to the beck and call of a creature. In case such practices succeed, there is the grave danger of being mislead and deceived by the evil spirit, who is often permitted, as the instrument of God, to punish guilty men. When resorted to, as a means of relieving fools of their earnings, it is sacrilegious; and those who support such impious humbugs can be excused from deadly sin only on the grounds of lunacy.

Hypnotism and Mesmerism differ from Spiritism in this, that their disciples account for the phenomena naturally and lay no claim to supernatural intervention. They produce a sleep in the subject, either as they claim, by the emanation of a subtile fluid from the operator's body, or by the influence of his mind over the mind of the subject They are agreed on this point, that natural laws could explain the phenomenon, if these laws were well understood.

With this sort of a thing, as belonging to the domain of science and outside her domain, the Church has nothing whatever to do. This is a theory upon which it behooves men of science to work; they alone are competent in the premises. But without at all encroaching on their domain, the Church claims the right to pronounce upon the morality of such practices and to condemn the evils that flow therefrom. So great are these evils and dangers, when unscrupulous and ignorant persons take to experimenting, that able and reliable physicians and statesmen have advocated the prohibition by law of all such indiscriminate practices. Crimes have been committed on hypnotized persons and crimes have been committed by them. It is a dangerous power exercised by men of evil mind and a sure means to their evil ends. It is likewise detrimental to physical and moral health. Finally, he who subjects himself to such influence commits an immoral act by giving up his will, his free agency, into the hands of another. He does this willingly, for no one can be hypnotized against his will; he does it without reason or just motive. This is an evil, and to it must be added the responsibility of any evil he may be made to commit whilst under this influence. Therefore is the Church wise in condemning the indiscriminate practice of hypnotism or mesmerism; and therefore will her children be wise if they leave it alone. It is not superstition, but it is a sin against man's individual liberty over which he is constituted sole guardian, according to the use and abuse of which he will one day be judged.

CHAPTER 35

CHRISTIAN SCIENCE

A recently discovered sin against the First Commandment is the worship of Mrs. Eddy, and it is commonly called Christian Science. This sacrilegious humbug was conceived in the brain of an old woman up in New Hampshire and, like the little demon of error that it is, it leaped forth, after a long period of travail, full-fledged and panoplied, and on its lips were these words: "What fools these mortals be!" Dame Eddy gets good returns from the sacrilegio-comic tour of her progeny around the country. Intellectual Boston is at her feet, and Boston pays well for its amusements.

It is remarkable for an utter lack of anything like Christianity or science. It is as Christian as Buddhism and as scientific as the notions of our early forefathers concerning the automobile. It is a parody on both and like the usual run of parodies, it is a success.

The average man should not attempt to delve down into the mysterious depths of mind and matter which form the basis of this system. In the first place, it is an impossible task for an ordinary intelligence; then, again, it were labor lost, for even if one did get down far enough one could get nothing satisfactory out of it. The force of Eddyism lies in its being mysterious, incomprehensible and contradictory. These qualities would kill an ordinary system, but this is no ordinary system. The only way to beat the Christian Scientist is to invite him to focus all the energy of his mind on a vulgar lamp-post and engrave thereon the name of the revered Eddy —this to show the power of mind. Then to prove the non-existence of matter, ask him to consent to your endeavoring to make a material impression on his head with an immaterial hammer.

Of course this is not what he meant; but what he did mean will become by no means clearer after the wearisome, interminable lengths to which he will go to elucidate. The fact is that he does not know it himself, and no one can give what he does not possess. True philosophy tells us to define terms and never to employ expressions of more than one meaning without saying in what sense we use them. Contempt of this rule is the salvation of Christian Science, and that is where we lose.

Yet there is something in this fad after all. Total insanity is never met with outside state institutions, and these people are at large. The ravings of a delirious patient are often a monstrous mass of wild absurdities; but, if you question the patient when convalescent, you will sometimes be surprised to find they were all founded on facts which had become exaggerated and distorted. There is no such thing as pure unadulterated error. All of which is meant to convey the idea that at the bottom of all fraud and falsehood there is some truth, and the malice of error is always proportionate with the amount of truth it has perverted.

The first truth that has been exaggerated beyond recognition is this, that a large proportion of human diseases are pure fiction of morbid imaginations, induced by the power of the mind. That such is the case, all medical men admit. Thus, the mind may often be used as a therapeutic agent, and clever physicians never fail to employ this kind of Christian Science. Mrs. Eddy is therefore no more the discoverer of the "malade imaginaire" than Moliere. When you' distort this truth and write books proclaiming the fact that all ills are of this sort, then you have Eddyism up to date. Mrs. Eddy gathers her skirts in her hand and leaps over the abyss between "some ills" and "all ills" with the agility of a gazelle. Yes, the mind has a wonderful power for healing, but it will make just as much impression on a broken leg as on a block of granite. So much for the scientific part of the theory.

The method of healing of Jesus Christ and that of the foundress of Christian Science are not one and the same method, although called by the name of faith they appear at first sight to the unwary to be identical. There is a preliminary act of the intelligence in both; there is the exercise of the will power; and a mention of God in Eddyism makes it look like a divine assistance. To the superficial there is no difference between a miracle performed at Lourdes by God at the intercession of the Blessed Virgin and a "cure" effected by the Widow of New Hampshire hills.

Yet there is a wide difference, as wide as the abyss between error and truth. In faith healing, God interposes and alone does the healing. It is a miracle, a suspension of the ordinary laws of nature. Faith is not a cause, but an essential condition. In Christian Science, it is the mind of the patient or of Mrs. Eddy that does the work. It is God only in the sense that God is one with the patient. Mind is the only thing that exists, and the human mind is one with the Mind which is God. Then again this cure instead of being in opposition to the normal state of things like a miracle, itself establishes a normal state, for disease is abnormal and in contradiction with the natural state of man. Mental healing, according to this system sets the machine going regularly; miracles put it out of order for the moment. Christian Science therefore, repudiates the healing method of Jesus by faith and sets up one of its own, thereby forfeiting all title to be called Christian.

Being, therefore, neither Christian nor scientific, this new cult is nothing but pure nonsense, like all superstitions; the product of a diseased mind swayed by the demon of pride, and should be treated principally as a mental disorder. The chief, and only, merit of the system consists in illustrating the truth, as old as the world, that when men wander from the House where they are fed with a celestial nourishment, they will be glad to eat any food offered them that has a semblance of food, even though it be but husks and refuse. Man is a religious animal; take away the true God, and he will adore anything or everything, even to a cucumber. However limited otherwise, there is no limit to his religious folly.

PART SIX

VOWS

CHAPTER 36

OATHS

The first quality of an oath is that it be true. It is evident that every statement we make, whether simple or sworn, must be true. If we affirm what we know to be false we lie, if we swear to what we know to be false, we perjure ourselves. Perjury is a sacrilegious falsehood, and the first sin against the Second Commandment.

If, while firmly believing it to be true, what we swear to happens to be false, we are not guilty of perjury, for the simple reason that our moral certitude places us in good faith, and good faith guarantees us against offending. The truth we proclaim under oath is relative not absolute, subjective rather than objective, that is to say, the statement we make is true as far as we are in a position to know. All this holds good before the bar of conscience, but it may be otherwise in the courts where something more than personal convictions, something more akin to scientific knowledge, is required.

He who swears without sufficient certitude, without a

prudent examination of the facts of the question, through ignorance that must be imputed to his guilt, that one takes a rash oath—a sin great or small according to the gravity of the circumstances. It is not infrequently grievous.

Some oaths, instead of being statements, are promises, sworn promises. That of which we call God to witness the truth is not something that is, but something that will be. If one promises under oath, and has no intention of redeeming his pledge; or if he afterwards revokes such an intention without serious reasons, and fails to make good his sworn promise, he sins grievously, for he makes a fool and a liar of Almighty God who acts as sponsor of a false pledge. Concerning temperance pledges, it may here be said that they are simple promises made to God, but not being sworn to, are not oaths in any sense of the word.

Then, again, to be lawful, an oath must be necessary or useful, demanded by the glory of God, our own or our neighbor's good; and it must be possible to fulfil the promise within the given time. Otherwise, we trifle with a sacred thing, we are guilty of taking vain and unnecessary oaths. There can be no doubt but that this is highly offensive to God, who is thus made little of in His holy name.

This is the most frequent offense against the Second Commandment, the sin of profane swearing, the calling upon God to witness the truth of every second word we utter. It betrays in a man a very weak sense of his own honesty when he cannot let his words stand for themselves. It betokens a blasphemous disrespect for God Himself, represented by that name which is made a convenient tool to further every vulgar end. It is therefore criminal and degrading, and the guilt thereby incurred cannot be palliated by the plea of habit. A sin is none the less a sin because it is one of a great many. Vice is criminal. The victim of a vice can be considered less guilty only on condition of seriously combating that vice. Failing in this, he must bear the full burden of his guilt.

Are we bound to keep our oaths? If valid, we certainly are. An oath is valid when the matter thereof is not forbidden or illicit. The matter is illicit when the statement or promise we make is contrary to right. He who binds himself under oath to do evil, not only does not sin in fulfiling his pledge, but would sin if he did redeem it. The sin he thus commits may be mortal or venial according to the gravity of the matter of the oath. He sinned in taking the oath; he sins more grievously in keeping it.

The binding force of an oath is also destroyed by fraud and deception. Fear may have a kindred effect, if it renders one incapable of a human act. Likewise a former oath may annul a subsequent oath under certain conditions.

Again, no man in taking an oath intends to bind himself to anything physically or morally impossible, or forbidden by his superiors; he expects that his promise will be accepted by the other party, that all things will remain unchanged, that the other party will keep faith, and that there will be no grave reason for him to change his mind. In the event of any of these conditions failing of fulfilment his intention is not to be held by his sworn word, and his oath is considered invalidated. He is to be favored in all doubts and is held only to the strict words of his promise.

The least therefore we have to do with oaths, the better.

They are things too sacred to trifle with. When necessity demands it, let our swearing honor the Almighty by the respect we show His holy name.

CHAPTER 37

VOWS

Vows are less common than oaths, and this is something to be thankful for, since being even more sacred than oaths, their abuse incidental to frequent usage would be more abominable. The fact that men so far respect the vow as to entirely leave it alone when they feel unequal to the task of keeping it inviolate, is a good sign—creditable to themselves and honorable to God.

People have become accustomed to looking upon vows as the exclusive monopoly of the Catholic Church and her religious men and women. Such things are rarely met with outside monasteries and convents, except in the case of secular priests. 'Tis true, one hears tell occasionally of a stray unfortunate who has broken away from a state voluntarily, deliberately, chosen and entered upon, and who struggles through life with a violated vow saddled upon him. But one does not associate the sacred and heroic character of the vow with such pitiable specimens of moral worth.

The besom of Protestant reform thought to sweep all vows off the face of the earth, as immoral, unlawful, unnatural or, at least, useless things. The first Coryphei broke theirs; and having learned from experience what troublesome things they are, instiled into their followers a salutary distaste for these solemn engagements that one can get along so well without. From disliking them in themselves, they came to dislike them in others, and it has come to this that the Church has been obliged to defend against the change of immorality an institution that alone makes perfection possible. Strange, this! More sad than strange.

First of all, what is a vow? It is a deliberate promise made to God by which we bind ourselves to do something good that is more pleasing to Him than its omission would be. It differs from a promissory oath in this, that an oath makes God a witness of a promise made to a third party, while in a vow there is no third party, the promise being made directly to God. In a violated oath, we break faith with man; in a broken vow, we are faithless to God. The vow is more intimate than the oath, and although sometimes the words are taken one for the other, in meaning they are widely different.

Resolutions or purposes, such as we make in confession never to sin again, or in moments of fervor to perform works of virtue, are not vows. A promise made to the Blessed Virgin or the saints is not a vow; it must be made directly to God Himself.

A promise made to God to avoid mortal sin is not a vow, in the strict sense of the word; or rather such a promise is outside the ordinary province of the vow, which naturally embraces works of supererogation and counsel. It is unnecessary and highly imprudent to make such promises under vow. A promise to commit sin is a blasphemous outrage. If what we promise to do is something indifferent, vain and useless, opposed to evangelical counsels or generally less agreeable to God than the contrary, our promise is null and void as far as the having the character of a vow is concerned.

Of course, in taking a vow we must know what we are doing and be free to act or not to act. If then the object of the vow is matter on which a vow may validly be taken, we are bound in conscience to keep our solemn engagement. What we forbid ourselves to do may be perfectly lawful and innocent, but by that vow we forfeit the right we had to do it, and for us it has become sinful. The peculiar position in which a vow places a man in relation to his fellow-men concerning what is right and wrong, is the characteristic of the vow that makes it the object of much attention. But it requires something lacking in the outfit of an intelligent man to perceive therein anything that savors of the unnatural, the unlawful or the immoral.

Concerning those whom a vow has constituted in a profession, we shall have a word to say later. Right here the folly, to say nothing stronger, of those who contract vows without thinking, must be apparent to all. No one should dare take upon himself or herself such a burden of his or her own initiative. It is an affair that imperiously demands the services of an outside, disinterested, experienced party, whose prudence will well weigh the conditions and the necessity of such a step. Without this, there is no end to the possible misery and dangers the taking of a vow may lead to.

If through an act of unthinking foolishness or rash

presumption, you find yourself weighed down with the incubus of a vow not made for your shoulders, the only way out is to make a clean breast of the matter to your confessor, and follow his directions.

CHAPTER 38

THE PROFESSIONAL VOWS

The professional vow is a triple one, and embraces the three great evangelical counsels of perfect chastity, poverty and obedience. The cloister is necessary for the observance of such engagements as these, and it were easier for a lily to flourish on the banks of the Dead Sea, or amid the fiery blasts of the Sahara, than for these delicate flowers of spirituality to thrive in the midst of the temptations, seductions and passions of the every day world of this life. Necessity makes a practice of these virtues a profession.

It is good to be chaste, good to be obedient, good to be voluntarily poor. What folly, then, to say that it is unlawful to bind oneself by promises of this kind, since it is lawful to be good—the only thing that is lawful! It is not unlawful, if you will, to possess riches, to enjoy one's independence, to wed; but there is virtue in foregoing these pleasures, and virtue is better than its defect, and it is no more unlawful to do better than to do good.

If it is lawful to contract a solemn engagement with man, why not with God? If it is lawful for a short time, why not for a long time? If it is lawful for two years, why not for ten, and a lifetime! The engagement is no more unlawful itself than that to which we engage ourselves.

The zealous guardians of the rights of man protest that, nevertheless, vows destroy man's liberty, and should therefore be forbidden, and the profession suppressed. It is along this line that the governmental machine is being run in France at present. If the vow destroys liberty, these fanatics are doing what appears dangerously near being the same thing.

There is a decided advantage in being your own slave-master over having another perform that service for you. If I do something which before God and my conscience I have a perfect right to do, if I do it with deliberate choice and affection, it is difficult to see wherein my liberty suffers. Again, if I decide not to marry—a right that every man certainly has—and in this situation engage myself by vow to observe perfect chastity—which I must do to retain the friendship of God—I do not see how I forfeit my liberty by swearing away a right I never had.

In all cases, the more difficult an enterprise a man enters upon and pursues to a final issue, the more fully he exercises his faculty of free will. And since the triple vow supposes nothing short of heroism in those who take it, it follows that they must use the very plenitude of their liberty to make the thing possible.

The "cui bono" is the next formidable opponent the vow has to contend with. What's the good of it? Where is the advantage in leading such an impossible existence when a person can save his soul without it? All are not damned who refuse to take vows. Is it not sufficient to be honest men and women?

That depends upon what you mean by an honest man. A great saint once said that an honest man would certainly not be hanged, but that it was by no means equally certain that he would not be damned. A man may do sundry wicked and crooked things and not forfeit his title to be called honest. The majority of Satan's subjects were probably honest people in their day.

The quality of being an honest man, according to many people, consists in having the privilege of doing a certain amount of wickedness without prejudice to his eternal salvation. The philosophy of this class of people is summed up in these words: "Do little and get much; make a success of life from the standpoint of your own selfishness, and then sneak into heaven almost by stealth and fraud." That is one way of doing business with the Lord. But, there are greater things in heaven and on earth than are dreamt of in your philosophy, Horatio.

Human natures differ as much as pebbles on the sea shore. One man's meat has often proven poison to another. In the religion of Jesus Christ there is something more than the Commandments given to Moses. Love of God has degrees of intensity and perfection. Such words as sacrifice, mortification, self-denial have a meaning as they have always had. God gives more to some, less to others; He demands corresponding returns. These are things Horatio ignores. Yet they are real, real as his own empty and conceited wisdom.

CHAPTER 39

THE PROFESSION

One of the advantages of the monastic life, created by vows, is that it is wholly in keeping with human nature such as God created it. Men differ in their spiritual complexion more widely even than they do in mental caliber and physical make-up. All are not fitted by character and general condition for the same 'career; we are "cut out" for our peculiar tasks. It is the calling of one to be a soldier, of another to be a statesman, because each is best fitted by nature for this particular walk of life. The born poet, if set to put together a machine, will, in the majority of cases, make a sorry mess of the job, and a bricklayer will usually prove to be an indifferent story-writer.

So also one is called to be a good Christian, while his brother may be destined for a more perfect life. If there are vocations in the natural life, why should there not be in the supernatural, which is just as truly a life? If variety of aptitudes and likes determine difference of calling, why should this not hold good for the soul as well as for the body and mind? If one should always follow the bent of one's legitimately natural inclinations, no fault can reasonably be found if another hearkens to the voice of his soul's aspirations and elect a career in harmony with his nature.

There are two roads on which all men must travel to their destiny. One is called the way of Precept, the other the way of Counsel. In each the advantages and inconveniences are about equally balanced. The former is wide and level with many joys and pleasures along the way; but there are many pitfalls and stumbling blocks, while on one side is a high, steep precipice over which men fall to their eternal doom. Those destined by Providence to go over this road are spiritually shod for the travel; if they slip and tumble, it is through their own neglect.

Some there are to whom it has been shown by experience —very little sometimes suffices—that they have, for reasons known alone to God, been denied the shoe that does not slip; and that if they do not wish to go over the brink, they must get off the highway and follow a path removed from this danger, a path not less difficult but more secure for them. Their salvation depends on it. This inside path, while it insures safety for these, might lead the others astray. Each in his respective place will be saved; if they exchange places, they are lost.

Then again, if you will look at it from another standpoint, there remains still on earth such a thing as love of God, pure love of God. And this love can be translated into acts and life. Love, as all well know, has its degrees of intensity and perfection. All well-born children love their parents, but they do not all love them in the same degree. Some are by nature more affectionate, some appreciate favors better, some receive more and know that more is expected of them.

In like manner, we who are all children of the Great Father are not all equally loving and generous. What therefore is more natural than that some should choose to give themselves up heart, soul and body to the exclusive service of God? What is there abnormal in the fact that they renounce the world and all its joys and legitimate pleasures, fast, pray and keep vigil, through pure love of God? There is only one thing they fear, and that is to offend God. By their vows they put this misfortune without the pale of possibility, as far as such a thing can be done by a creature endowed with free will.

Of course there are those for whom all this is unmitigated twaddle and bosh. To mention abnegation, sacrifice, etc., to such people is to speak in a language no more intelligible than Sanskrit. Naturally one of these will expect his children to appreciate the sacrifices he makes for their happiness, but with God they think it must be different.

There was once a young man who was rich. He had never broken the Commandments of God. Wondering if he had done enough to be saved, he came to the Messiah and put the question to Him. The answer he received was, that, if he were sinless, he had done well, but that there was a sanctity, not negative but positive, which if he would acquire, would betoken in him a charity becoming a follower of a Crucified God. Christ called the young man to a life of perfection. "If thou wilt be perfect, go, sell what thou hast, give to the poor, then come, and follow me." It is not known whether this invitation was accepted by the young man; but ever since then it has been the joy of men and women in the Catholic Church to accept it, and to give up all in order to serve the Maker.

Scoffers and revilers of monasticism are a necessary evil. Being given the course of nature that sometimes runs to freaks, they must exist. Living, they must talk, and talking they must utter ineptitudes. People always do when they discourse on things they do not comprehend. But let this be our consolation: monks are immortal. They were, they are, they ever shall be. All else is grass.

CHAPTER 40

THE RELIGIOUS

Owing to the disturbance over things religious in France, vows and those who exemplify them in their lives are receiving of late a large share of public attention. On this topic, it seems, every one is qualified to speak; all sorts of opinions have been ventilated in the religious, the non-religious, and the irreligious press, for the benefit of those who are interested in this pitiful spasm of Gallic madness against the Almighty and His Church. The measure of unparalleled tyranny and injustice, in which antipathy to religious orders has found expression, is being favorably and unfavorably commented upon. But since monks, friars and nuns seldom find favor with the non Catholic world, the general verdict is that the religious, like the anarchist, must go; society is afraid of both and is safe from neither.

To Catholics who understand human nature and have read history, this condition of things is not surprising; it is, we might venture to say, the normal state of mind in relation to things so intensely Catholic is religious vows. Antagonism against monasticism was born the day Luther decided to take a wife; and as long as that same spirit lingers on earth we shall expect this antagonism to thrive and prosper. Not only that, but we shall never expect the religious to get a fair hearing for their cause. The hater, open or covert, of the habit and cowl is whole-souled or nothing in his convictions. And he believes the devil should be fought with his own weapons.

We do not expect all men to think as we do concerning the merits of the religious profession. To approve it without restriction would be to approve the Church. To find no wrong in it would be indicative of a dangerous Romish tendency. And we are not prepared to assert that any such symptoms exist to an alarming extent in those who expatiate on religious topics these latter days. There will be differences of opinion on this score, as on many others, and one fellow's opinion is as good, to himself, as another's.

There are even objections, to many an honest man, serious objections, that may be brought up and become legiti-mate matter for discussion. We take it for granted that intelli-gent men do not oppose an institution as venerable as monasticism without reasons. Contention between people who respect intelligence is always based on what has at least a semblance of truth, and has for its object to detect reality and label it as distinct from appearance.

We go farther, and admit that there have been abuses in this system of perfection, abuses that we were the first to detect, the first to deplore and feel the shame of it. But before we believed it, we investigated and made sure it was so. We found out very often that the accusations were false. Scandalmongers and dishonest critics noted the charges, but forgot to publish the verdict, and naturally with the public these charges stand. No wonder then that such tales breed antipathy and hatred among those who are not in position to control facts.

A queer feature about this is that people do not give religious credit for being human. That they are flesh and blood, all agree; that they should err, is preposterous. A hue-and-cry goes up when it becomes known that one of these children of Adam has paid the penalty of being human. One would think an angel had fallen from heaven. We notice in this attitude an unconscious recognition of the sanctity of the religious state; but we see behind it a Pharisaic spirit that exaggerates evil at the expense of justice.

Now, if the principle that abuse destroys use is applied to all things, nothing will remain standing, and the best will go first. Corruptio optimi pessima. Everything human is liable to abuse; that which is not, is divine. Religious and laymen, mortals all, the only time it is beyond our power to do wrong is when we are dead, buried, and twenty-four hours underground. If in life we make mistakes, the fault lies, not in our being of this or that profession, but in being human. Whatever, therefore, the excesses that religious can be proven guilty of, the institution itself must not be held responsible, unless it can be shown that there exists a relation of cause and effect. And whoever reasons otherwise, abuses the intelligence of his listeners.

We desire, in the name of honesty and fairness, to see less of that spirit that espies all manner of evil beneath the habit of a religious; that discovers in convents and monasteries plotting against the State in favor of the Papacy, the accumulation of untold wealth by oppression and extortion for the satisfaction of laziness and lust, iniquity of the deepest dye allied to general worthlessness. Common sense goes a long way in this world. If it were only a less rare commodity, and if an effective tribunal could be erected for the suppression of mendacity, the religious would appear for the first time in history in their true colors before the world, and light would shine in darkness.

Chapter 41

The Vow of Poverty

One objection to the vow of poverty that has a serious face on it, and certainly looks wicked, is that it does not prevent the accumulation of great wealth, as may be seen in the cases of the Philippine Friars and the French orders. This is one difficulty; here is another and quite different: the wealth of the religious is excessive, detrimental to the well-being of the people and a menace to the State. Taken separately, it is easy to dispose of these charges and to explain them away. But if you put them together in one loose, vague, general imputation of avarice, extortion and injustice, and hurl the same at a person unable to make distinctions, the shock is apt to disconcert him for a moment.

The first indictment seems to hint at a contradiction, or at least an incompatibility, between the profession of poverty and the fact of possessing wealth. We claim that the one does not affect the' other, that a religious may belong to a rich order and still keep his vow inviolate. The vow in the religious is individual and personal; the riches collective. It is the physical person that is poor; the moral being has the wealth. Men may club together, put their means into a common fund, renounce all personal claim thereto, live on a meagre revenue and employ the surplus for various purposes other than their needs. The personal poverty of such as these is real.

This is the case of the religious. Personally they do not own the clothes on their backs. The necessaries of life are furnished them out of a common fund. What remains, goes through their hands for the glory of God and in charity to fellow-man. The employment to which these men devote their lives, such as prayer, charity, the maintenance and conducting of schools and hospitals, is not lucrative to any great extent. And since very few Orders resort to begging, the revenue from capital is the only means of assuring existence. It is therefore no more repugnant for religious to depend on funded wealth than it was for the Apostolic College to have a common purse. The secret reason for this condition of things is that works of zeal rarely yield abundant returns, and man cannot live on the air of heaven.

As to the extent of such wealth and its dangers, it would seem that if it be neither ill gotten nor employed for illegitimate purposes, in justice and equity, there cannot be two opinions on the subject. Every human being has a right to the fruit of his industry and activity. To deny this is to advocate extreme socialism and anarchy and, he who puts this doctrine into practice, destroys the principle on which society rests. The law that strikes at religious corporations whose wealth accrues from centuries of toil and labor, may to-morrow consistently confiscate the goods and finances of every other corporation in the realm. If you force the religious out of land and home, why not force Morgan, Rockefeller & Co., out of theirs! The justice in one case is as good as in the other.

It is difficult to see how the people suffer from accumulated wealth, the revenues from which are almost entirely devoted to the relief of misery and the instruction of the ignorant. The people are the sole beneficiaries. There is here none of the arrogance and selfishness that usually characterize the possession of wealth to the embitterment of misery and misfortune. The religious, by their vow and their means, can share the condition of the poor and relieve it. If there is any institution better calculated to promote the well-being of the common people, it should be put to work. When the moneyed combinations whose rights are respected, show themselves as little prejudicial to the welfare of the classes, the religious will be prepared to go out of existence.

Everyone is inclined to accept as true the statement, on record as official, that the wealth of the Religious Orders in France is at the bottom of the trouble. We are not therefore a little astonished to learn from other sources that it is rather their poverty, which is burdensome to the people. The religious are not too rich, but too poor. They cannot support themselves, and live on the enforced charity of the laborer. French parents, not being equal to the task of maintaining monasteries and supporting large families, limited the number of their children. The population fell off in consequence. The government came to the relief of the people and cast out the religious.

And here we have the beautiful consistency of those who believe that any old reason is better than none at all. The religious are too poor, their poverty is a burden on the people; the religious are too rich, their riches are prejudicial to the welfare of the people. One reason is good; two are better. If they contradict, it is only a trifling matter. As for us, we don't know quite where we stand. We can hear well enough, amid the din of denunciation, the conclusion that the religious must go; but we cannot, for the life of us, catch the why and wherefore. Is it because they are too poor? or because they are too rich? or because they are both? We might be justified in thinking: because they are neither, but because they are what they are— religious, devoted to the Church and champions of Her cause. This reason is at least as good as the two that contradict and destroy each other. In this sense, is monastic poverty a bad and evil thing?

CHAPTER 42

THE VOW OF POVERTY

One objection to the vow of poverty that has a serious face on it, and certainly looks wicked, is that it does not prevent the accumulation of great wealth, as may be seen in the cases of the Philippine Friars and the French orders. This is one difficulty; here is another and quite different: the wealth of the religious is excessive, detrimental to the well-being of the people and a menace to the State. Taken separately, it is easy to dispose of these charges and to explain them away. But if you put them together in one loose, vague, general imputation of avarice, extortion and injustice, and hurl the same at a person unable to make distinctions, the shock is apt to disconcert him for a moment.

The first indictment seems to hint at a contradiction, or at least an incompatibility, between the profession of poverty and the fact of possessing wealth. We claim that the one does not affect the' other, that a religious may belong to a rich order and still keep his vow inviolate. The vow in the religious is individual and personal; the riches collective. It is the physical person that is poor; the moral being has the wealth. Men may club together, put their means into a common fund, renounce all personal claim thereto, live on a meagre revenue and employ the surplus for various purposes other than their needs. The personal poverty of such as these is real.

This is the case of the religious. Personally they do not own the clothes on their backs. The necessaries of life are furnished them out of a common fund. What remains, goes through their hands for the glory of God and in charity to fellow-man. The employment to which these men devote their lives, such as prayer, charity, the maintenance and conducting of schools and hospitals, is not lucrative to any great extent. And since very few Orders resort to begging, the revenue from capital is the only means of assuring existence. It is therefore no more repugnant for religious to depend on funded wealth than it was for the Apostolic College to have a common purse. The secret reason for this condition of things is that works of zeal rarely yield abundant returns, and man cannot live on the air of heaven.

As to the extent of such wealth and its dangers, it would seem that if it be neither ill gotten nor employed for illegitimate purposes, in justice and equity, there cannot be two opinions on the subject. Every human being has a right to the fruit of his industry and activity. To deny this is to advocate extreme socialism and anarchy and, he who puts this doctrine into practice, destroys the principle on which society rests. The law that strikes at religious corporations whose wealth accrues from centuries of toil and labor, may to-morrow consistently confiscate the goods and finances of every other corporation in the realm. If you force the religious out of land and home, why not force Morgan, Rockefeller & Co., out of theirs! The justice in one case is as good as in the other.

It is difficult to see how the people suffer from accumulated wealth, the revenues from which are almost entirely devoted to the relief of misery and the instruction of the ignorant. The people are the sole beneficiaries. There is here none of the arrogance and selfishness that usually characterize the possession of wealth to the embitterment of misery and misfortune. The religious, by their vow and their means, can share the condition of the poor and relieve it. If there is any institution better calculated to promote the well-being of the common people, it should be put to work. When the moneyed combinations whose rights are respected, show themselves as little prejudicial to the welfare of the classes, the religious will be prepared to go out of existence.

Everyone is inclined to accept as true the statement, on record as official, that the wealth of the Religious Orders in France is at the bottom of the trouble. We are not therefore a little astonished to learn from other sources that it is rather their poverty, which is burdensome to the people. The religious are not too rich, but too poor. They cannot support themselves, and live on the enforced charity of the laborer. French parents, not being equal to the task of maintaining monasteries and supporting large families, limited the number of their children. The population fell off in consequence. The government came to the relief of the people and cast out the religious.

And here we have the beautiful consistency of those who believe that any old reason is better than none at all. The religious are too poor, their poverty is a burden on the people; the religious are too rich, their riches are prejudicial to the welfare of the people. One reason is good; two are better. If they contradict, it is only a trifling matter. As for us, we don't know quite where we stand. We can hear well enough, amid the din of denunciation, the conclusion that the religious must go; but we cannot, for the life of us, catch the why and wherefore. Is it because they are too poor? or because they are too rich? or because they are both? We might be justified in thinking: because they are neither, but because they are what they are— religious, devoted to the Church and champions of Her cause. This reason is at least as good as the two that contradict and destroy each other. In this sense, is monastic poverty a bad and evil thing?

CHAPTER 43

THE VOW OF OBEDIENCE

What kind of obedience is that which makes religious "unwilling to acknowledge any superior but the Pope?" We have been confidently informed this is the ground given in several instances for their removal. And we confess that, if the words "acknowledge" and "superior" are used in certain of the meanings they undoubtedly have, there is good and sufficient ground for such removal. At the same time we submit that the foregoing phrase is open to different interpretations of meaning, several of which would make out this measure of repression to be one of rank injustice.

The studied misrule and abuse of language serves a detestable purpose that is only too evident. A charge like the above is true and false, that is to say, it is neither true nor false; it says nothing, unless explained, or unless you make it say what you wish. It is a sure, safe, but cowardly way of destroying an enemy without being obliged to admit the guilt to oneself.

Now the religious, and Catholic laity as well, never think of acknowledging, in the full acceptation of the word, any other spiritual superior than the Pope, and there can be nothing in this deserving repression. Again, no Catholic may consistently with Catholic principles, refuse to accept as legitimate the legally constituted authority of the country in which he resides. As to a man's views on the different forms of government, that is nobody's business but his own. But whether he approves or disapproves in theory, his life and conduct must conform with the laws justly enacted under the form of Government that happens to be accepted. To depart from this rule is to go counter to Catholic teaching, and no religious order does so without incurring strict censure.

The vow of obedience in a religious respects Caesar as well as God. It cannot validly bind one to violate the laws of State any more than to violate the law of God. This vow does not even concern itself with civil and political matters; by it the religious alone is affected, the citizen looks out for himself. But the citizen is already bound by his conscience and the laws of the Church to respect and obey lawful authority.

A good religious is a good citizen, and he cannot be the former, if he is not the latter. As a mere Catholic, he is more liable to be always found on the side of good citizenship, because in his religion he is taught, first of all, to respect authority on which all his religious convictions are based. There is a natural tendency in a Protestant, who will have nothing to do with authority in spiritual matters, to bring this state of mind over with him into temporary affairs; being self-willed in greater things, he is fore-inclined to be self-willed in lesser. The Catholic and, for a greater reason, the religious knows less of this temptation; and the better Catholic and religious he is, the farther removed he is from possible revolt against, or even disrespect of, authority.

Against but one Order of all those repressed can the charge of insubordination be brought with any show of truth. The Assumptionists made the mistake of thinking that they could with impunity criticise the doings of the Government, just as it is done in Paris every day by the boulevard press. It is generally conceded that, considering the well-known attitude of the Government towards the order, this was a highly imprudent course for a religious paper to pursue. But their right to do so is founded on the privilege of free speech. It takes very little to find abuse of free speech in the utterances of the clergy or religious in France. They are safe only when they are silent. If there were less docility and more defiance in their attitude, if the French Catholics relied less on God and more on man for redress, they would receive more justice than they have been receiving.

The punishment meted out to the religious for their insubordination has had, we are told, a doleful effect on the temporal power of the Pope, an interesting patch of which has been broken up by the new French law. It is a mystery to us how this law can affect the temporal power of the Pope any more than the political status of Timbuctoo. It is passably difficult to make an impression on what has ceased to exist these thirty years. We thought the temporal power was dead. This bit of news has been dinned into our ears until we have come to believe. No conference, synod or council is considered by our dissenting friends without a good strong sermon on this topic. Strange that it should resurrect just in time to lose "an interesting patch" of itself! This is cruelty. Why not respect the grave? We recommend the perusal of the obituary of the temporal power written in Italian politics since the year 1870. We believe the tomb is carefully guarded.

CHAPTER 44

THE VOW OF CHASTITY

Religious are sometimes called celibates. Now, a celibate, one of the bachelor persuasion, is a person who considers himself or herself good enough company in this life, and chooses single blessedness in preference to the not unmixed joys of wedlock. This alone is sufficient to make one a celibate, and nothing more is required. Religious do not wed; but, specifically, that is all there is in common between them. All celibates are not chaste; celibacy is not necessarily chastity, by a large majority. Unless something other than selfishness suggests this choice of life, the word is apt to be a misnomer for profligacy. And one who takes the vow of celibacy does not break it by sinning against the Sixth Commandment; he is true to it until he weds. The religious vow is something more than this.

Again, chastity, by itself, does not properly designate the state of religious men and women. Chastity is moral purity, but purity is a relative term, and admits of many degrees. It is perfect or imperfect. There is a conjugal chastity; while in single life, it may concern itself with the body, with or without reference to the mind and heart. Chastity reaches its highest form when it excludes everything carnal, what is lawful as well as what is unlawful, thoughts and desires as well as deeds.

This is the chastity that is proper to religious, and it is more correctly called virginity. This is the natural state of spirits who have no bodies; cultivated in the frail flesh of children of Adam, it is the most delicate flower imaginable. Considering the incessant struggle it supposes in those who take such a vow against the spirit within us that is so strong, the taking and keeping of it indicate a degree of fortitude little short of heroism. Only the few, and that few relying wholly on the grace of God, can aspire to this state.

From a spiritual point of view, there can be no question as to the superiority of this state of life over all others. The teaching of St. Paul to the Corinthians is too plain to need any comment, not to mention the example of Christ, His Blessed Mother, His disciples and all those who in the course of time have loved God best and served Him most generously.

Prescinding from all spiritual considerations and looking at things through purely human eyes, vows of this sort must appear prejudicial to the propagation of the species. In fact, they go against the law of nature which says: increase and multiply, so we are told.

If that law is natural as well as positive, it is certain that it applies to man collectively, and not individually. It is manifested only in the instinct that makes this duty a pleasure. Where the inclination is lacking, the obligation is not obvious. That which is repugnant is not natural, in any true sense of the word; whether this repugnance be of the intellectual or spiritual order, it matters not, for our nature is spiritual as truly as it is animal. The law of nature forces no man into a state that is not in harmony with his sympathies and affections.

Nevertheless, it must be admitted that to a certain extent the race suffers numerically from an institution that fosters abstention from marriage. To what extent, is an entirely different question. Not all laymen marry. It is safe to say that the vast majority of religious men, vow or no vow, would never wed; so that the vow is not really to blame for their state, and the consequences thereof. As for women, statistics show it to be impossible for all to marry since their number exceeds that of men.

Now, marriage with the fair sex, is very often a matter of competition. Talent, beauty, character, disposition and accomplishments play a very active role in the acquisition of a husband. Considering that the chances of those who seek refuge under the veil are not of the poorest, since they are the fairest and best endowed of our daughters, it would seem to follow that their act is a charity extended to their less fortunate sisters who are thereby aided to success, instead of being doomed to failure by the insufficiency of their own qualifications.

Be this as it may, what we most strenuously object to, is that vows be held responsible for the sins of others. In some countries and sections of countries, the population is almost stationary in marked contrast to that of others. Looking for the cause for this unnatural phenomenon, there are who see it in the spread of monasticism, with its vow of chastity. They fail to remark that not numerous, but large families are the best sign of vigor in a nation. Impurity, not chastity, is the enemy of the race. Instead of warring against those whose lives are pure, why not destroy that monster that is gnawing at the very vitals of the race, sapping its strength at the very font of life, that modern Moloch, to whom fashionable society offers sacrifice more abominable than the hecatombs of Carthage. This iniquity, rampant wherever the sense of God is absent, and none other, is the cause which some people do not see because they have good reasons for not wanting to see. It is very convenient to have someone handy to accuse of one's own faults. It is too bad that the now almost extinct race of Puritans did not have a few monks around to blame for the phenomenon of their failure to keep abreast of the race.

If celibacy, therefore, means untrammeled vice, and marriage degenerates into New Englandism, the world will get along better with less of both. Vows, if they have no other merit, respect at least the law of God, and this world is run according to that law.

SPEECH

CHAPTER 45

SWEARING

"Thou shalt not take the name of the Lord, thy God in vain."

A name is a sign, and respect for God Himself, as prescribed by the First Commandment through faith, hope, charity, prayer and religion, naturally implies respect for the name that stands for and signifies God. Your name may, of itself, be nothing more than mere sound; but used in relation to what it represents, it is as sacred, and means as much to you, as your very person, for whatever is addressed to your name, whether of praise or blame, is intended to reach, and does effectively reach, yourself, to your honor or dishonor. You exact therefore of men, as a right, the same respect for your name as for your person; and that is what God does in the Second Commandment.

The name of God represents all that He is. He who profanes that name profanes a sacred thing, and is guilty of what is, in reality, a sacrilege. To use it with respect and piety is an act of religion which honors God. Men use and abuse this holy name, and first of all, by swearing, that is, by taking oaths.

In the early history of mankind, we are told, swearing was unknown. Men were honest, could trust each other and take each other's word. But when duplicity, fraud and deception rose out of the corrupt heart of man, when sincerity disappeared, then confidence disappeared also, no man's word was any longer good. Then it was that, in order to put an end to their differences, they called upon God by name to witness the truth of what they affirmed. They substituted God's unquestioned veracity for their own questioned veracity, and incidentally paid homage to His truth; God went security for man. Necessity therefore made man swear; oaths became a substitute for honesty.

A reverent use of the name of God, for a lawful purpose, cannot be wrong; on the contrary, it is good, being a public recognition of the greatest of God's attributes—truth. But like all good things it is liable to be abused. A too frequent use of the oath will easily lead to irreverence, and thence to perjury. It is against this danger, rather than against the fact itself of swearing, that Christ warns us in a text that seems at first blush to condemn the oath as evil. The common sense of mankind has always given this interpretation to the words of Christ.

An oath, therefore, is a calling upon God to witness the truth of what we say, and it means that we put our veracity on a par with His and make Him shoulder the responsibility of truthfulness.

To take an oath we must swear by God. To swear by all

the saints in the calendar would not make an oath. Properly speaking, it is not even sufficient to simply say: "I swear," we must use the name of God. In this matter, we first consider the words. Do they signify a swearing, by God, either in their natural sense or in their general acceptation? Or is there an intention of giving them this signification? In conscience and before God, it is only when there is such an intention that there is a formal oath and one is held to the conditions and responsibilities thereof.

Bear in mind that we are here dealing for the moment solely with lawful swearing. There are such things as imprecation, blasphemy, and general profanity, of which there will be question later, and which have this in common with the oath, that they call on the name of God; the difference is the same that exists between bad and good, right and wrong. These must therefore be clearly distinguished from religious and legal swearing.

There is also a difference between a religious and a legal oath. The religious oath is content with searching the conscience in order to verify the sincerity or insincerity of the swearer. If one really intends to swear by God to a certain statement, and employs certain words to express his intention, he is considered religiously to have taken an oath. If he pronounces a formula that expresses an oath, without the intention of swearing, then he has sworn to nothing. He has certainly committed a sin, but there is no oath. Again, if a man does not believe in God, he cannot swear by Him; and in countries where God is repudiated, all attempts at administering oaths are vain and empty. You cannot call, to attest the truth of your words, a being that does not exist, and for him who does not believe in God, He does not exist.

The purely legal oath considers the fact and supposes the intention. If you swear without deliberation, then, with you lies the burden of proving it; since the law will allow it only on evidence and will hold you bound until such evidence is shown. When a person is engaged in a serious affair, he is charitably supposed to know what he is talking about; if it happens that he does not, then so much the worse for him. In the case of people who protest beforehand that they are infidels or agnostics, or who being sworn on the New Testament, disclaim all belief in Christ, there is nothing to be done, except it be to allow them to attest by the blood of a rooster or by the Great Horn Spoon. Then, whatever way they swear, there is no harm done.

CHAPTER 46

BLASPHEMY

To blaspheme is to speak ill of God; blasphemy is an utterance derogatory to the respect and honor due to God. Primarily, it is a sin of the tongue; but, like all other sins, it draws its malice from the heart. Thus, a thought may be blasphemous, even though the blasphemy remain unexpressed; and a gesture, oftentimes more expressive than a word, may contain all the malice of blasphemy. This impiety therefore may be committed in thought, in word and in deed.

Blasphemy addresses itself directly to God, to His attributes and perfections which are denied, or ridiculed; to Jesus Christ and the Blessed Sacrament; indirectly, through His Mother and His saints, through Holy Scripture and religion, through the Church and her ministers in their quality of ministers,—all of which, being intimately and inseparably connected with the idea of God, cannot be vilified without the honor of God being affected; and, consequently, all contempt and irreverence addressed to them, takes on the nature of blasphemy. An indirect sin of blasphemy is less enormous than a direct offense, but the difference is in degree, not in kind.

All error that affects God directly, or indirectly through sacred things, is blasphemy whether the error consist in a denial of what is true, or an attribution of what is false. Contempt, ridicule, scoffing and sneering, where are concerned the Holy and things holy, are blasphemous. He also blasphemes who attributes to a creature what belongs to God alone, or can be said only of holy things, who drags down the sacred to the level of the profane.

Revilings against God are happily rare; when met with, they are invariably the mouthings of self-styled atheists or infidels whose sanity is not always a patent fact. Heretics are usually blasphemous when they treat of anything outside Jesus Christ and the Bible; and not even Christ and Scripture escape, for often their ideas and utterances concerning both are as injurious to God as they are false and erroneous. Finally, despair and anger not infrequently find satisfaction in abusing God and all that pertains to Him.

Nothing more abominable can be conceived than this evil, since it attacks, and is in opposition to, God Himself. And nothing shows up its malice so much as the fact that blasphemy is the natural product and offspring of hate; it goes to the limit of human power in revolt against the Maker. It is, however, a consolation to know that, in the majority of cases, blasphemy is found where faith is wanting or responsibility absent, for it may charitably be taken for granted that if the blasphemer really knew what he was saying, he would rather cut out his tongue than repeat it. So true is it that the salvation of many depends almost as much on their own ignorance as on the grace of God.

There is a species of blasphemy, not without its degree of malice, found sometimes in people who are otherwise God-fearing and religious. When He visits them with affliction and adversity, their self-conscious righteousness goes out and seeks Comparison with prosperous ungodliness, and forthwith comments on strange fact of the deserving suffering while the undeserving are spared. They remark to themselves that the wicked always succeed, and entertain a strong suspicion that if they were as bad as others certain things would not happen.

All this smacks dangerously of revolt against the Providence of God. Job's problem is one that can be solved only by faith and a strong spiritual sense. He who has it not is liable to get on the wrong side in the discussion; and it is difficult to go very far on that side without finding Providence at fault and thus becoming guilty of blasphemy. For, to mention partiality in the same breath with God's care of the universe, is to deny Him.

The daily papers, a few years ago, gave public notoriety to two instances of blasphemy, and their very remarkable punishment, for it is impossible not to see the hand of God in what followed so close upon the offending. A desperate gambler called upon the Almighty to strike him dumb, if in the next deal a certain card turned up. It did turn up, and at the last accounts the man had not yet spoken. Another cast from his door a vendor of images and crucifixes with a curse and the remark that he would rather have the devil in his house than a crucifix. The very next day, he became the father of what came as near being the devil as anything the doctors of that vicinity ever saw. These are not Sunday-school stories invented to frighten children; the facts occurred, and were heralded broadcast throughout the land.

Despair urged the first unfortunate to defy the Almighty. In the other 'twas hatred for the Church that honors the image of Christ crucified as one honors the portrait of a mother. The blasphemy in the second case reached God as effectively as in the first, and the outrage contained in both is of an order that human language is incapable of qualifying.

CHAPTER 47

CURSING

To bless one is not merely to wish that one well, but also to invoke good fortune upon his head, to recommend him to the Giver of all goods. So, too, cursing, damning, imprecation, malediction—synonymous terms— is stronger than evil wishing and desiring. He who acts thus invokes a spirit of evil, asks God to visit His wrath upon the object cursed, to inflict death, damnation, or other ills. There is consequently in such language at least an implicit calling upon God, for the evil invoked is invoked of God, either directly or indirectly. And that is why the Second Commandment concerns itself with cursing.

Thus it will be seen that this abuse of language offends against religion and charity as well. To the malice of calling down evil upon a brother's head is added the impiety of calling upon God to do it, to curse when He should be prayed to bless.

Of course all depends on what is the object of our imprecations. One species of this vice contains blasphemy pure and simple, that is, a curse which attains something that refers to God in an especial manner, and as such is cursed. The idea of God cannot be separated from that of the soul, of faith, of the Church, etc. Malediction addressed to them reaches God, and contains all the malice of blasphemy.

When the malediction falls on creatures, without any reference to their relationship to God, we have cursing in its proper form with a special malice of its own. Directly, charity alone is violated, but charity has obligations which are binding under pain of mortal sin. No man can sin against himself or against his neighbor without offending God.

A curse may be, and frequently is, emphasized with a vow or an oath. One may solemnly promise God in certain contingencies that he will damn another to hell; or he may call upon God to witness his execrations. The malice of two specific sins is here accumulated, the offense is double in this one abominable utterance; nothing can be conceived more horrible, unless it be the indifferent frequency with which it is perpetrated.

The guilt incurred by those who thus curse and damn, leaving aside the scandal which is thereby nearly always given, is naturally measured by the degree of advertence possessed by such persons. Supposing full deliberation, to curse a fellow-man or self, if the evil invoked be of a serious nature, is a mortal sin.

Passion or habit may excuse, if the movement is what is called "a first movement," that is, a mechanical utterance without reflection or volition; also, if the habit has been retracted and is in process of reform. If neither damnation nor death nor infamy nor any major evil is invoked, the sin may be less grievous, but sin it always is. If the object anathematized is an animal, a thing, a vice, etc., there may be a slight sin or no sin at all. Some things deserved to be cursed. In damning others, there may be disorder enough to constitute a venial sin, without any greater malice.

Considering the case of a man who, far removed from human hearing, should discover too late, his forgetfulness to leave the way clear between a block and a fast-descending and ponderous ax, and, in a fit of acute discomfort and uncontrollable feeling consequential to such forgetfulness, should consign block, ax, and various objects in the immediate vicinity to the nethermost depths of Stygian darkness: in such a case, we do not think there would be sin.

On the other hand, they in whose favor such attenuating circumstances do not militate, do the office of the demons. These latter can do nothing but curse and heap maledictions upon all who do not share their lot. To damn is the office of the damned. It is therefore fitting that those who cease not to damn while on earth be condemned to damn eternally and be damned in the next life. And if it is true that "the mouth speaks out of the abundance of the heart," to what but to hell can be compared the inner soul of him whose delight consists in vomiting forth curses and imprecations upon his fellowmen?

CHAPTER 48

PROFANITY

Profanity is not a specific sin. Under this general head come all blasphemy, false, rash, unjust and unnecessary oaths, rash and violated vows, and cursing:—called profanity, because in each case the name of God is profaned, that is to say, is made less holy, by its application to unworthy objects and in unbecoming circumstances; profanity, because it has to do with the Holy Name, and not profanation, which looks to sacred things. Although language lends itself to many devices and is well nigh inexhaustible in its resources, this category of sins of profanity embraces about all modes of offending against the Holy Name, and consequently against the Second Commandment.

We have already examined the different species of profanity. But it is not always easy to classify certain utterances and expressions that savour of profanity, to determine the specific nature of their malice, especially the guilt incurred by the speaker. First of all, the terms used are often distorted from their original signification, or require that words left understood be supplied; as they stand, they are often as meaningless to the speaker as to the general uniniti- ated public. To get at the formal malice of such utterances is still more difficult, for it becomes necessary to interpret the intentions of the speaker. Thus, in one case, words that contain no evident insult to God may be used with all the vehemence of profanity, to which guilt is certainly attached; in another, the most unholy language may be employed in ignorance of its meaning, with no evil intent, the only danger of malice being from habit, passion or scandal.

This brings us to consider certain ejaculatory or exclama- tory expressions such as: God! good God! Lord! etc., employed by persons of very different spiritual complexion. Evidently, these words may be employed in good and in evil part; whether in one or the other, depends on the circum- stances of their using. They may proceed from piety and true devotion of the heart, out of the abundance of which the mouth speaks. Far from being wrong, this is positively good and meritorious.

If this is done through force of habit, or is the result of levity, without the least interior devotion or affection, it is a mitigated form of profanity. To say the least, no honor accrues to God from such language and such use of His name; and where He is concerned, not to honor Him is dangerously near dishonoring Him. If contempt of God or scandal result from such language, the offense may easily be mortal.

Finally, excited feelings of passion or wrath vent them- selves in this manner, and here it is still more easy to make it a grievous offending. About the only thing that can excuse from fault is absolute indeliberation.

Again, without implying any malediction, prescinding altogether from the supernatural character of what they represent, as ejaculations only, we come across the use of such words as hell, devil, damnation, etc. Good ethics condemn such terms in conversation; hearing them used people may be scandalized, especially the young; if one uses them with the mistaken idea that they contain blasphemy, then that one is formally guilty of blasphemy; finally, it is vulgar, coarse and unmannerly to do so. But all this being admitted, we do not see any more moral iniquity in the mention of these words than of their equivalents: eternal fire, Satan, perdition, etc. We do not advise or encourage the use of such terms, but it sometimes jars one's sense of propriety to see people hold up their hands in holy horror at the sound of these words, as if their mention were something unspeakably wicked, while they themselves would look fornication, for instance, straight in the face without a shudder or a blush.

Profanity is certainly a sin, sometimes a grievous sin; but in our humble opinion, the fiat of self-righteous Pharisaism to the contrary notwithstanding, it is a few hundred times oftener no sin at all, or a very white sin, than the awful crime some people see in it. If a fellow could quote classical "Mehercule," and Shakespearean cuss-words, he would not perhaps be so vulgar as to say "hell." But not having such language at his command, and being filled with strong feelings that clamor for a good substantial expression, if he looks around and finds these the strongest and only available ones, and uses them,—it is necessity and human nature, we wot, more than sacrilegious profanity. It were better if his speech were aye, aye and nay, nay; but it does not make it look any better to convict him of the blackest sin on the calendar just because he mentioned a place that really exists, if it is hot, and which it is well to have ever before our eyes against the temptations of life.

PART EIGHT

REST

CHAPTER 49

THE LAW OF REST

The last of the three Commandments that refer directly to God, prescribes a rest from toil, and profane works; and in commemoration of the mystical repose of the Lord after the six days' creation, designates the Sabbath or seventh day as a day that shall be set apart and made sacred to God. The peculiarity of the commandment is that it interferes with the occupations of man, intrudes upon his individual affairs and claims a worship of works. The others do not go thus far, and are satisfied with a worship of the heart and tongue, of affections and language.

Leaving aside for the moment the special designation of a day devoted to this worship, the law of rest itself deserves attention. Whether the Saturday or Sunday be observed, whether the rest be long or brief, a day or an hour, depends entirely on the positive will of God. More than this must be said of the command of rest; that law grows out of our relations with God, is founded in nature, is according to the natural order of things.

This repose means abstention from bodily activity.. The law does not go so far as to prescribe stagnation and sloth, but it is satisfied with such abstention as is compatible with the reasonable needs of man. Of its nature, it constitutes an exterior, public act of religion. The question is: Does the nature of our relations with God demand this sort of worship? Evidently, yes. Else God, who created the whole man, would not receive a perfect worship. If God made man, man belongs to Him; if from that possession flows a natural obligation to worship with heart and tongue, why not also of the body? God has a Maker's right over us, and without some acknowledgment on the part of the body of this right, there would be no evidence that such a right existed. There is no doubt but that the law of our being requires of us an interior worship. Now, if that spirit of homage within us is sincere, it will naturally seek to exteriorize itself; if it is to be preserved, it must "out." We are not here speaking of certain peculiarly ordered individuals, but of the bulk of common humanity. Experience teaches that what does not come out either never existed or is not assured of a prolonged existence. Just as the mind must go out of itself for the substance of its thoughts, so must the heart go out to get relief from the pressure of its feelings. God commanded this external worship because it alone could preserve internal affections.

Again, there are many things which the ordinary man ignores concerning God, which it is necessary for him to know, and which do not come by intuition. In other words, he must be taught a host of truths that he is incapable of finding out by himself. Education and instruction in religious matters are outside the sphere of his usual occupations. Where will he ever get this necessary information, if he is not taught? And how can he be taught, if he does not lay aside occupations that are incompatible with the acquisition of intellectual truths? He is therefore forced by the law of his being, and the obligation he owes his Maker, to rest from his every-day labors, once in awhile, in order to learn his full duty, if for nothing else.

Pagans, who never knew the law of Moses, serve neither Saturday nor Sunday; neither do they give an entire day, at fixed intervals to the exterior worship of the Deity, as we do. But a case will not be found where they did not on certain occasions rest from work in order to offer the homage of their fidelity to their gods, and to listen, to instruction and exhortation from their holy men. These pagans follow the natural law written in their souls, and it is there they discover the obligation they are under to honor God by rest from labor and to make holy unto Him a certain space of time.

CHAPTER 50

THE DAY OF REST

The third article of the Mosaic Code not only enunciates the law of rest, but says just how much time shall be given to its observance; it prescribes neither a week nor a few hours, but one day in seven. If you have a taste for such things and look well, you will find several reasons put forth as justifying this special designation of one day in seven. The number seven the Jews regarded as a sacred number; the Romans, as the symbol of perfection. Students of antiquity have discovered that among nearly all peoples this number in some way or other refers to the Deity. Science finds that nature prefers this number; light under analysis reveals seven colors, and all colors refer to the seven orders of the solar spectrum; the human voice has seven tones that constitute the scale of sound; the human body is renewed every seven years. Authorities on hygiene and physiology teach that one day in six is too much, one day in eight is too little, but that one day in seven is sufficient and necessary for the physical needs of man.

These considerations may or may not carry conviction to the average mind. On the face of it, they confirm rather than prove. They do not reveal the necessity of a day of rest so much as show its reasonableness and how it harmonizes with nature in its periodicity, its symmetry and its exact proportion to the strength of man. As for real substantial reasons, there is but one,—a good and sufficient,— and that is the positive will of God. He said: keep this day holy; such is His command; no man should need a better reason.

The God-given law of Moses says Saturday, Christians say Sunday. Protestants and Catholics alike say Sunday, and Sunday it is. But this is not a trifling change; it calls for an explanation. Why was it made? What is there to justify it? On what authority was it done? Can the will of God, unmistakably manifested, be thus disregarded and put aside by His creatures? This is a serious question.

One of the most interesting things in the world would be to hear a Protestant Christian, on Protestant grounds, justify his observance of the Sunday instead of the Sabbath, and give reasons for his conduct. "Search the Scriptures." Aye, search from Genesis to Revelations, the Mosaic prescriptions will hold good in spite of all your researches. Instead of justification you will find condemnation. "The Bible, the Bible alone" theory hardly fits in here. Are Papists the only ones to add to the holy writings, or to go counter to them? Suppose this change cannot be justified on Scriptural grounds, what then? And the fact is, it cannot.

It is hardly satisfactory to remark that this is a disciplinary injunction, and Christ abrogated the Jewish ceremonial. But if it is nothing more than this, how came it to get on the table of the Law? Its embodiment in the Decalogue makes it somewhat different from all other ceremonial prescriptions; as it stands, it is on a par with the veto to kill or to steal. Christ abolished the purely Jewish law, but he left the Decalogue intact.

Christ rose from the dead on Sunday, 'tis true; but nowhere in writing can it be found that His resurrection on that day meant a change in the Third Commandment. In the nature of the event, there is absolutely no relation between it and the observance of Sunday.

Where will our friend find a loop-hole to escape? Oh! as usual, for the Sunday as for the Bible, he will have to fall back on the old Church. What in the world could he do without her? He will find there an authority, and he is obliged to recognize it, even if he does on ordinary occasions declaim against and condemn it. Incidentally, if his eyes are open, he will discover that his individually interpreted Bible has failed most woefully to do its work; it condemns the Protestant Sunday.

This day was changed on the sole authority of the Holy Roman Catholic Church, as the representative of God on earth, to whose keeping was confided the interpretation of God's word, and in whose bosom is found that other criterion of truth, called tradition. Tradition it is that justifies the change she made. Deny this, and there is no justification possible, and you must go back to the Mosaic Sabbath. Admit it, and if you are a Protestant you will find yourself in somewhat of a mess.

A logical Protestant must be a very uneasy being. If the Church is right in this, why should she not be right in defining the Immaculate Conception? And if she errs here, what assurance is there that she does not err there? How can he say she is right on one occasion, and wrong on another? What kind of nonsense is it that makes her truthful or erring according to one's fancy and taste? Truly, the reformer blundered when he did not treat the Sunday as he treated the Pope and all Church authority, for it is papistical to a degree.

CHAPTER 51

KEEPING THE LORD'S DAY HOLY

The Third Commandment bids us sanctify the Lord's day; but in what that sanctification shall consist, it does not say. It is certain, however, that it is only by worship, of one kind or another, that the day can be properly kept holy to the Lord; and since interior worship is prescribed by the First Commandment, exterior and public worship must be what is called for. Then, there are many modes of worship; there is no end to the means man may devise of offering homage to the Creator.

The first element of worship is abstention from profane labor; rest is the first condition of keeping the Sabbath. The word Sabbath itself means cessation of work. You cannot do two things at the same time, you cannot serve God and Mammon. Our everyday occupations are not, of their nature, a public homage of fidelity to God. If any homage is to be offered, as a preliminary, work must cease. This interruption of the ordinary business of life alone makes it possible to enter seriously into the more important business of God's service, and in this sense it is a negative worship.

Yet, there is also something positive about it, for the simple fact of desisting from toil contains an element of direct homage. Six days are ours for ourselves. What accrues from our activity on those days is our profit. To God we sacrifice one day and all it might bring to us, we pay to Him a tithe of our time, labor and earnings. By directing aright our intentions, therefore, our rest assumes the higher dignity of explicit, emphatic religion and reverence, and in a fuller manner sanctifies the day that is the Lord's.

We should, however, guard ourselves against the mistaken notion that sloth and idleness are synonymous of rest. It is not all activity, but the ordinary activity of common life, that is forbidden. It were a sacrilegious mockery to make God the author of a law that fosters laziness and favors the sluggard. Another extreme that common sense condemns is that the physical man should suffer martyrdom while the soul thus communes with God, that promenades and recreation should be abolished, and social amenities ignored, that dryness, gloom, moroseness and severity are the proper conditions of Sabbatical observance.

In this respect, our Puritan ancestors were the true children of Pharisaism, and their Blue Laws more properly belong in the Talmud than in the Constitution of an American Commonwealth. God loves a cheerful giver, and would you not judge from appearances that religion was painful to these pious witch-burners and everything for God most grudgingly done? Sighs, grimaces, groans and wails, this is the homage the devils in hell offer to the justice of God; there is no more place for them in the religion of earth than in the religion of heaven.

Correlative with the obligation of rest is that of purely positive worship, and here is the difficulty of deciding just what is the correct thing in religious worship. The Jews had their institutions, but Christ abolished them. The Pagans had their way—sacrifice; Protestants have their preaching and hymn-singing. Catholics offer a Sacrifice, too, but an unbloody one. Later on, we shall hear the Church speak out on the subject. She exercised the right to change the day itself; she claims naturally the right to say how it should be observed, because the day belongs to her. And she will impose upon her children the obligation to attend mass. But here the precepts of the Church are out of the question.

The obligation, however, to participate in some act of worship is plain. The First Commandment charges every man to offer an exterior homage of one kind or another, at some time or another. The Third sets aside a day for the worship of the Divinity. Thus the general command of the first precept is specified. This is the time, or there is no time. With the Third Commandment before him, man cannot arbitrarily choose for himself the time for his worship, he must do it on Sunday.

Public worship being established in all Christian communities, every Christian who cannot improve upon what is offered and who is convinced that a certain mode of worship is the best and true, is bound by the law to participate therein. The obligation may be greater if he ignores the principles of religion and cannot get information and instruction outside the temple of religion. For Catholics, there is only one true mode of public worship, and that is the Sacrifice of the Mass. No layman is sufficient unto himself to provide such an act of religion. He has, therefore, no choice, he must assist at that sacrifice if he would fulfil the obligation he is under of Sunday worship.

CHAPTER 52

WORSHIP OF SACRIFICE

W e Catholics contend, and our contention is based on a law of nature that we glean from the history of man, that sacrifice is the soul of religion, that there never was a universally and permanently accepted religion—and that there cannot be any such religion —without an altar, a victim, a priest, and a sacrifice. We claim that reason and experience would bear us out in this contention, even without the example and teaching and express commands of Jesus Christ, who, in founding a new and the only true religion, Himself offered sacrifice and left a sacrifice to be perpetually offered in His religion; and that sacrifice constitutes the high worship we owe to the Creator.

It is our conviction that, when man came into the presence of the Almighty, his first impulse was to speak to Him, and his first word was an act of adoration. But human language is a feeble medium of communication with the Almighty. Man talks to man. To talk with God, he sought out another language; and, as in the case of Adam's sons, he discovered in sacrifice a better and stronger mode of expressing his religious feelings. He therefore offered sacrifice, and sacrifice became the language of man in his relations with the Deity.

In its simplest definition, sacrifice is the offering to God of a victim, by one authorized for that task. It supposes essentially the destruction of the victim; and the act is an eloquent acknowledgment, in language that is as plain as it possibly can be made, that God is the supreme Lord of life and death, that all things that exist come from Him, and revert to Him as to their natural end.

The philosophy of sacrifice is that man, in some manner or other, had incurred the wrath of the Almighty. The pagan could not tell hi just what his offense consisted; but there is nothing plainer than the fact that he considered himself under the ban of God's displeasure, and that sin had something to do with it; and he feared the Deity accordingly. We know that original sin was the curse under which he labored.

Whatever the offense was, it was in the flesh, the result of weakness rather than malice. There was something in his nature that inclined to evil and was responsible for sin. The better part tried to serve, but the inferior man revolted. Flesh, therefore, was wicked and sinful; and since all offense must be atoned for, the flesh should pay the penalty of evil. The wrath of God could be appeased, and sacrifice was the thing that could do it.

Another thing most remarkable among those who worshiped by sacrifice in the early times, is that they believed firmly in the reversibility of merit, that is, that the innocent could atone for the wicked. Somehow, they acquired the notion that stainless victims were more agreeable to God than others. God sanctioned this belief among the Jews, and most strikingly on the hill of Calvary.

This being the case, man being guilty and not having the right to inflict the supreme penalty upon himself, the natural thing to do was to substitute a victim for himself, to put the flesh of another in the place of his own and to visit upon it the punishment that was due to himself. And he offered to God this vicarious atonement. His action spoke in this wise: "My God, I am a sinner and deserve Thy wrath. But look upon this victim as though it were myself. My sins and offenses I lay upon its shoulders, this knife shall be the bolt of Thy vengeance, and it shall make atonement in blood." This is the language of sacrifice. As we have said, it supposes the necessity of atonement and belief in the reversibility of merit.

Now, if we find in history, as we certainly do find,—that all peoples offered sacrifice of this kind, we do not think we would be far from the truth if we deduced therefrom a law of nature; and if it is a law of nature, it is a law of God. If there is no religion of antiquity that did not offer sacrifice, then it would seem that the Almighty had traced a path along which man naturally trod and which his natural instinct showed him.

We believe in the axiom of St. Augustine: "securus judicet orbis terrarum, a universally accepted judgment can be safely followed." Especially do we feel secure with the history of the chosen people of God before us arid its sacrifice ordained by the law; with the sanction of Christ's sacrifice in our mind, and the practice of the divinely inspired Church which makes sacrifice the soul of her worship.

The victim we have is Jesus Christ Himself, and none other than He. He gave us His flesh and blood to consume, with the command to consume. Our sacrifice, therefore, consists in the offering up of this Victim to God and the consuming of it. Upon the Victim of the altar, as upon the Victim of the Cross, we lay our sins and offenses, and, in one case as in the other, the sacred blood, in God's eyes, washes our iniquity away.

Of course, it requires faith to believe, but religion is nothing if it is not whole and entire a matter of faith. The less faith you have, the more you try to simplify matters. Waning faith began by eliminating authority and sacrifice and the unwritten word. Now the written word is going the same way. Pretty soon we shall hear of the Decalogue's being subjected to this same eliminating process. After all, when one gets started in that direction, what reason is there that he should ever stop!

CHAPTER 53

WORSHIP OF REST

Participation in public worship is the positive obligation flowing from the Third Commandment; abstention from labor is what is negatively enjoined. Now, works differ as widely in their nature as differ in form and dimension the pebbles on the sea-shore. There are works of God and works of the devil, and works which, as regards spirituality, are totally indifferent, profane works, as distinguished from sacred and sinful works. And these latter may be corporal or intellectual or both. Work or labor or toil, in itself, is a spending of energy, an exercise of activity; it covers a deal of ground. And since the law simply says to abstain from work, it falls to us to determine just what works are meant, for it is certain that all works, that is, all that come under the general head of work, do not profane the Lord's day.

The legislation of the Church, which is the custodian of the Sunday, on this head commends itself to all thoughtful men; while, for those who recognize the Church as the true one, that legislation is authority. The Church distinguishes three kinds of profane works, that is, works that are neither sacred nor iniquitous of their nature. There is one kind which requires labor of the mind rather than of the body. These works tend directly to the culture or exercise of the mind, and are called liberal works, because under the Romans, freemen or "liberi" almost exclusively were engaged therein. Such are reading, writing, studying, music, drawing —in general, mental occupations in whole, or more mental than corporal. These works the Church does not consider the law includes in its prohibition, and they are consequently not forbidden.

It is impossible here to enumerate all that enters into this class of works; custom has something to say in determining what is liberal in our works; and in investigating, we must apply to each case the general principle. The labor in question may be gratuitous or well paid; it may cause fatigue or afford recreation: all this is not to the point. The question is, outside the danger of omitting divine service, scandal or circumstances that might lead to the annoyances and distraction of others—the question is: does this work call for exercise of the mind more than that of the body? If the answer is affirmative, then the work is liberal, and as such it is not forbidden on Sunday, it is not considered a profanation of the Lord's day.

On the other extreme are what go by the name of servile works, which call forth principally bodily effort and tend directly to the advantage of the body. They are known also as works of manual labor. Before the days of Christianity, slaves alone were thus employed, and from the word "servi" or slaves these are called servile works.

Here again it is the nature of the work that makes it servile. It may be remunerative or not, recreative or not, fatiguing or not; it may be a regular occupation, or just taken up for the moment; it may be, outside cases of necessity, for the glory of God or for the good of the neighbor. If it is true that the body has more part therein than the mind, then it is a servile work and it is forbidden. Of course there are serious reasons that dispense us from our obligation to this law, but we are not talking about that just at present.

The reason of the proscription is, not that such works are evil, but that they interfere with the intention we should give to the worship we owe to God, and that, without this cessation of labor, our bodily health would be impaired: these are the two motives of the law. But even if it happened, in an individual case, that these inconveniences were removed, that neither God's reverence nor one's own health suffered from such occupations as the law condemns, the obligation would still remain to abstain therefrom, for it is general and absolute, and when there is question of obeying a law, the subject has a right to examine the law, but not the motives of the law.

We shall later see that there are other works, called common, which require activity of the mind and of the body in about an equal measure or which enter into the common necessities of life. These are not forbidden in themselves, although in certain contingencies they may be adjudged unlawful; but, in the matter of servile works, nothing but necessity, the greater glory of God, or the good of the neighbor, can allow us to consider the law non-binding. To break it is a sin, slight or grievous, according to the nature of the offense.

CHAPTER 54

SERVILE WORKS

B ut, if servile works are prohibited on the Lord's day, it must be remembered that "the Sabbath was made for man, and not man for the Sabbath," that, for certain good and sufficient reasons, the law ceases to oblige; and, in these circumstances, works of a purely servile nature are no longer unlawful. This is a truth Christ made very clear to the straight-laced Pharisees of the old dispensation who interpreted too rigorously the divine prohibition; and certain Pharisees of the new dispensation, who are supposed assiduously to read the Bible, should jog their memories on the point in order to save themselves from the ridicule that surrounds the memory of their ancestors of Blue-Law fame. The Church enters into the spirit of her divine Founder and recognizes cases in which labor on Sunday may be, and is, more agreeable to God, and more meritorious to ourselves, than rest from labor.

The law certainly does not intend to forbid a kind of works, specifically servile in themselves, connected with divine worship, required by the necessities of public religion, or needed to give to that worship all the solemnity and pomp which it deserves; provided, of course, such things could not well be done on another day. All God's laws are for His greater glory, and to assert that works necessary for the honoring of God are forbidden by His law is to be guilty of a contradiction in terms. All things therefore needed for the preparation and becoming celebration of the rites of religion, even though of a servile nature, are lawful and do not come under the head of this prohibition.

The law ceases likewise to bind when its observance would prevent an act of charity towards the neighbor in distress, necessity, or pressing need. If the necessity is real and true charity demands it, in matters not what work, not intrinsically evil, is to be done, on what day or for how long a time it is to be done; charity overrides every law, for it is itself the first law of God. Thus, if the neighbor is in danger of suffering, or actually suffers, any injury, damage or ill, God requires that we give our services to that neighbor rather than to Himself. As a matter of fact, in thus serving the neighbor, we serve God in the best possible way.

Finally, necessity, public as well as personal, dispenses from obligation to the law. In time of war, all things required for its carrying on are licit. It is lawful to fight the elements when they threaten destruction, to save crops in an interval of fine weather when delay would mean a risk; to cater to public conveniences which custom adjudges necessary,—and by custom we mean that which has at least the implicit sanction of authority,—such as public conveyances, pharmacies, hotels, etc. Certain industries run by steam power require that their fires should not be put out altogether, and the labor necessary to keep them going is not considered illicit. In general, all servile work that is necessary to insure against serious loss is lawful.

As for the individual, it is easier to allow him to toil on Sunday, that is, a less serious reason is required, if he assists at divine worship, than in the contrary event. One can be justified in omitting both obligations only in the event of inability otherwise to provide for self and family. He whose occupation demands Sunday labor need not consider himself guilty so long as he is unable to secure a position with something like the same emoluments; but it is his duty to regret the necessity that prevents him from fulfiling the law, and to make efforts to better his condition from a spiritual point of view, even if the change does not to any appreciable extent better it financially; a pursuit equally available should be preferred. Neglect in seeking out such an amelioration of situation would cause the necessity of it to cease and make the delinquent responsible for habitual breach of the law.

If it is always a sin to engage without necessity in servile works on Sunday, it is not equally sinful to labor little or labor much. Common sense tells us that all our failings are not in the same measure offensive to God, for they do not all contain the same amount of malice and contempt of authority. A person who resolves to break the law and persists in working all day long, is of a certainty more guilty than he who after attending divine service fails so far as to labor an hour. The question therefore is, how long must one work on Sunday to be guilty of a mortal sin.

The answer to this question is: a notable time; but that

does not throw a very great abundance of light on the subject. But surely a fourth of the whole is a notable part. Now, considering that a day's work is, not twenty-four hours, but ten hours, very rarely twelve, frequently only eight, it will be seen to follow that two hours' work would be considered a notable breach of the law of rest. And this is the decision of competent authority. Not but that less might make us grievously guilty, but we may take it as certain that he who works during two full hours, at a labor considered servile, without sufficient reason, commits a mortal sin.

CHAPTER 55

COMMON WORKS

There is a third sort of works to be considered in relation to Sunday observance, which, being of their nature neither liberal nor servile, go by the specific name of common works. This class embraces works of two kinds, viz., those which enter into the common, daily, inevitable necessities of life, and those in which the mind and body are exerted in an equal measure.

The former are not considered servile because they are necessary, not in certain circumstances, but at all times, for all persons, in all conditions of life. Activity of this kind, so universally and imperiously demanded, does not require dispensation from the law, as in the case of necessary servile works properly so-called; but it stands outside all legislation and is a law unto itself.

These works are usually domestic occupations, as cooking and the preparation of victuals, the keeping of the house in becoming tidiness, the proper care of children, of beasts of burden and domestic animals. People must eat, the body must be fed, life requires attention on Sunday as well as on the other six days; and in no circumstances can this labor be dispensed with. Sometimes eatables for Sunday consumption may be prepared on the previous day; if this is not done, whether through forgetfulness, neglect or indifference, it is lawful on Sunday to prepare a good table, even one more sumptuous than on ordinary days. For Sunday is a day of festival, and without enthusing over the fact, we must concede that the words feast and festival are synonymous in human language, that the ordinary and favorite place for human rejoicing is the table, and in this man differs not from the other animals of creation. This may not be aesthetic but it is true.

In walking, riding, games, etc., the physical and mental forces of man are called into play in about equal proportion, or at least, these occupations can be called neither liberal arts nor manual labor; all manners of persons engage therein without respect to condition or profession. These are also called common works; and to them may be added hunting and fishing, when custom, rightly understood, does not forbid them, and in this region custom most uniformly does so forbid.

These occupations are looked upon as innocent pastime, affording relief to the body and mind, and in this respect should be likened to the taking of food. For it is certain that sanitary conditions often as imperiously demand recreation as nourishment. Especially is this the case with persons given to sedentary pursuits, confined during the week to shops, factories and stores, and whose only opportunity this is to shake off the dull monotony of work and to give the bodies and minds necessary relaxation and distraction. It is not physical rest that such people require so much as healthy movement of a pleasing kind, and activity that will draw their attention from habitual channels and thus break the strain that fatigues them. Under these conditions, common works are not only allowed, but they are to be encouraged.

But it must not be lost sight of that these pursuits are permitted as long as they remain common works, that is, as long as they do not accidentally become servile works, or go contrary to the end for which they are allowed. This may occur in three different manners, and when it does occur, the works known as common are forbidden as servile works.

1. They must not expose us to the danger of omitting divine service. The obligation to positively sanctify the day remains intact. Sin may be committed, slight or grievous, according as the danger to which we expose ourselves, by indulging in these pursuits, of missing public worship, is more or less remote, more or less probable.

2. These works become illicit when they are excessive, when too much time is given to them, when the body receives too large a share of the exercise, when accompanied by overmuch application, show or fatigue. In these cases, the purpose of the law is defeated, the works are considered no longer common and fall under the veto that affects servile works. An aggravating circumstance is that of working for the sole purpose of gain, as in the case of professional baseball, etc.

3. Lastly, there are exterior circumstances that make these occupations a desecration of the Lord's day, and as such evidently they cannot be tolerated. They must not be bois-

terous to the extent of disturbing the neighbor's rest and quiet, or detracting from the reverence due the Sabbath; they must not entice others away from a respectful observance of the Lord's day or offer an opportunity or occasion for sin, cursing, blasphemy and foul language, contention and drunkenness; they must not be a scandal for the community. Outside these contingencies of disorder, the Sabbath rest is not broken by indulgence in works classified as common works. Such activity, in all common sense and reason, is compatible with the reverence that God claims as His due on His day.

PART NINE

PARENTING

CHAPTER 56

PARENTAL DIGNITY

We have done with the three commandments that refer directly to God. The second Table of the Law contains seven precepts that concern themselves with our relations to God, indirectly, through the creature; they treat of our duties and obligations toward the neighbor. As God may be honored, so He may be dishonored, through the works of His hand; one may offend as effectively by disregard for the law that binds us to God's creatures as for that which binds us to the Creator Himself.

Since parents are those of God's creatures that stand nearest to us, the Fourth Commandment immediately orders us to honor them as the authors of our being and the representatives of divine authority, and it prescribes the homage we owe them in their capacity of parents. But that which applies to fathers and mothers, applies in a certain degree to all who have any right or authority to command; consequently, this law also regulates the duties of superiors and inferiors in general to one another.

The honor we owe to our parents consists in four things: respect for their dignity, love for their beneficence, obedience to their authority and assistance in their needs. Whoever fails in one of these requirements, breaks the law, offends God and sins. His sin may be mortal, if the quality of the offense and the malice of the offender be such as to constitute I serious breach of the law.

'Tis the great fault of our age to underrate parental dignity. In the easy-going world, preference is given to profligate celibacy over honorable wedlock; marriage itself is degraded to the level of a purely natural contract, its bond has lost its character of indissolubility and its obligations are shirked to meet the demands of fashion and convenience. When parents, unworthy ones, do not appreciate their own dignity, how will others, their children, appreciate it? And parenthood will never be esteemed while its true nature and sanctity are ignored and contemned; there is no dignity where the idea of God is excluded.

After God had created man, He left him to work out his destiny in a natural way; and immediately man assumed towards his offspring the relation that God first held towards himself—he assumed the prerogatives of paternity and of authority. All paternity belongs to God, and to Him alone; yet man is delegated to that lofty, quasi-divine function. God alone can create; yet so near does the parental office approach to the power of creation that we call it pro-creation.

Tis true, this privilege man holds in common with the rest of animated nature, but with this difference: that the fruit of his loins is a child of God, with an immortal soul, an heir to heaven where its destiny is to glorify the Eternal during all eternity. And thus, man, in his function of parent, is as far differentiated from the rest of animal nature as the act by which God created man is superior to all His other creative acts.

If the tempter, when working out his plan for the fall of our first parents, had simply and unconditionally said: "Ye shall be as gods," his utterance would have in it more truth than he intended, for the mantle of parenthood that was soon to fall upon them made them like unto God. The children that romped around them, looked up to them even, almost, as they were accustomed to look up to the Creator. And little the wonder, since to their parents they owed their very existence.

As depositaries of authority, there is no human station, however exalted, comparable to theirs. Children are not merely subjects, they belong to their parents. Church and State, under God, may see to it that that authority is not abused; but within the bounds of right, they are held to respect it; and their acts that go contrary to the exercise of parental authority are, by the fact of such opposition, null and void. Before the State or Church, the family was; its natural rights transcend theirs, and this bowing, as it were, of all constituted human authority before the dominion of parents is evidence enough of their dignity.

"God could not be everywhere, therefore he made parents—fathers and mothers"—that is how the pagans used to put it. However theologically unsound this proposition may appear, it is a beautiful attempt at a great truth, viz., that parents towards us stand in God's stead. In consequence of this eminent dignity that is theirs, they deserve our respect. They not only deserve it, but God so ordains it.

CHAPTER 57

FILIAL RESPECT

Worthy of honor are they whom the Lord sees fit to honor. In the exalted station to which they have been called and in the express command made by the Lord to honor them, we see evidence of the dignity of parents; and the honor we owe them for this dignity is the honor of respect. By respect, we mean the recognition of their superiority, the reverence, veneration and awe all well-born men instinctively feel for natural worth that transcends their own, the deference in tone, manner and deportment that naturally belongs to such worth.

It is much easier to say in what respect does not consist than to define the term itself. If it really exists in the heart—and there it must exist, to be at all—it will find expression in a thousand different ways, and will never be at a loss to express itself. Books will give you the laws of etiquette and will tell you how to be polite; but the laws that govern respect are graven on the heart, and he whose heart is in the right place never fails to read and interpret them correctly. Towards all, at all times and in all places, he will conform the details of his life with the suggestions of his inner consciousness—this is respect.

Respect has no substitute; neither assistance nor obedience nor love can supply it or take its place It may happen that children are no longer obliged to help their parents; they may be justified in not obeying them; the circumstances may be such that they no longer have love or affection for them; but respect can never be wanting without serious guilt. The reason is simple: because it is due in justice, because it is founded on natural rights that can never be forfeited, even when parents themselves lose the sense of their own dignity.

Sinful, wicked and scandalous parents there have been, are, and will be. But just as they do not owe the excellence to any deed of their own, but to the free choice of the Almighty, so it depends not on themselves to forfeit it. God made them parents without respect for their personal worth. He is the custodian of their dignity. Good or bad, they are parents and remain parents. Woe unto those who despise the authors of their days!

Respect overlooks an innocent joke at the expense of a parent, when absolutely no malice is intended, when on both sides it is looked upon as a matter of good-natured pleasantry. It brooks humor. Not all familiarity breeds contempt.

But contempt, which is directly opposed to respect, is a sin that is never anything but mortal. It refuses honor, belittles dignity and considers parents beneath esteem. It is contempt to laugh at, to mock, to gibe and insult parents; it is contempt to call them vile, opprobrious names, to tell of their faults; it is contempt, and the height of contempt, to defy them, to curse them or to strike them. It is bad enough when this sort of thing is directed against an equal; but when parents are made the objects of contempt, it acquires a dignity that is infernal.

The malediction of Heaven, the almighty wrath of God follows him or her who despises a parent. We are repeatedly told in Holy Writ that such offenders "shall die the death." Scorn of parents is looked upon as a crime almost on a par with hatred of God. Pagans frequently punished it with death. Among Christians it is left to the avenging wrath of God who is pledged to defend the dignity of His delegated paternity.

It is not a rare occurrence to see just retribution visited upon parents who in their day were undutiful, unworthy and unnatural children. The justice of Heaven often permits it to be done unto us as we do unto others. Our children will treat us as we shall have treated our parents; their hands will be raised against us and will smite us on the cheek to avenge the grandsire's dishonor and tears, and to make us atone in shame for our sins against our parents. If we respect others, they will respect us; if we respect our parents, our children will respect us.

CHAPTER 58

FILIAL LOVE

He who has a heart, and has it properly located, will not fail to love that which is good; he will have no difficulty in so doing, it will require neither command nor persuasion to make him do so. If he proves refractory to this law of nature, it is because he is not like the rest of mortals, because he is inhuman; and his abnormal condition is due, not to nature's mistakes, but to his own. And no consideration under heaven will be equal to the task of instilling affection into a stone or a chunk of putty.

That is good which is desirable, or which is the source of what is desirable. God alone is absolutely good, that is to say, good in Himself and the cause of all good. Created things are good in the proportion of their furnishing us with things desirable, and are for that reason called relatively good. They confer benefits on one and not perhaps on another. When I· say: this or that is good, I mean that it is useful to me, and is productive of comfort, happiness and other desirable things.

Because we are naturally selfish, our appreciation of what is good depends on what we get out of it.

Therefore, it is that a child's first, best and strongest love should be for its parents, for the greatest good it enjoys, the thing of all others to be desired, the essential condition of all else, namely its existence, it owes to its parents. Life is the boon we receive from them; not only the giving, but the saving in more than one instance, the fostering and preserving and sustaining during long years of helplessness, and the adorning of it with all the advantages we possess. Nor does this take into account the intimate cost, the sufferings and labors, the cares and anxieties, the trouble and worriment that are the lot of devoted parenthood. It is life spent and given for life. Flesh and blood, substance, health and comfort, strength of body and peace of soul, lavished with unstinted generosity out of the fulness of parental affection—these are things that can never be repaid in kind, they are repaid with the coin of filial piety and love, or they remain dead debts.

Failure to meet these obligations brands one a reprobate. There is not, in all creation, bird or beast, but feels and shows instinctive affection towards those to whom it owes its being. He, therefore, who closes his heart to the promptings of filial love, has the consolation of knowing that, not only he does not belong to the order of human beings, but he places himself outside the pale of animal nature itself, and exists in a world of his own creation, which no human language is able to properly qualify.

The love we owe to our parents is next in quality to that which we owe to God and to ourselves. Love has a way of identifying its object and its subject; the lover and the beloved become one, their interests are common, their purpose alike. The dutiful child, therefore, looks upon its parent as another self, and remains indifferent to nothing that for weal or for woe affects that parent. Love consists in this community of feeling, concern and interest. When the demon of selfishness drives gratitude out of the heart and the ties of natural sympathy become strained, and love begins to wane; when they are snapped asunder, love is dead.

The love of God, of course, primes all other love. "He who loves father or mother more than me," says the Saviour, "is not worthy of me." Filial love, therefore, must not conflict with that which we owe to God; it must yield, for it draws its force from the latter and has no meaning without it. In normal conditions, this conflict never occurs; it can occur only in the event of parents overriding the law that governs their station in life. To make divine love wait on the human is criminal.

It may, and no doubt does, happen that parents become unlovable beings through disregard for the moral law. And because love is not a commodity that is made to order, children may be found who justify on these grounds their absence of affection or even their positive hatred for such parents. A drunken parent, one who attacks the life, virtue or reputation of his offspring, a low brute who has neither honor nor affection, and whose office it is to make home a living hell, such a one can hardly be loved.

But pity is a form of love; and just as we may never despise a fallen parent, just so do we owe him or her, even in the depths of his or her degradation, a meed of pity and commiseration. There is no erring soul but may be reclaimed; every soul is worth the price of its redemption, and there is no unfortunate, be he ever so low, but deserves, for the sake of his soul, a tribute of sympathy and a prayer for his betterment. And the child that refuses this, however just the cause of his aversion, offends against the law of nature, of charity and of God.

CHAPTER 59

AUTHORITY AND OBEDIENCE

Authority means the right to command; to command is to exact obedience, and obedience is submission of one's will to that of another, will is a faculty that adores its own independence, is ambitious of rule and dominion, and can hardly bear to serve. It is made free, and may not bend; it is proud, and hates to bend; some will add, it is the dominant faculty in man, and therefore should not bend.

Every man for himself; we are born free; all men are equal, and no one has the right to impose his will upon another; we are directly responsible to God, and "go-betweens" are repudiated by the common sense of mankind, —this is good Protestant theory and it is most convenient and acceptable to the unregenerate heart of man. We naturally like that kind of talk; it appeals to us instinctively. It is a theory that possesses many merits besides that of being true in a sense in which only one takes it out of fifty who advocate it.

But these advocates are careful—and the reason of their solicitude is anything but clear—to keep within the religious lines, and they never dare to carry their theory into the domain of political society; their hard common sense forbids. And they are likewise careful to prevent their children from practicing the doctrine within the realm of paternal authority, that is, if they have any children. Society calls it anarchy, and parents call it "unnatural cussedness;" in religion it is "freedom of the children of God!"

If there is authority, there must be obedience; if one has the right to command, there arises in others the correlative duty and obligation to submit. There is no question of how this will suit us; it simply does not, and will not, suit us; it is hard, painful and humiliating, but it is a fact, and that is sufficient.

Likewise, it is a fact that if authority was ever given by God to man, it was given to the parent; all men, Protestants and anarchists alike, admit this. The social being and the religious being may reject and repudiate all law, but the child is subject to its parents, it must obey. Failing in this, it sins.

Disobedience is always a sin, if it is disobedience, that is, a refusal to submit in things that are just, to the express command of paternal authority. The sin may be slight or grievous, the quality of its malice depending on the character of the refusal, of the things commanded and of the command itself. In order that the offense may be mortal, the refusal must be deliberate, containing an element of contempt, as all malicious disobedience does. The command must be express, peremptory, absolute. And nothing must be commanded done that may not reasonably be accomplished or is not within the sphere of parental jurisdiction or is contrary to the law of God.

An order that is unreasonable or unlawful is invalid. Not only it may, but it should be, disregarded. It is not sufficient for a parent, wishing to oblige under pain of grievous sin, that he ask a thing done, that he express his mind on the matter; he must order it and leave no room to doubt that he means what he says. There may be disobedience without this peremptoriness of command, but it cannot be a serious fault. It is well also to make certain allowance for the levity and thoughtlessness of youth, especially in matters whose importance is beyond their comprehension.

It is generally admitted that parental authority, exercised in things that concern good morals and the salvation of the soul, can scarcely ever be ignored without mortal offending. This means that besides the sin committed—if the prohibition touches matters of sin—there is a sin specifically different and a grievous one, of disobedience; by reason of the parental prohibition, there are two sins, instead of one. This should be remembered by those who, against the express command of their parents, frequent bad companions, remain on the street at night, neglect their religious duty, etc.

Parents have nothing to say in the choice their children make of a state in life, that is, they may suggest, but must not coerce. This is a matter that depends on personal tastes and the inner voicings of the spirit; having come to the age of manhood or womanhood, the party interested knows best what walk of life will make him or her happy and salvation easier. It is therefore for them to choose, and their choice must be respected. In this they are not bound to obey the will of their parents, and if disinclined to do so, should not.

CHAPTER 60

SHOULD WE HELP OUR PARENTS?

There are few things more evident to natural reason than the obligation children are under to assist their parents when necessity knocks at their door, and finding them unable to meet its harsh demands, presses them with the goad of misery and want. Old age is weak and has to lean on strength and youth for support; like childhood, it is helpless. Accidentally, misfortune may render a parent dependent and needy. In such contingencies, it is not for neighbors, friends or relatives to come in and lend a helping hand; this duty devolves on the offspring, on them first and on them alone.

Charity is not alone to prescribe this office of piety. A stronger law than charity has a claim in the matter, and that is the law of justice. Justice demands a "quid pro quo," it exacts a just compensation for services rendered. Even though there be no agreement between parents and offspring, and the former gave without a thought of return, nature records a contract, by the terms of which parents in want are entitled to the same support from their children as the latter received from them in the days of their helplessness.

Those who do not live up to the terms of this natural contract stand amenable to the justice of Heaven. The obligation follows them during life, wherever they go; and they can no more shirk it than they can efface the characters that declare it, graven on their hearts. Nothing but sheer impossibility can dispense them.

So sacred and inviolable is this obligation that it passes before that of assisting wife and children, the necessity being equal; for filial obligations enjoy the distinction of priority. Not even engagements contracted before God hold against the duty of relieving parental distress and want, for vows are of counsel and must yield to the dictates of natural and divine law.

Of course, the gravity of this obligation is proportionate to the stress of necessity under which parents labor. To constitute a mortal sin of neglect, it is not necessary that a parent be in the extreme of privation and beggary. It is not easy to draw the line between slight and grievous offending in this matter, but if some young men and women examined their conscience as carefully as they do their new spring suits and hats, they would find material for confession the avowal of which might be necessary to confessional integrity.

It has become the fashion with certain of the rising generation, after draining the family exchequer for some sixteen or eighteen years, to emancipate themselves as soon as their wages cover the cost of living, with a little surplus. They pay their board, that is to say, they stand towards their parents as a stranger would, and forgetting the debt their younger years have piled up against them, they hand over a miserable pittance just enough to cover the expenses of bed and board. This might, and possibly does, make them "feel big," but that feeling is a false one, and the "bigness" experienced is certainly not in their moral worth, in many cases such conduct is a prevarication against the law of God. This applies with equal force to young women whose vanity over-rides the claims of charity and justice, and who are said to "put all their earnings on their backs," while they eat the bread that another earns.

Frequently children leave home and leave all their obligations to their parents behind them at home. If their letters are rare, enclosed checks are still rarer. They like to keep the old folks informed of the fact that it costs a good deal to live away from home. They sometimes come home on a visit; but these are visits; and visitors, even if they do stay quite a while, do not pay board.

But pecuniary assistance is not all; it is occasionally care and attention an aged parent requires, the presence of a daughter who prefers the gaiety of the city to the quiet of the old homestead that is imperiously demanded. If the parent be feeble or sick, the undutiful child is criminally negligent; the crime is still greater if there be danger through that absence of the parent's dying without religious consolation.

I have said nothing of that unnatural specimen of humanity, sometimes called a "loafer," and by still more ignoble names, who, to use a vulgar term, "grubs" on his parents, drinks what he earns and befouls the home he robs, with his loathsome presence and scandalous living. The least said of him the better. He exists: 'tis already too much said.

Chapter 61

Disinterested Love in Parents

Love seems to resume all the obligations of parents toward their offspring; certainly, it directs all their actions, and they fulfil these obligations ill or well according to the quality of that love. But love is not sufficient; love is of two kinds, the right and the wrong; nothing good comes of an affection that is not properly ordered. In itself, parental love is natural, instinctive; therefore it is not meritorious to any high degree. But there is much merit in the proper kind of parental affection, because it requires sacrifice.

There may be too little love, to the neglect and misfortune of children. There may be too much, to their spoiling and utter perversion. Again there may be affection that is partial, that singles out one for caresses and favors to the exclusion of the others; hence discord and dissensions in the family. The first two forms of inordinate affection are equally bad, while the last combines both and contains the double evil thereof. It is hard to say which is the worse off, the child that receives too much or the one that receives too little of that love which to be correct should avoid extremes.

Parents are apt, under the sway of natural affection, to overlook the fact that God has rights over the children, and that the welfare and interests of the children must not be left outside all consideration: herein lies the root of all the evil that befalls the family through degenerate love. What is commonly, but improperly, called love is either pagan fondness or simon-pure egotism and self-love.

When a vain person looks into a mirror, she (if it be a "she") will immediately fall in love with the image, because it is an image of herself. And a selfish parent sees in his child, not another being, but himself, and he loves it for himself. His affection is not an act of generosity, as it should be, but an act of self-indulgence. He does not seek to please another, he seeks to please himself. His love, therefore, is nothing but concentrated vanity—and that is the wrong kind.

Such a parent will neglect a less favored child, and he will so far dote on the corporal and physical object of his devotion as to forget there is a soul within. He will account all things good that flatter his conceit, and all things evil that disturb the voluptuousness of his attachment. He owns that child, and he is going to make it the object of his eternal delights, God's rights and the child's own interests to the contrary notwithstanding. This fellow is not a parent; he is a pure animal, and the cub will, one day make good returns for services rendered.

A parent with a growing-up family, carefully reared and expensively educated, will often lay clever plans and dream elaborate dreams of a golden future from which it would almost be cruelty to awake him. He sees his pains and toils requited a thousand fold, his disbursements yielding a high rate of interest and the name his children bear—his name—respected and honored. In all this there is scarcely anything blameworthy; but the trouble comes when the views of the Almighty fail to square with the parental views.

Symptoms of the malady then reveal themselves. Misfortunes are met with complaints and murmurings against Providence and the manner in which it runs the cosmic machine. Being usually self-righteous, such parents bring up the old discussion as to the justice of the divine plan by which the good suffer and the wicked prosper in this world. Sorrow in bereavement is legitimate and sacred, but when wounded love vents its wrath on the Almighty, the limit is passed, and then we say: "Such love is love only in name, love must respect the rights of God; if it does not, it is something else." The Almighty never intended children to be a paying investment; it belongs to Him to call children to Himself as well as parents themselves, when He feels like it. Parents who ignore this do not give their children the love the latter have a right to expect.

Intelligent and Christian parents, therefore, need to understand the true status of the offspring, and should make careful allowance for children's own interests, both material and spiritual, and for the all-supreme rights of God in the premises. Since true love seeks to do good, in parents it should first never lose sight of the child's soul and the means to help him save it. Without this all else is labor lost. God frowns on such unchristian affection, and He usually sees to it that even in this world the reaping be according to the sowing.

The rearing of a child is the making or unmaking of a man or woman. Love is the motive power behind this enterprise. That is why we insist on the disinterestedness of parental love, before touching on the all-important question of education.

CHAPTER 62

EDUCATE THE CHILDREN

Before reaching the age of reason, the child's needs are purely animal; it requires to be fed, clothed and provided with the general necessities of life. Every child has a natural right that its young life be fostered and protected; the giver must preserve his gift, otherwise his gift is vain. To neglect this duty is a sin, not precisely against the fourth, but rather against the fifth, commandment which treats of killing and kindred acts.

When the mind begins to open and the reasoning faculties to develop, the duty of educating the child becomes incumbent on the parent. As its physical, so its intellectual, being must be trained and nourished. And by education is here meant the training of the young mind, the bringing out of its mental powers and the acquisition of useful knowledge, without reference to anything moral or religious. This latter feature— the most important of all deserves especial attention.

Concerning the culture of the mind, it is a fact, recognized by all, that in this era of popular rights and liberties, no man can expect to make anything but a meagre success of life, if he does that much, without at least a modicum of knowledge and intellectual training. This is an age in which brains are at a high premium; and although brains are by no means the monopoly of the cultured class, they must be considered as non-existent if they are not brought out by education. Knowledge is what counts nowadays. Even in the most common walks of life advancement is impossible without it. This is one reason why parents, who have at heart the future success and well-being of their children, should strive to give them as good an education as their means allow.

Their happiness here is also concerned. If he be ignorant and untaught, a man will be frowned at, laughed at, and be made in many ways, in contact with his fellow-men, to feel the overwhelming inferiority of his position. He will be made unhappy, unless he chooses to keep out of the way of those who know something and associate with those who know nothing—in which case he is very liable to feel lonesome.

He is moreover deprived of the positive comforts and happiness that education affords. Neither books nor public questions will interest him; his leisure moments will be a time of idleness and unbearable tedium; a whole world—the world of the mind—will be closed to him, with its joys, pleasures and comforts which are many.

Add to this the fact that the Maker never intended that the noble faculty of the intelligence should remain an inert element in the life of His creature, that this precious talent should remain buried in the flesh of animal nature. Intelligence alone distinguishes us from the brute; we are under obligation to perfect our humanity. And since education is a means of doing this, we owe it to our nature that we educate ourselves and have educated those who are under our care.

How long should the child be kept at school? The law provides that every child attend school until it reaches the age of fourteen. This law appears to be reasonable and just, and we think that in ordinary circumstances it has the power to bind in conscience. The parent therefore who neglects to keep children at school we account guilty of sin, and of grievous sin, if the neglect be notable.

Outside this provision of the law, we think children should be kept at school as long as it is possible and prudent to do so. This depends, of course, on the means and resources of the parents. They are under no obligation to give to their children an education above what their means allow. Then, the aptitudes, physical and mental, of the child are a factor to be considered. Poor health or inherited weakness may forbid a too close application to studies, while it may be a pure waste of time and money to keep at school a child that will not profit by the advantage offered. It is better to put such a child at work as soon as possible. As says the philosopher of Archey Road: "You may lead a young man to the university, but you cannot make him learn."

Outside these contingencies, we think every child has a right to a common school education, such as is given in our system under the high school, whether it be fourteen years of age or over. Reading and writing, grammar and arithmetic, history and geography, these are the fundamental and essential elements of a common school education; and in our time and country, a modicum of information on these subjects is necessary for the future well-being, success and happiness of our children. And since parents are bound to care for the future of their children, we consider them likewise bound to give them such an education as will ensure these blessings.

Chapter 63

Educational Extravagance

Our public educational system is made up of a grammar and a high school course, the latter consisting of a four years term of studies, devoted in part, to a more thorough grounding in the essentials of education; the other part—by far the more considerable, according to the consensus of opinion—is expended on educational frills and vanities. These "trimmings" are given gratis, the public bearing the burden of expense, which foots up to a very respectable total.

For a certain class of people—the people of means—this sort of a thing has not many disadvantages; it is in a line with the future occupation or profession of their offspring. But for the bulk of the children who attend our free schools and on whose parents educational taxes are levied, it has serious inconveniences, is not in line with their future occupation or profession, is not only superfluous, but detrimental. It is for them so much time lost—precious time, that were better spent learning a trade or otherwise fitting themselves for their life work. Herein therefore we discover a double extravagance: that of parents who provide unwisely for their children's future and that of the municipality which offers as popular an education that is anything but popular, since only the few can enjoy it while all must bear the burden alike.

There is much in getting a start in life, in beginning early; a delay is often a handicap hard to overcome. With very few exceptions, our children gain their livelihood with their hands and eyes and ears, and not solely with their brains; they therefore require the most practical education imaginable. They need intellectual tools to work with, and not a smattering of science, botany, drawing and political philosophy to forget as soon as possible. Pure culture studies are not a practical gain for them, while the time consumed in pursuing these is so much taken away from a thorough training in the essentials. Lectures on science, elementary experiments in chemistry, kindergarten instructions in water color painting, these are as much in their place in the education of the average child as an ivory-handled gold pen in the hand that wields the pick-ax.

A boy is better off learning a trade than cramming his head full of culture fads; he is then doing something useful and profitable on which the happiness and success of his life will depend. By the time his companions have done dabbling in science and have come to the conclusion that they are simply being shown how ignorant they are—not a very consoling conclusion after all—he will have already laid the foundation of his career and be earning enough to settle down in life. He may not be able to talk on an infinity of subjects about which he knows nothing at all, but he will be able to earn his own living, which is something worth while.

If the free high school were more of a business school, people would get better returns for their money. True, some would then be obliged to pay for the expensive fads that would be done away with; but since they alone enjoy these things, why should others be made to pay for them who cannot enjoy them? Why should the poor be taxed to educate the rich? Why not give the poor full value for their share of the burden? Why not provide them with intellectual tools that suit their condition, just as the rich are being provided for in the present system? The parochial high school has, in several places we know of, been made to serve as a protest against such evils and as an example that has already been followed in more than one instance by the public schools. Intelligent and energetic pastors, knowing full well the conditions and needs of their people, offer the children a course in business methods as being more suitable, more profitable and less extravagant than four years spent in acquiring a smattering of what they will never possess thoroughly and never need in their callings in life. It is better to fill young minds with the useful than with the agreeable, when it is impossible to furnish both. Results already bespeak the wisdom of this plan and reflect no small honor on its originators.

Parents therefore should see to it that their children get the kind of education they need, the kind that will serve them best in after life. They should not allow the precious time of youth to be whiled away in trifles and vanities. Children have a right: to be educated in a manner in keeping with their conditions in life, and it is criminal in parents to neglect the real needs of their children while trying: to fit them for positions they will never occupy.

In the meantime, let them protest against the extravagance of educational enthusiasts and excessive State paternalism. Let them ask that the burden of culture studies be put where it belongs, that is, on the shoulders of those who are the sole beneficiaries; and that free popular education be made popular, that is, for all, and not for an elite of society. The public school system was called into existence to do one work, namely, to educate the masses: it was never intended to furnish a college education for the benefit of the rich men's sons at the expense of the poor. As it stands to-day, it is an unadulterated extravagance.

CHAPTER 64

GODLESS EDUCATION

The other defect, respecting education as found in the public schools of the land, is that it leaves the soul out of all consideration and relegates the idea of God to a background of silent contempt. On this subject we can do no better than quote wisdom from the Fathers of the Third Plenary Council of Baltimore.

"Few, if any, will deny that a sound civilization must depend upon sound popular education." But education, in order to be sound and to produce "beneficial results, must develop what is best in man, and make him not only clever, but good. A one-sided education will develop a one-sided life; and such a life will surely topple over, and so will every social system that is built up of such lives. True civilization requires that not only the physical and intellectual, but also the moral and religious, well-being of the people should be improved, and at least with equal care.

"It cannot be desirable or advantageous that religion

should be excluded from the school. On the contrary, it ought to be there one of the chief agencies for moulding the young life to all that is true and virtuous, and holy. To shut religion out of the school, and keep it for home and the Church, is, logically, to train up a generation that will consider religion good for home and the Church, but not for the practical business of real life. A life is not dwarfed, but ennobled, by being lived in the presence of God.

"The avowed enemies of Christianity in some European countries are banishing religion from the schools (they have done it since) in order to eliminate it gradually from among the people. In this they are logical. Take away religion from the school, and you take it away from the people. Take it away from the people, and morality will soon follow; morality gone, even their physical condition will ere long degenerate into corruption which breeds decrepitude, while their intellectual attainments would only serve as a light to guide them to deeper depths of vice and ruin. A civilization without religion would be a civilization of 'the struggle for existence, and the survival of the fittest,' in which cunning and strength would become the substitutes for principle, virtue, conscience and duty."

One of the things the Catholic Church fears least in this country is Protestantism. She considers it harmless, moribund, in the throes of disintegration. It never has, cannot and never will thrive long where it has to depend on something other than wealth and political power. It has unchurched millions, is still unchurching at a tremendous rate, and will end by unchurching itself. The godless school has done its work for Protestantism, and done it well. Its dearest enemy could not wish for better results.

Popular education comes more and more to mean popularized irreligion. The future struggles of the Church will be with Agnosticism and Infidelity—the product of the godless public school. And without pretending to be prophets or sons of prophets, we Catholics can foresee the day when godless education, after making bad Christians, will make bad citizens. And because no civilization worthy of the name has ever subsisted, or can subsist, without religion, the maintenance of this system of popular and free government will devolve on the product of Christian education, and its perpetuity will depend upon the generations turned out of the religious school.

The most substantial protest the Catholic Church offers against godless education is the system of her parochial schools; and this alone is sufficient to give an idea of the importance of this question. From headquarters comes the order to erect Catholic schools in every parish in this land as soon as the thing can be done. This means a tremendous amount of work, and a tremendous expense. It means a competition on educational grounds with the greatest, richest and most powerful nation in the world. The game must be worth the candle; there must be some proportion between the end and the means.

The Catholic Church has the wisdom of ages to learn from; and when she embarks on an enterprise of this kind, even her bitterest enemies can afford to take it for granted that there is something behind it. And there is. There is her very life, which depends on the fidelity of her children. And her children are lost to her and to God unless she fosters religion in her young. Let parents share this solicitude of the Church for the little ones, and beware of the dangers of the godless school.

Chapter 65

Correction

Among the many things that are good for children and that parents are in duty bound to supply is—the rod! This may sound old-fashioned, and it unfortunately is; there is a new school of home discipline in vogue nowadays.

Slippers have outgrown their usefulness as implements of persuasion, being now employed exclusively as foot-gear. The lissom birch thrives ungarnered in the thicket, where grace and gentleness supply the whilom vigor of its sway. The unyielding barrel-stave, that formerly occupied a place of honor and convenience in the household, is now relegated, a harmless thing, to a forgotten corner of the cellar, and no longer points a moral but adorns a wood-pile. Disciplinary applications of the old type have fallen into innocuous desuetude; the penny now tempts, the sugar candy soothes and sugar-coated promises entice when the rod should quell and blister. Meanwhile the refractory urchin, with no fear to stimulate his sluggish conscience, chuckles, rejoices and is glad, and bethinks himself of some uninvented methods of devilment.

Yes, it is old-fashioned in these days to smite with the rattan as did the mighty of yore. The custom certainly lived a long time. The author of the Proverbs spoke of the practise to the parents of his generation, and there is no mistaking the meaning of his words. He spoke with authority, too; if we mistake not, it was the Holy Ghost that inspired his utterances. Here are a few of his old-fashioned sayings: "Spare the rod and spoil the child; he who loves his child spares not the rod; correction gives judgment to the child who ordinarily is incapable of reflection; if the child be not chastised, it will bring down shame and disgrace upon the head of its parent." It is our opinion that authority of this sort should redeem the defect of antiquity under which the teaching itself labors. There are some things "ever ancient, ever new;" this is one of them.

The philosophy of correction may be found in the doctrine of original sin. Every child of Adam has a nature that is corrupted; it is a soil in which pride in all its forms and with all its cortege of vices takes strong and ready root. This growth crops out into stubbornness, selfishness, a horror of restraint, effort and self-denial; mischief, and a spirit of rebellion and destruction. In its native state, untouched by the rod of discipline, the child is wild. Now, you must force a crooked tree to grow straight; you must break a wild colt to domesticate it, and you must whip a wild boy to make him fit for the company of civilized people. Being self-willed, he will seek to follow the bent of his own inclinations; without intelligence or experience and by nature prone to evil, he will follow the wrong path; and the habits acquired in youth, the faults developed he will carry through life to his own and the misery of others. He therefore requires training and a substitute for judgment; and according to the Holy Ghost, the rod furnishes both. In the majority of cases nothing can supply it.

This theory has held good in all the ages of the world, and unless the species has "evolved" by extraordinary leaps and bounds within the last fifty years, it holds good to-day, modern nursery milk-and-honey discipline to the contrary notwithstanding. It may be hard on the youngster—it was hard on us!—but the difficulty is only temporary; and difficulty, some genius has said, is the nurse of greatness, a harsh nurse, who roughly rocks her foster-children into strength and athletic proportions.

The great point is that this treatment be given in time, when it is possible to administer it with success and fruit. The ordinary child does not need Oft-repeated doses; a firm hand and a vigorous application go a long way, in most cases. Half-hearted, milk-and-water castigation, like physic, should be thrown to the dogs. Long threatenings spoil the operation; they betray weakness which the child is the first to discover. And without being brutal, it is well that the chastisement be such as will linger somewhat longer in the memory than in the sensibility.

The defects that deserve this corrective especially are insubordination, sulkiness and sullenness; it is good to stir up the lazy; it is necessary to instil in the child's mind a saving sense of its own inferiority and to inculcate lessons of humility, self-effacement and self-denial. It should scourge dishonesty and lying. The bear licks its cub into shape; let the parent go to the bear, inquire of its ways and be wise. His children will then have a moral shape and a form of character that will stand them in good stead in after life; and they will give thanks in proportion to the pain inflicted during the process of formation.

JUSTICE

CHAPTER 66

JUSTICE AND RIGHTS

J
ustice is a virtue by which we render unto every man that which to him is due. Among equals, it is called commutative justice, the which alone is here in question. It protects us in the enjoyment of our own rights, and imposes upon us the obligation of respecting the rights of our fellow-men. This, of course, supposes that we have certain rights and that we know what a right is. But what is a right?

The word itself may be clearer in the minds of many than its definition; few ignore what a right is, and fewer still perhaps could say clearly and correctly what they mean by the word. A right is not something that you can see and feel and smell: it is a moral faculty, that is, a recognized, inviolable power or liberty to do something, to hold or obtain possession of something. Where the right of property is concerned, it supposes a certain relation or connection between a person and an object; this may be a relation of natural possession, as in the case of life or reputation, a relation of lawful acquisition, as that of the goods of life, etc. Out of this relation springs a title, just and proper, by which I may call that object "mine," or you, "yours;" ownership is thereby established of the object and conceded to the party in question. This party is therefore said to have a right to the object; and the right is good, whether he is in possession or not thereof. Justice respects this right, respects the just claims and titles of the owner, and forbids every act injurious thereto.

All this pre-supposes the idea of God, and without that idea, there can be no justice and no rights, properly so-called. Justice is based on the conformity of all things with the will of God. The will of God is that we attain to everlasting happiness in the next world through the means of an established order of things in this life. This world is so ruled, and our nature is such, that certain means are either absolutely or relatively necessary for the attaining of that end; for example, life, reputation, liberty, the pursuit of happiness in the measure of our lawful capacity. The obligation therefore to reach that end gives us the right to use these means; and God places in every soul the virtue of justice so that this right may be respected.

But it must be understood that the rights of God towards us transcend all other rights that we may have towards our fellow-men; ours we enjoy under the high dominion of Him who grants all rights. Consequently, in the pursuit of justice for ourselves, our rights cease the moment they come into antagonism with the superior rights of God as found in His Law. No man has a right to do what is evil, not even to preserve that most inalienable and sacred of all rights, his right to life. To deny this is to destroy the very notion of justice; the restrictions of our rights are more sacred than those rights themselves.

Violation of rights among equals is called injustice. This sin has a triple malice; it attacks the liberty of fellow-men and destroys it; it attacks the order of the world and the basis of society; it attacks the decree and mandate of the Almighty who wills that this world shall be run on the plan of justice. Injustice is therefore directly a sin against man, and indirectly a crime against God.

So jealous is God of the rights of His creatures that He never remains satisfied until full justice is done for every act of injustice. Charity may be wounded, and the fault condoned; but only reparation in kind will satisfy justice. Whatever is mine is mine, and mine it will ever remain, wherever in this world another may have betaken himself with it. As long as it exists it will appeal to me as to its master and owner; if justice is not done in this world, then it will appeal to the justice of Heaven for vengeance.

The six last commandments treat of the rights of man and condemn injustice. We are told to respect the life, the virtue, the goods and the reputation of our fellow-men; we are commanded to do so not only in act, but also in thought and desire. Life is protected by the fifth, virtue by the sixth and ninth, property by the seventh and tenth, and reputation by the eighth. To sin against any of these commandments is to sin against justice in one form or another.

The claims, however, of violated justice are not such as to exact the impossible in order to repair an injury done. A dead man cannot be brought back to life, a penniless thief cannot make restitution unless he steals from somebody else, etc., etc. But he who finds himself thus physically incapable of undoing the wrongs committed must have at least the will and intention of so doing: to revoke such intention would be to commit a fresh sin of injustice. The alternative is to do penance, either willingly in this life, or forcibly in the purging flames of the suffering Church in the next. In that way, some time or other, justice, according to the plan of God, will be done; but He will never be satisfied until it is done.

CHAPTER 67

HOMICIDE

To kill is to take life, human or animal. It was once thought by a sect of crazy fanatics, that the Fifth Commandment applied to the killing of animals as well as of men. When a man slays a man, he slays an equal; when he kills an animal, he kills a creature made to serve him and to be his food; and raw meat is not always palatable, and to cook is to kill. "Everything that moves and lives," says Holy Writ, "shall be unto you as food."

The killing therefore herein question is the taking of human life, or homicide. There can be no doubt but that life is man's best and most precious possession, and that he has an inborn right to live as long as nature's laws operate in his favor. But man is not master of that gift of life, either in himself or in others. God, who alone can give, alone may take it away. Sole master of life, He deals it out to His creatures as it pleases Him; and whoever tampers with human life intrudes upon the domain of the Divinity, violating at the some time the first right of his fellow-man.

We have an instinctive horror of blood, human blood. For the ordinary individual the Mosaic enactment that forbids murder is almost superfluous, so deeply has nature graven on our hearts the letter of that law. Murder is abominable, for the very reason that life is precious; and no reasonable being, civilized or savage, dealing death unjustly unto a fellow-man, can have any other conviction in his soul than that he is committing a crime and incurring the almighty wrath of the Deity. If such killing is done by a responsible agent, and against the right of the victim, the crime committed is murder or unjustifiable homicide.

Which supposes that there is a kind of homicide that is justifiable, in seeming contradiction of the general law of God and nature, which specifies no exception. But there is a question here less of exception than of distinction. The law is a general one, of vast comprehension. Is all killing prohibited? Evidently no. It is limited to human beings, in the first place; to responsible agents, in the next; and thirdly, it involves a question of injustice. What is forbidden is the voluntary and unjust killing of a human being. Having thus specified according to the rules of right reasoning, we find we have a considerable margin left for the taking of life that is justifiable. And the records of Divine revelation will approve the findings of right reason.

We find God in the Old Law, while upholding His fifth precept, commanding capital punishment and sanctioning the slaughter of war; He not only approved the slaying of certain persons, but there are instances of His giving authority to kill. By so doing He delegated His supreme right over life to His creatures. "Whoever sheds human blood, let his blood be shed." In the New Testament the officer of the law is called the minister of God and is said not without cause to carry the sword; and the sword is the symbol of the power to inflict death.

The presence of such laws as that of capital punishment, of war and of self-defense, in all the written codes of civilized peoples, as well as in the unwritten codes of savage tribes, can be accounted for only by a direct or indirect commission from the Deity. A legal tradition so universal and so constant is a natural law, and consequently a divine law. In a matter of such importance all mankind could not have erred; if it has, it is perfectly safe to be with it in its error.

These exceptions, if we may call them exceptions, suppose the victim to have forfeited his right to live, to have placed himself in a position of unjust aggression, which aggression gives to the party attacked the right to repel it, to protect his own life even at the cost of the life of the unjust aggressor. This is an individual privilege in only one instance, that of self-defence; in all others it is invested in the body politic or society which alone can declare war and inflict death on a capital offender.

Of course it may be said that in moral matters, like does not cure like, that to permit killing is a strange manner of discouraging the same. But this measure acts as a deterrent; it is not a cure for the offender, or rather it is, and a radical one; it is intended to instil a salutary dread into the hearts of those who may be inclined to play too freely with human life. This is the only argument assassins understand; it is therefore the only one we can use against them.

Chapter 68

Is Suicide a Sin?

Most people no doubt remember how, a short time previous to his death, Col. Robert Ingersoli, the agnostic lecturer, gave out a thesis with the above title, offering a negative conclusion. Some discussion ensued in public print; the question was debated hotly, and whole columns of pros and cons were inflicted on the suffering public by the theologues who had taken the matter seriously.

We recall, too, how, in the height of the discussion, a poor devil of an unfortunate was found in one of the parks of the Metropolis with an empty pistol in his clinched fist, a bullet in his head and in his pocket a copy of the thesis: Is suicide a sin?

To a Christian, this theorizing and speculation was laughable enough; but when one was brought face to face with the reality of the thing, a grim humor was added to the situation. Comedy is dangerous that leads to tragedy.

The witty part of the matter was this: Ingersoli spoke of

sin. Now, what kind of an intelligible thing could sin be in the mind of a blasphemous agnostic? What meaning could it have for any man who professes not to know, or to care, who or what God is?

If there is no Legislator, there is no Law; if no Law, then no violation of the Law. If God does not exist, there can be no offending Him. Eliminate the notion of God, and there is no such thing as sin. Sin, therefore, had no meaning for Ingersoli; his thesis had no meaning, nothing he said had any meaning. Yet, people took him seriously! And at least one poor wretch was willing to test the truth of the assertion and run his chances.

Some people, less speculative, contend that the fact of suicide is sufficient evidence of irresponsibility, as no man in his right senses would take his own life. This position is both charitable and consoling; unfortunately, certain facts of premeditation and clear mindedness militate so strongly against such a general theory that one can easily afford to doubt its soundness. That this is true in many cases, perhaps in the majority of cases, all will admit; in all cases, few will admit it. However, the question here is one of principle, and not of fact.

THE PRIME EVIL at the bottom of all killing is that of injustice; but in self-destruction where the culprit and the victim are one and the same person, there can be no question of injustice. Akin to, and a substitute for, the law of justice is that of charity, by which we are bound to love ourselves and do ourselves no harm or injury. The saying "charity begins at home" means that we ourselves are the first objects of our charity. If therefore we must respect the life of our neighbor, the obligation is still greater to respect our own.

Then there is the supreme law of justice that reposes in God. We should remember that God is the supreme and sole Master of life. Man has a lease of life, but it does not belong to him to destroy at his own will. He did not give it to himself; and he cannot take it away. Destruction supposes an authority and dominion that does not belong to any man where life is concerned. And he who assumes such a prerogative commits an act of unquestionable injustice against Him whose authority is usurped.

By indirect killing we mean the placing of an act, good or at least morally indifferent, from which may result a benefit that is intended, but also an evil—death—which is not intended but simply suffered to occur. In this event there is no sin, provided there be sufficient reason for permitting said evil effect. The act may be an operation, the benefit intended, a cure; the evil risked, death. The misery of ill health is a sufficient reason for risking the evil of death in the hope of regaining strength and health. To escape sure death, to escape from grave danger or ills, to preserve one's virtue, to save another's life, to assure a great public benefit, etc., these are reasons proportionate to the evil of risking life; and in these and similar cases, if death results, it is indirect suicide, and is in nowise criminal.

The same cannot be said of death that results from abuses or excesses of any kind, such as dissipation or debauchery; from risks that are taken in a spirit of bravado or with a view to winning fame or lucre. For a still better reason this cannot be said of those who undergo criminal operations: it is never permitted to do what is intrinsically evil that good may come therefrom.

All this applies to self-mutilation as well as to self-destruction; as parts of the whole, one's limbs should be the objects of one's charity, and God's law demands that we preserve them as well as the body itself. It is lawful to submit to the maiming process only when the utility of the whole body demands it; otherwise it is criminal.

One word more. What about those who call upon, and desire death? To desire evil is sinful. Yes, but death is a moral evil when its mode is contrary to the laws of God and of nature. Thus, with perfect acquiescence to order of Divine Providence, if one desire death in order to be at rest with God, that one desires a good and meritorious thing and with perfect regularity; it is less meritorious to desire death with the sole view of escaping the ills and troubles of life; it would even be difficult to convict one of mortal offending if he desired death for a slight and futile reason, if there be due respect for the will of God. The sin of such desires consists in rebellion against the divine Will and opposition to the providence of God; in such cases the sin is never anything but grievous.

CHAPTER 69

SELF-DEFENSE

The thought is a terrible one—and the act is desperate in itself—of a man, however justified his conduct may be, slaying with his own hand a fellow being and sending his soul, unprepared perhaps, before its Maker. But it is a still more desperate thing, because it strikes us nearer home, to yield up one's life into the hands of an agent of injustice. There is here an alternative of two very great evils; it is a question of two lives, his and mine; I must slay or I must die without having done anything to forfeit my life.

But the law of charity, founded in nature, makes my life more precious to me than his, for charity begins at home. Then, to save his life, I must give mine; and he risks his to take mine! I do not desire to kill my unjust aggressor, but I do intend, as I have a perfect right, to protect my own life. If he, without cause, places his existence as an obstacle to my enjoyment of life, then I shall remove that obstacle, and to do it, I shall kill. Again, a desperate remedy, but the situation is most terribly desperate. Being given law of my being, I can not help the inevitable result of conditions of which I am nowise responsible. The man who attacks my life places his own beyond the possibility of my saving it.

This, of course, supposes a man using the full measure of his rights. But is he bound to do this, morally? Not if his charity for another be greater than that which he bears towards himself, if he go beyond the divine injunction to love his neighbor as himself and love him better than himself; if he feel that he is better prepared to meet his God than the other, if he have no one dependent on him for maintenance and support. Even did he happen to be in the state of mortal sin, there is every reason to believe that such charity as will sacrifice life for another, greater than which no man has, would wash away that sin and open the way of mercy; while great indeed must be the necessity of the dependent ones to require absolutely the death of another.

The aggression that justifies killing must be unjust. This would not be the case of a criminal being brought to justice or resisting arrest. Justice cannot conflict with itself and can do nothing unjust in carrying out its own mandates. The culprit therefore has no grounds to stand upon for his defense.

Neither is killing justifiable, if wounding or mutilation would effect the purpose. But here the code of morals allows much latitude on account of the difficulty of judging to a nicety the intentions of the aggressor, that is, whether he means to kill or not; and of so directing the protecting blow as to inflict just enough, and no more disability than the occasion requires.

Virtue in woman is rightly considered a boon greater than life; and for that matter, so is the state of God's friendship in the soul of any creature. Then, here too applies the principle of self-defense. If I may kill to save my life, I may for a better reason kill to save my soul and to avoid mortal offense. True, the loss of bodily integrity does not necessarily imply a staining of the soul; but human nature is such as to make the one an almost fatal consequence of the other. The person therefore who kills to escape unjust contamination acts within his or her rights and before God is justified in the doing.

We would venture to say the same thing of a man who resorts to this extreme in order to protect his rightly gotten goods, on these two conditions, however: that there be some kind of proportion between the loss and the remedy he employs to protect himself against it; and that he have well grounded hope that the remedy will be effective, that it will prevent said loss, and not transform itself into revenge.

And here a last remark is in order. The killing that is permitted to save, is not permitted to avenge loss sustained; the law sanctions self-defense, but not vengeance. If a man, on the principle of self-defense, has the right to kill to save his brother, and fails to do so, his further right to kill ceases; the object is past saving and vengeance is criminal. If a woman has been wronged, once the wrong effected, there can be no lawful recourse to slaying, for what is lost is beyond redemption, and no reason for such action exists except revenge. In these cases killing is murder, pure and simple, and there is nothing under Heaven to justify it.

Remembering the injunction to love our neighbor as

ourself, we add that we have the same right to defend our neighbor's life as we have to defend our own, even to protect his or her innocence and virtue and possessions. A husband may defend the honor of his wife, which is his own, even though the wife be a party to the crime and consent to the defilement; but the right is only to prevent, and ceases on the event of accomplishment, even at the incipient stage.

CHAPTER 70

MURDER OFTEN SANCTIONED

All injury done to another in order to repair an insult is criminal, and if said injury result in death, it is murder.

Here we consider an insult as an attack on one's reputation or character, a charge or accusation, a slurring remark, etc., without reference to the truth or falsity thereof. It may be objected that whereas reputation, like chastity and considerable possessions, is often valued as high as life itself, the same right exists to defend it even at the cost of another's life. But it must be remembered that the loss of character sustained in consequence of an insult of this kind is something very ephemeral and unsubstantial; and only to a mind abnormally sensitive can any proportion be perceived between the loss and the remedy. This is especially true when the attack is in words and goes no farther than words: for "sticks and stones will break your bones, but names will never hurt you," as we used to say when we were boys. Then, words are such fleeting things that the harm is done, whatever harm there is, before any remedy can be brought to bear upon it; which fact leaves no room for self-defense.

In such a case, the only redress that can be had is from the courts of justice, established to undo wrongs as far as the thing can be done. The power to do this belongs to the State alone, and is vested in no private individual. To assume the prerogative of privately doing oneself justice, when recourse can be had to the tribunals of justice, is to sin, and every act committed in this pursuit of justice is unlawful and criminal.

This applies likewise to all the other cases of self-defense wherein life, virtue and wealth are concerned, if the harm is already done, or if legal measures can prevent the evil, or undo it. It may be that the justice dealt out by the tribunal, in case of injury being done to u's, prove inferior to that which we might have obtained ourselves by private methods. But this is not a reason for one to take the law into one's own hands. Such loss is accidental and must be ascribed to the inevitable course of human things.

Duelling is a form of murder and suicide combined, for which there can possibly be no justification. The code of honor that requires the reparation of an insult at the point of the sword or the muzzle of a pistol has no existence outside the befogged intelligence of godless men. The duel repairs nothing and aggravates the evil it seeks to remedy. The justice it appeals to is a creature dependent on skill and luck; such justice is not only blind, but crazy as well.

That is why the Church anathematizes duelling. The duel she condemns is a hand-to-hand combat prearranged as to weapons, time and place, and it is immaterial whether it be to the death or only to the letting of first blood. She fulminates her major excommunication against duellists, even in the event of their failing to keep their agreement. Her sentence affects seconds and all those who advise or favor or abet, and even those whose simple presence is an incentive and encouragement. She refuses Christian burial to the one who falls, unless before dying he shows certain dispositions of repentance.

Prize fighting, however brutal and degrading, must not be put in the category of duelling. Its object is not to wipe out an insult, but to furnish sport and to reap the incidental profits. In normal conditions there is no danger to life or limb. Sharkey might stop with the point of his chin a blow that would send many another into kingdom come; but so long as Sharkey does the stopping the danger remains non-existent. If, however, hate instead of lucre bring the men together, that motive would be sufficient to make the game one of blood if not of death.

Lynching, is another kind of murder, and a cowardly, brutal kind, at that. No crime, no abomination on the part of the victim, however great, can justify such an inhuman proceeding. It brands with the crime of wilful murder every man or woman who has a hand in it. To defend the theory of lynching-is as bad as to carry it out in practice. And it is greatly to be feared that the Almighty will one day call this land to account for the outrageous performances of unbridled license and heartless cruelty that occur so frequently in our midst.

The only plea on which to ground an excuse for such exhibitions of brutality and disrespect for order and justice would be the inability of established government to mete out justice to the guilty; but this is not even the case, for government is defied and lawful authority capable and willing to punish is spurned; the culprit is taken from the hands of the law and delivered over to the vengeance of a mob. However popular the doctrine of Judge Lynch may be in certain sections of the land, it is nevertheless reprobated by the law of God and stands condemned at the bar of His justice.

CHAPTER 71

ON THE ETHICS OF WAR

In these days, since we have evolved into a fighting nation, our young men feel within them the instinct of battle, which, like Job's steed, "when it heareth the trumpet, saith: 'ha, ha'; that smelleth the battle afar off, the encouraging of the captains, the shouting of the army." Military trappings are no longer looked upon as stage furniture, good only for Fourth-of-July parades and sham manoeuvers. War with us has become a stern reality, and promises to continue such, for people do not yield up willingly their independence, even to a world-power with a providential "destiny" to fulfil. And since war is slaughter, it might be apropos to remark on the morality of such killing as is done on the field of battle and of war in general.

In every war there is a right side and a wrong side; sometimes, perhaps, more frequently, there is right and wrong on both sides, due to bungling diplomacy and the blindness of prejudice. But in every case justice demands the triumph of one cause and the defeat of the other. To determine in any particular case the side of right and justice is a very difficult matter. And perhaps it is just as well that it is so; for could this be done with truth and accuracy, frightful responsibilities would have to be placed on the shoulders of somebody; and we shrink instinctively from the thought of any one individual or body of individuals standing before God with the crime of war on his or their souls.

Therefore it is that grave men are of the opinion that such a tremendous event as war is not wholly of man's making, but rather an act of God, like earthquakes, volcanic eruptions and the like; which things He uses as flails to chastise His people, or to bring them to a sense of their own insignificance in His sight. Be this as it may, it is nevertheless true that a private individual is rarely, if ever, competent to judge rightly by himself of the morality of any given cause, until such time at least as history has probed the matter and brought every evidence to light. In case, therefore, of doubt, every presumption should favor the cause of one's own country. If, in my private opinion, the cause of my country is doubtfully wrong, then that doubt should yield to the weight of higher authoritative opinion. Official or popular judgment will be authority for me; on that authority I may form a strong probable opinion, at least; and this will assure the morality of my taking up my country's cause, even though it be doubtful from my personal point of view. If this cannot be done and one's conscience positively reprove such a cause, then that one cannot, until a contrary conviction is acquired, take any part therein. But he is in no wise bound to defend with arms the other side, for his convictions are subjective and general laws do not take these into account.

Who are bound to serve? That depends on the quality of danger to which the commonwealth is exposed. First, the obligation is for those who can do so easily; young men, strong, unmarried, with a taste for such adventure as war affords. The greater the general peril, the less private needs should be considered. The situation may be such as to call forth every able-bodied man, irrespective of family necessities. To shirk this duty when it is plainly a duty—a rare circumstance, indeed—is without doubt a sin.

Obedience to orders is the alpha and omega of army discipline; without it a cause is lost from the beginning. Numbers are nothing compared to order; a mob is not a fighting machine; it is only a fair target. The issue of a battle, or even of a whole war, may depend on obedience to orders. Army men know this so well that death is not infrequently the penalty of disobedience. Consequently, a violation of discipline is usually a serious offense; it may easily be a mortal sin.

War being slaughter, the soldier's business is to kill or rather to disable, as many of the enemy as possible on the field of battle. This disabling process means, of course, and necessarily, the maiming unto death of many. Such killing is not only lawful, but obligatory. War, like the surgeon's knife, must often lop off much in order to save the whole. The best soldier is he who inflicts most damage on the enemy.

But the desire and intention of the soldier should not be primarily to kill, but only to put the enemy beyond the possibility of doing further harm. Death will be the result of his efforts in many cases, and this he suffers to occur rather than desires and intends. He has no right to slay outside of battle or without the express command of a superior officer; if he does so, he is guilty of murder. Neither must there be hate behind the aim that singles out a foe for destruction; the general hatred which he bestows on the opposing cause must respect the individual enemy.

It is not lawful to wantonly torture or maim an enemy, whoever or whatever he may be, however great his crime. Not even the express command of a superior officer can justify such doings, because it is barbarity, pure and unmitigated. In war these things are morally just what they would be if they were perpetrated in the heart of peace and civilization by a gang of thugs. These are abominations that, not only disgrace the flag under which they are committed, but even cry to Heaven for vengeance.

CHAPTER 72

THE MASSACRE OF THE INNOCENTS

Herod, the Bloody, slew all under two. A modern Moloch, a creature of lust and blood, disguised often under the cloak of respectability, stalks through a Christian land denying the babe the right to be born at all, demanding that it be crushed as soon as conceived. There is murder and murder; but this is the most heartless, cowardly and brutal on the catalogue of crime.

It is bad enough to cut down an enemy, to shoot him in the back; but when it comes to slaying a victim as helpless as a babe, incapable of entering a protest, innocent of all wrong save that of existing; when even baptism is denied it, and thereby the sight of God for all eternity; when finally the victim is one's own flesh and blood, the language of hell alone is capable of qualifying such deeds.

Do not say there is no injustice. Every innocent human being, at every stage of its existence, from the first to the last, born or unborn, has a natural and inalienable right to live, as long as nature's laws operate in its favor. Being innocent it cannot forfeit that right. God is no exceptor of persons; a soul is a soul, whether it be the soul of a pontiff, a king or a sage, or the soul of the unborn babe of the last woman of the people. In every case, the right to live is exactly the same.

The circumstances, regular or irregular, of its coming into life, not being of its own making, do not affect the right in the least. It obeyed the law by which every man is created; it could not disobey, for the law is fatal. Its presence therefore, cannot be morally obnoxious, a crime on its part. Whether its presence is a joy or a shame, that depends solely on the free act of others than itself; and it is for them to enjoy the privilege or bear the disgrace and burden. That presence may occasion poverty, suffering, it may even endanger life; what if it does! Has a person in misfortune the right to strike down another who has had no part in making that misfortune?

Life does not begin at birth, but precedes it; prenatal life is truly life. That which is conceived, is; being, it lives as essentially as a full-grown man in the prime of life. Being the fruit of humanity it is human at every instant of its career; being human, it is a creature of God, has an immortal soul with the image of the Maker stamped thereon. And the veto of God, "Thou shalt not kill," protects that life, or it has no meaning at all.

The psychological moment of incipient life, the instant marked by the infusion of soul into body, may furnish a problem of speculation for the savant; but even when certitude ends and doubt begins, the law of God fails not to protect. No man who doubts seriously that the act he is about to perform is a crime, and is free to act or not to act, is anything but a criminal, if he goes ahead notwithstanding and does the deed. If I send a bullet into a man's head doubting whether or not he be dead, I commit murder by that act, and it matters not at all in point of fact whether said person were really dead or not before I made sure. In the matter, therefore, which concerns us here, doubt will not make killing justifiable. The law is: when in doubt, do not act.

Then, again, as far as guilt is concerned, it makes not a particle of difference whether results follow or not. Sin, you know, is an act of the will; the exterior deed completes, but does not make, the crime. If I do all in my power to effect a wrong and fail in the attempt through no fault of my own, I am just as guilty before God as if I perpetrated the crime in deed. It is more than a desire to commit sin, which is sinful; it is a specific sin in itself, and in this matter, it is murder pure and simple.

This applies with equal force to the agent who does the deed, to the principal who has it done or consents to its being done, to those who advise, encourage, urge or co-operate in any way therein, as well as to those who having authority to prevent, neglect to use it. The stain of blood is on the soul of every person to whom any degree of responsibility or complicity can be attached.

If every murderer in this enlightened Christian land of ours received the rope which is his or her due, according to the letter of the law, business would be brisk for quite a spell. It is a small town that has not its professional babe-slaughterer, who succeeds in evading the law even when he contrives to kill two at one time. He does not like to do it, but there is money in it, you know; and he pockets his unholy blood money without a squirm. Don't prosecute him; if you do, he will make revelations that will startle the town.

As for the unnatural mother, it is best to leave her to listen in the dead of night to the appealing voice of her murdered babes before the tribunal of God's infinite justice. Their blood calls for vengeance.

CHAPTER 73

ENMITY

Killing is not the only thing forbidden by the Fifth Commandment: thereby are prescribed all forms of enmity, of which killing is one, that attack either directly or indirectly, in thought or desire, as well as in deed, the life, limbs or health of the neighbor. The fifth precept protects the physical man; everything therefore that partakes of the nature of a design on the body of another is an offense against this commandment. All such offenses are not equally grievous, but each contains a malice of its own, which is prescribed under the head of killing.

Enmity that takes the form of fighting, assault and battery, is clearly a breach of the law of God. It is lawful to wound, maim and otherwise disable an assailant, on the principle of self-defense, when there is no other means of protecting oneself against attack. But outside this contingency, such conduct is ruffianism before man, and sin before God. The State alone has the right to inflict penalties and avenge wrongs; to turn this right over to every individual would be destructive of society. If this sort of a thing is unlawful and criminal when there might be some kind of an excuse for it on the ground of injury received, the malice thereof is aggravated considerably by the fact of there being no excuse at all, or only imaginary ones.

There is another form of enmity or hatred that runs not to blows but to words. Herein is evil, not because of any bodily injury wrought, of which there is none, but because of the diabolical spirit that manifests itself, a spirit reproved by God and which, in given circumstances, is ready to resort to physical injury and even to the letting of blood. There can be no doubt that hatred in itself is forbidden by this commandment, for "whosoever hateth his brother is a murderer," according to St. John. It matters little, therefore, whether such hatred be in deeds or in words; the malice is there and the sin is consummated. A person, too weak to do an enemy bodily harm, may often use his or her tongue to better effect than another could his fists, and the verbal outrage thus committed may be worse than a physical one.

It is not even necessary that the spirit of enmity show itself at all on the outside for the incurring of such guilt as attends the violation of this commandment. It is sufficient that it possess the soul and go no farther than a desire to do harm. This is the spirit of revenge, and it is none the less sinful in the eyes of God because it lacks the complement of exterior acts. It is immoral to nourish a grudge against a fellow-man. Such a spirit only awaits an occasion to deal a blow, and, when that occasion shows itself, will be ready, willing and anxious to strike. The Lord refuses the gifts and offerings and prayers of such people as these; they are told to go and become reconciled with their brother and lay low the spirit that holds them; then, and only then, will their offerings be acceptable.

Even less than this suffices to constitute a breach of the Fifth Commandment. It is the quality of such passions as envy and jealousy to sometimes be content with the mere thought of injury done to their object, without, even going so far as to desire to work the evil themselves. These passions are often held in check for a time; but, in the event of misfortune befalling the hated rival, there follows a sense of complacency and satisfaction which, if entertained, has all the malice of mortal sin. If, on the contrary, the prosperity of another inspire us with a feeling of regret and sadness, which is deliberately countenanced and consented to, there can be no doubt as to the grievous malice of such a failing.

Finally recklessness may be the cause of our harming another. It is a sound principle of morals that one is responsible for his acts in the measure of his foreseeing, and consenting to, the results and consequences. But there is still another sound principle according to which every man is accountable, at least indirectly, for the evil consequences of his actions, even though they be unforeseen and involuntary, in the measure of the want of ordinary human prudence shown in his conduct. A man with a loaded revolver in his hand may not have any design on the lives of his neighbors; but if he blazes away right and left, and happens to fill this or that one with lead, he is guilty, if he is in his right mind; and a sin, a mortal sin, is still a sin, even if it is committed indirectly. Negligence is often culpable, and ignorance frequently a sin.

Naturally, just as the soul is superior to the body, so evil example, scandal, the killing of the soul of another is a crime of a far greater enormity than the working of injury unto the body. Scandal comes properly under the head of murder; but it is less blood than lust that furnishes it with working material. It will therefore be treated in its place and time.

CHAPTER 74

OUR ENEMIES

What is an enemy? A personal, an individual enemy is he who has done us a personal injury. The enemy, in a general or collective sense, are they—a people, a class or party—who are opposed to our interests, whose presence, doings or sayings are obnoxious to us for many natural reasons. Concerning these latter, it might be said that it is natural, oftentimes necessary and proper, to oppose them by all legitimate means. This opposition, however lawful, is scarcely ever compatible with any high degree of charity or affection. But whatever of aversion, antipathy or even hatred is thereby engendered, it is not of a personal nature; it does not attain the individual, but embraces a category of beings as a whole, who become identified with the cause they sustain and thereby fall under the common enmity. The law that binds us unto love of our enemy operates only in favor of the units, and not of the group as a group.

Hatred, aversion, antipathy, such as divides peoples,

races and communities, is one, though not the highest, characteristic of patriotism; it may be called the defect of a quality. When a man is whole-souled in a cause, he will brook with difficulty any system of ideas opposed to, and destructive of, his own. Anxious for the triumph of what he believes the cause of right and justice, he will rejoice over the discomfiture of his rivals and the defeat of their cause. Wars leave behind an inheritance of hatred; persecution makes wounds that take a long time to heal. The descendants of the defeated, conquered or persecuted will look upon the generations of their fathers' foes as typifying oppression, tyranny and injustice, will wish them all manner of evil and gloat over their downfall. Such feelings die hard. They spring from convictions. The wounds made by injustice, fancied or real, will smart; and just as naturally will men retain in their hearts aversion for all that which, for them, stands for such injustice. This is criminal only when it fails to respect the individual and become personal hate.

Him who has done us a personal injury we must forgive. Pardon drives hatred out of the heart. Love of God is incompatible with personal enmity; therefore such enmity must be quelched. He who says he loves God and hates his brother is a liar, according to divine testimony. What takes the place of this hate? Love, a love that is called common love, to distinguish it from that special sort of affection that we have for friends. This is a general kind of love that embraces all men, and excludes none individually. It forbids all uncharity towards a man as a unit, and it supposes a disposition of the soul that would not refuse to give a full measure of love and assistance, if necessity required it. This sort of love leaves no room for hatred of a personal nature in the heart.

Is it enough to forgive sincerely from the heart? It is not enough; we must manifest our forgiveness, and this for three good reasons: first, in order to secure us against self-illusion and to test the sincerity of our dispositions; secondly, in order to put an end to discord by showing the other party that we hold no grudge; lastly, in order to remove whatever scandal may have been given by our breach of friendship. The disorder of enmity can be thoroughly cured and healed only by an open renewal of the ties of friendship; and this is done by the offering and acknowledgment of the signs of friendship.

The signs of friendship are of two sorts, the one common, the other special. Common tokens of friendship are those signs which are current among people of the same condition of life; such as saluting, answering a question, dealing in business affairs, etc. These are commonly regarded as sufficient to take away any reasonable suspicion of hatred, although, in matter of fact, the inference may be false. But the refusal to give such tokens of pardon usually argues the presence of an uncharitable feeling that is sinful; it is nearly always evidence of an unforgiving spirit. There are certain cases wherein the offense received being of a peculiar nature, justifies one in deferring such evidence of forgiveness; but these cases are rare.

If we are obliged to show by unmistakable signs that we forgive a wrong that has been done, we are in nowise bound to make a particular friend of the person who has been guilty of the wrong. We need not go out of our way to meet him, receive or visit him or treat him as a long lost brother. He would not expect it, and we fulfil our obligations toward him by the ordinary civilities we show him in the business of life.

If we have offended, we must take the first step toward reconciliation and apologize; that is the only way we have of repairing the injury done, and to this we are held in conscience. If there is equal blame on both sides, then both are bound to the same duty of offering an apology. To refuse such advances on the part of one who has wronged us is to commit an offense that might very easily be grievous.

All this, of course, is apart from the question of indemnification in case of real damage being sustained. We may condone an offense and at the same time require that the loss suffered be repaired. And in case the delinquent refuse to settle amicably, we are justified in pursuing him before the courts. Justice is not necessarily opposed to charity.

CHAPTER 75

IMMORALITY

The natural order of things brings us to a consideration of the Sixth Commandment, and at the same time, of the Ninth, as treating of the same matter—a matter so highly immoral as to deserve the specific appellation of immorality.

People, as a rule, are tolerably well informed on this subject. It is a knowledge acquired by instinct, the depraved instinct of our fallen nature, and supplemented by the experiences weaned from the daily sayings and doings of common life. Finally, that sort of journalism known as the "yellow," and literature called pornographic, serve to round off this education and give it the finishing touches.

But, on the other hand, if one considers the innocent, the young and inexperienced, who are not a few; and likewise the morbidly curious of sensual tendencies, who are many, this matter must appear as a high explosive, capable of doing any amount of damage, if not handled with the utmost care and caution.

Much, therefore, must be left unsaid, or half-said; suggestion and insinuation must be trusted to go far enough, in order that, while the knowing understand, the ignorant may be secure in the bliss of their ignorance and be not prematurely informed.

They, for whom such language is insufficient, know where to go for fuller information. Parents are the natural teachers; the boy's father and the girl's mother know what to say, how and when to say it; or at least should know. And if parents were only more careful, in their own way, to acquaint their children with certain facts when the time comes for it, much evil would be avoided, both moral and physical.

But there are secrets too sacred even for parents' ears, that are confided only to God, through His appointed minister. Catholics know this man is the confessor, and the place for such information and counsel, the holy tribunal of penance. These two channels of knowledge are safe; the same cannot be said of others.

As a preliminary, we would remark that sins, of the sort here in question as well as all kinds of sin, are not limited to deeds. Exterior acts consummate the malice of evil, but they do not constitute such malice; evil is generated in the heart. One who desires to do wrong offends God as effectively as another who does the wrong in deed. Not only that, but he who makes evil the food of his mind and ponders complacently on the seductive beauty of vice is no less guilty than he who goes beyond theory into practice. This is something we frequently forget, or would fain forget, the greed of passion blinding us more or less voluntarily to the real moral value of our acts.

As a consequence of this self-illusion many a one finds himself far beyond his depth in the sea of immorality before he fully realizes his position. It is small beginnings that lead to lasting results; it is by repeated acts that habits are formed; and evil grows on us faster than most of us are willing to acknowledge. All manner of good and evil originates in thought; and that is where the little monster of uncleanness must be strangled before it is full-grown, if we would be free from its unspeakable thralldom.

Again, this is a matter the malice and evil of which very, very rarely, if ever, escapes us. He who commits a sin of impurity and says he did not know it was wrong, lies deliberately, or else he is not in his right frame of mind. The Maker has left in our souls enough of natural virtue and grace to enable us to distinguish right and wrong, clean and unclean; even the child with no definite knowledge of the matter, meeting it for the first time, instinctively blushes and recoils from the moral hideousness of its aspect. Conscience here speaks in no uncertain accents; he alone does not hear who does not wish to hear.

Catholic theologians are even more rigid concerning the matter itself, prescinding altogether from our perception of it. They say that here no levity of matter is allowed, that is to say, every violation, however slight, of either of these two commandments, is a sin. You cannot even touch this pitch of moral defilement without being yourself defiled. It is useless therefore to argue the matter and enter a plea of triviality and inconsequence; nothing is trivial that is of a nature to offend God and damn a soul.

Weakness has the same value as an excuse as it has elsewhere in moral matters. Few sins are of pure malice; weakness is responsible for the damnation of all, or nearly all, the lost. That very weakness is the sin, for virtue is strength. To make this plea therefore is to make no plea at all, for we are all weak, desperately weak, especially against the demon of the flesh, and we become weaker by yielding. And we are responsible for the degree of moral debility under which we labor just as we are for the degree of guilt we have incurred.

Finally, as God, is no exceptor of persons, He does not distinguish between souls, and sex makes no difference with Him. In this His judgment differs from that of the world which absolves the man and condemns the woman. There is no evident reason why the violation of a divine precept should be less criminal in one human creature than in another. And if the reprobation of society does not follow both equally, the wrath of God does, and He will render unto every one according to his and her works.

CHAPTER 76

THE SINK OF INIQUITY

The malice of lust consists in the abuse of a natural, a quasi-divine faculty, which is prostituted to ignoble purposes foreign to the ends by the Creator established. The lines along which this faculty may be legitimately exercised, are laid down by natural and divine laws, destined to preserve God's rights, to maintain order in society and to protect man against himself. The laws result in the foundation of a state, called matrimony, within which the exercise of this human prerogative, delegated to man by the Creator, receives the sanction of divine authority, and becomes invested with a sacred character, as sacred as its abuse is abominable and odious.

To disregard and ignore this condition of things and to seek satisfaction for one's passions outside the domain of lawful wedlock, is to revolt against this order of creative wisdom and to violate the letter of the law. But the intrinsic malice of the evil appears in the nature of this violation. This abuse touches life; not life in its being, but in its source, in the principle that makes all vitality possible, which is still more serious. Immorality is therefore a moral poisoning of the wells of life. It profanes and desecrates a faculty and prerogative so sacred that it is likened to the almighty power of the Creator.

A manifold malice may attach to a single act in violation of the law of moral purity. The burden of a vow in either party incurring guilt, whether that vow be matrimonial or religious, is a circumstance that adds injustice or sacrilege to the crime, according to the nature of that vow; and the double guilt is on both parties. If the vow exists in one and the other delinquent, then the offense is still further multiplied and the guilt aggravated. Blood-relationship adds a specific malice of its own, slight or grievous according to the intimacy of said relationship. Fornication, adultery, sacrilege and incest—these, to give to things their proper names, are terms that specify various degrees of malice and guilt in this matter; and although they do not sound well or look well in print, they have a meaning which sensible folks should not ignore.

A lapse from virtue is bad; the habit or vice, voluntarily entertained, is infinitely worse. If the one argues weakness, even culpable, the other betrays a studied contempt for God and the law, an utter perversion of the moral sense that does not even esteem virtue in itself; an appalling thralldom of the spirit to the flesh, an appetite that is all ungodly, a gluttony that is bestial. Very often it supposes a victim held fast in the clutches of unfeeling hoggishness, fascinated or subjugated, made to serve, while serviceable; and then cast off without a shred of respectability for another. It is an ordinary occurrence for one of these victims to swallow a deadly potion on being shown her folly and left to its consequences; and the human ogre rides triumphantly home in his red automobile.

But the positions may be reversed; the victim may play the role of seductress, and displaying charms that excite the passions, ensnare the youth whose feet are not guided by the lamp of experience, wisdom and religion. This is the human spider, soulless and shameless, using splendid gifts of God to form a web with which to inveigle and entrap a too willing prey. And the dead flies, who will count them!

The climax of infamy is reached when this sort of a thing is made, not a pastime, but a business, when virtue is put on the market with its fixed value attached and bartered for a price. There is no outrage on human feeling greater than this. We are all born of woman; and the sight of womanhood thus degraded and profaned would give us more of a shock if it were less common. The curse of God is on such wretches as ply this unnatural trade and live by infamy; not only on them, but on those also who make such traffic possible and lucrative. Considering all things, more guilty the latter than the former, perhaps. Active co-operation in evil makes one a joint partner in guilt; to encourage infamy is not only to sin, but also to share all the odium thereof; while he who contributes to the perpetuation of an iniquity of this nature is, in a sense, worse than the unfortunates themselves.

The civil law which seeks to eliminate the social evil of prostitution by enactment and process, gives rise, by enactment and process, to another evil almost as widespread. Divorce is a creature of the law, and divorce opens the door to concubinage, legalized if you will, but concubinage just the same. The marriage tie is intact after as well as before the decree of divorce; no human power can break that bond. The permission therefore to re-marry is permission to live in adultery, and that permission is, of its very nature, null and void. They who avail themselves of such a permission and live in sin, may count on the protection of the law, but the law will not protect them against the wrath of the Almighty who condemns their immoral living.

CHAPTER 77

WHEREIN NATURE IS OPPOSED

Certain excesses, such as we have already alluded to, however base and abominable in themselves and their effects, have nevertheless this to their credit that, while violating the positive law of God, they respect at least the fundamental laws of nature, according to which the universe is constructed and ordered. To satisfy one's depraved appetites along forbidden but natural lines, is certainly criminal; but an unnatural and beastly instinct is sometimes not-satisfied with such abuse and excess; the passion becomes so blinded as to ignore the difference of sex, runs even lower, to the inferior order of brutes. This is the very acme of ungodliness.

There are laws on the statute books against abominations of this sort; and be it said to the shame of a Christian community, said laws find an only too frequent application. Severe as are the penalties, they are less an adequate punishment than a public expression of the common horror inspired by the very mention of crimes they are destined to chastise. To attain this depth of infamy is at one and the same time to sin and to receive the penalty of sin. Here culminates repeated violence to the moral law. When one is sated with ordinary lusts and is bent on sweeping the whole gamut of mundane experiences and excitations, that one invariably descends to the unnatural and extraordinary, and lives a life of protest against nature.

St. Paul confirms this. According to him, God, in punishment for sin delivers over people to shameful affections, to a reprobate sense; he suffers them to be a hell unto themselves. And nature seldom fails to avenge herself for the outrages suffered. She uses the flail of disease and remorse, of misery and disgust, and she scourges the culprit to the verge of the grave, often to the yawning pit of hell.

People shudder at the very thought of such unmentionable things: but there are circles in society in which such sanctimonious shuddering is a mighty thin veil of hypocrisy. Infinitely more common, and little, if any, less unnatural and abominable are the crimes that are killing off the old stock that once possessed the land and making the country dependent for increase of population on the floods of immigration. The old Puritan families are almost extinct; Boston is more Irish than Dublin. The phenomenon is so striking here that it is called New Englandism. Why are there so few large families outside the Irish and Canadian elements? Why are there seen so few children in the fashionable districts of our large cities? Why this blast of sterility with which the land is cursed? Look behind the phenomenon, and you will find the cause; and the finding will make you shudder. And if only those shudder who are free from stain, the shuddering will be scarcely audible. Onan and Malthus as household gods are worse than the gods of Rome.

Meanwhile, the unit deteriorates alongside the family, being given over to a reprobate sense that is centered in self, that furnishes, against all law, its own satisfactions, and reaps, in all justice, its inevitable harvest of woe. To what extent this vice is common it would serve no purpose to examine; students of criminology have more than once made known their views on the matter. The character of its malice, both moral and physical, needs no comment; nature is outraged. But it has this among its several features; the thralldom to which it subjects its victim has nothing outside itself to which it may be compared. Man's self is his own greatest tyrant; there are no tortures so exquisite as those we provide for ourselves. While therefore we reprove the culprit, we commiserate with the unfortunate victim, and esteem that there is none more worthy of sympathy, conditioned, of course, on a state of mind and soul on his part that seeks relief and freedom; otherwise, it were pity wasted.

We have done with this infernal category of sin and filth. Yet we would remark right here that for the most part, as far as they are general and common, these excesses are the result of one cause; and that cause is everyday systematic Godlessness such as our public schools are largely responsible for. This system is responsible for a want of vital Christianity, of a lack of faith and religion that penetrates the human fibre and makes God and morality a factor in every deed. Deprived of this, youth has nothing to fall back on when the hour of temptation comes; and when he falls, nothing to keep him from the bottom of the pit.

It is impossible to put this argument in detail before the Christian and Catholic parent. If the parent docs not see it, it is because that parent is deficient in the most essential quality of a parent. Nothing but the atmosphere of a religious school can save our youth from being victims of that maelstrom of impurity that sweeps the land. And that alone, with the rigid principles of morality there inculcated, can save the parents of to-morrow from the blight and curse of New Englandism.

CHAPTER 78

SCANDAL

On only rare occasions do people who follow the bent of their unbridled passions bethink themselves of the double guilt that frequently attaches to their sins. Seemingly satisfied with the evil they have wrought unto their own souls, they choose to ignore the wrong they may have done unto others as a consequence of their sinful doings. They believe in the principle that every soul is personally responsible for its own damnation: which is true; but they forget that many elements may enter as causes into such a calamity. We are in nowise isolated beings in this world; our lives may, and do, affect the lives of others, and influence them sometimes to an extraordinary extent. We shall have, each of us, to answer one day for results of such influence; there is no man but is, in this sense, his brother's guardian.

There are, who deny this, like Cain. Yet we Icnow that Jesus Christ spoke clearly His mind in regard to scandal, and the emphasis He lays on His anathemas leaves no room to doubt of His judgment on the subject. Scandal, in fact, is murder; not corporal murder, which is a vengeance-crying abomination, but spiritual murder, heinous over the other in the same measure as the soul's value transcends that of the body. Kill the body, and the soul may live and be saved; kill the soul and it is lost eternally.

Properly speaking, scandal is any word or deed, evil or even with an appearance of evil, of a nature to furnish an occasion of spiritual downfall, to lead another info sin. It does not even matter whether the results be intended or merely suffered to occur; it does not even matter if no results follow at all. It is sufficient that the stumbling-block of scandal be placed in the way of another to his spiritual peril, and designed by nature to make him fall; on him who placed it, is the guilt of scandal.

The act of scandal consists in making sin easier to commit—as though it were not already easy enough to sin— for another. Natural grace, of which we are not totally bereft, raises certain barriers to protect and defend the weak and feeble. Conspicuous among these are ignorance and shame; evil sometimes offers difficulties, the ones physical, the others spiritual, such as innate delicacy, sense of dignity, timidity, instinctive repugnance for filth, human respect, dread of consequences, etc. These stand on guard before the soul to repel the first advances of the tempter which are the most dangerous; the Devil seldom unmasks his heavy batteries until the advance-posts of the soul are taken. It is the business of scandal to break down these barriers, and for scandal this work is as easy as it is nefarious. For curiosity is a hungering appetite, virtue is often protected with a very thin veil, and vice can be made to lose its hideousness and assume charms, to untried virtue, irresistible. There is nothing doing for His Satanic Majesty while scandal is in the field; he looks on and smiles.

There may be some truth in the Darwinian theory after all, if we judge from the imitative propensities of the species, probably an inherited trait of our common ancestor, the monkey. At any rate, we are often more easily led by example than by conviction; example leads us against our convictions. Asked why we did this or that, knowing we should not have done it, we answer with simian honesty, "because such a one did it, or invited us to do it." We get over a good many old-fashioned notions concerning modesty and purity, after listening to the experiences of others; we forget to be ashamed in the presence of the brazen, the unabashed and the impudent. We feel partially justified in doing what we see done by One to whom we are accustomed to look up. "If he acts thus," we say, "how can it be so very wrong in me; and if everybody—and everybody sometimes means a very few— if everybody does so, it cannot be so bad as I first imagined." Thus may be seen the workings of scandal in the mind and soul of its victim. Remembering our natural proneness to carnal indulgence, it is not surprising that the victims of scandal are so many. But this cannot be taken as an apology for the scandal-giver; rather the contrary, since the malice of his sin has possibilities so unbounded.

Scandal supposes an inducement to commit sin, which is not the case when the receiver is already all disposed to sin and is as bad as the giver. Nor can scandal be said properly to be given when those who receive it are in all probability

immune against the evil. Some people say they are scandalized when they are only shocked; if what shocked them has
nothing in it to induce them into sinning, then their received
scandal is only imaginative, nor has any been given. Then,
the number of persons scandalized must be considered as an
aggravating circumstance. Finally, the guilt of scandal is
greater or less according to the helplessness of the victim or
intended victim, and to the sacredness of his or her right to
immunity from temptation, children being most sacred in
this respect.

Of course God is merciful and forgives us our offenses
however great 'they may be. We may undo a deal of wrong
committed by us in this life, and die in the state of grace, even
after the most abominable crimes. Theologically, therefore,
the idea has little to commend itself, but it must have
occurred to more than one: how does one feel in heaven,
knowing that there is in hell, at that moment, one or many
through his or her agency! How mysterious is the justice of
God to suffer such a state of affairs! And although theoretically possible, how can anyone count on such a contingency
in his or her particular case! If the scandalous would reflect
seriously on this, they would be less willing to take the
chances offered by a possibility of this nature.

CHAPTER 79

OCCASIONS

Occasions of sin are persons, places or things that may easily lead us into sin: this definition of the little catechism is simple and clear and requires no comment. It is not necessary that said places or things, or even said persons, be evil in themselves; it is sufficient that contact with, or proximity to, them induce one to commit an evil. It may happen, and sometimes does, that a person without any evil design whatever become an occasion of sin for another. The blame therefore does not necessarily lie with objects, but rather with the subject.

Occasions are of two kinds: the remote or far and the proximate or near; they differ in the degree of facility with which they furnish temptation, and in the quality and nature of such temptation. In the former, the danger of falling is less, in the latter it is more, probable. In theory, it is impossible to draw the line and say just when an occasion ceases to be proximate and becomes remote; but in the concrete the thing is easy enough. If I have a well-grounded fear, a fear made prudent by experience, that in this or that conjuncture I shall sin, then it is a near occasion for me. If, however, I can feel with knowledge and conviction that I am strong enough to overcome the inevitable temptation arising from this other conjunction of circumstances, the occasion is only remote.

Thus, since danger in moral matters is nearly always relative; what is a remote occasion for one may be a proximate occasion for another. Proneness to evil is not the same in us all, for we have not all the same temperament and the same virtue. Two individuals may assist at a ball or a dance or a play, the one secure from sin, immune against temptation, the other a manifold victim of his or her folly. The dance or spectacle may not be bad in itself, it is not bad in fact for one, it is positively evil for the other and a near occasion of sin.

Remote occasions cannot always be avoided, they are so numerous and frequent; besides the evil they contain is a purely imaginative, and therefore negligible, quantity. There may be guilt however, in seeking such occasions and without reason exposing ourselves to their possible dangers; temerity is culpable; he that loves danger shall perish.

With the other kind, it is different. The simple fact of embracing a proximate occasion of sin is a grievous fault, even in the event of our accidentally not succumbing to the temptation to which we are exposed. There is an evil in such rashness independent of its consequences. He therefore who persists in visiting a place where there is every facility for sinning and where he has frequently sinned, does a deed of crime by going there; and whatever afterwards occurs, or does not occur, affects that crime not in the least. The same is true of reading certain books, novels and love-stories, for people of a certain spiritual complexion. The same is true of company-keeping, street-walking, familiarity and loose conversation. Nor can anything different be said of such liberties, consented to or merely tolerated, as embracing and kissing, amorous effusions and all perilous amusements of this nature. When experience shows these things to be fraught with danger, then they become sinful in themselves, and can be indulged in only in contempt of the law of God and to our own serious spiritual detriment.

But suppose I cannot avoid the occasion of sin, cannot remove it. What then?

If it is a clear case of proximate occasion of sin, and all means fail to change it, then the supposition of impossibility is a ridiculous one. It is paramount to asserting that sin and offense of God is sometimes necessary; and to talk thus is to talk nonsense. Sin is a deliberate act of a free will; mention necessity in the same breath, and you destroy the notion of sin. There can never be an impossibility of avoiding sin; consequently, there can never be an impossibility of avoiding a near occasion of sin.

It may be hard, very difficult; but that is another thing. But, as we have already said, the difficulty is rather within than without us, it arises from a lack of will power. But hard or easy, these occasions must nevertheless be removed. Let the suffering entailed be what it may, the eye must be plucked out, the arm must be lopped off, to use the Saviour's figurative language, if in no other way the soul can be saved from sin. Better to leave your father's house, better to give up your very life, than to damn your soul for all eternity. But extremes are rarely called for; small sacrifices often cost more than great ones. A good dose of ordinary, everyday mortification and penance goes a long way toward producing the necessary effect. An ounce of self-denial will work miracles in a sluggard, cowardly soul.

It would be well on occasion to remember this, especially when one in such a state is thinking seriously of going to confession: if he is not prepared to make the required effort, then he had better stay away until such a time as he is willing. For if he states his case correctly, he will not receive absolution; if his avowal is not according to fact, his confession is void, perhaps sacrilegious. Have done with sin before you can expect to have your sins forgiven.

PART ELEVEN

MARRIAGE

CHAPTER 80

HEARTS

The heart, the seat of the affections, is, after the mind whose authority and direction it is made to obey, man's noblest faculty; but it may, in the event of its contemning reason's dictates, become the source and fountain-head of inordinate lust and an instrument of much moral disaster and ruin. When the intelligence becomes powerless to command and to say what and when and how the affections shall disport themselves, then man becomes a slave to his heart and is led like an ass by the nose hither and thither; and when nature thus runs unrestrained and wild, it makes for the mudholes of lust wherein to wallow and besot itself.

The heart is made to love what is good; now, good is real or apparent. Love is blind, and needs reason to discern for it what is good and what is not, reason to direct its affections into their legitimate channels. But the heart may refuse to be thus controlled, swayed by the whisperings of ignorant pride and conceit; or it may be unable to receive the impulse of the reason on account of the unhealthy fumes that arise from a too exuberant animal nature unchastened by self-denial. Then it is that, free to act as it lists, it accepts indiscriminately everything with an appearance of good, in which gets mixed up much of that which appeals to the inferior appetites. And in the end it gets lost.

Again, the heart is a power for good or evil; it may be likened to a magazine, holding within its throbbing sides an explosive deposit of untold energy and puissance, capable of all things within the range of the human. While it may lift man to the very pinnacle of goodness, it may also sink him to the lowest level of infamy. Only, in one case, it is spiritualized love, in the other, it is carnal; in one case it obeys the spirit, in the other, the flesh; in one case its true name is charity, in the other, it is animal, sexual instinct, and it is only improperly called love. For God is love. Love therefore is pure. That which is not pure is not love.

People who trifle with the affections usually come to woe sooner or later, sooner rather than later; affairs of the heart are always morally malodorous affairs. Frequently there is evil on one side at least, in intention, from the start. The devil's game is to play on the chaste attachment, and in an unguarded moment, to swing it around to his point. If the victim does not balk at the first shock and surprise, the game is won; for long experience has made him confident of being able to make the counterfeit look like the real; and it requires, as a general rule, little argument to make us look at our faults in their best light.

Many a pure love has degenerated and many a virtue fallen, why? because people forget who and what they are, forget they are human, forget they are creatures of flesh and blood, predisposed to sin, saturated with concupiscence and naturally frail as a reed against the seductions of the wily one. They forget this, and act as though theirs were art angelic, instead of a human, nature. They imagine themselves proof against that which counts such victims as David and Solomon, which would cause the fall of a Father of the desert, or even of an angel from heaven encumbered with the burden we carry, if he despised the claims of ordinary common sense.

And this forgetfulness on their part, let it be remembered, is wholly voluntary and culpable, at least in its cause. They may not have been attentive at the precise moment that the flames of passion reached the mine of their affections; but they were well aware that things would come inevitably to such a pass. And when the mine went up, as it was natural, what wonder if disaster followed! Who is to blame but themselves? People do not play with matches around a powder magazine; and if they do, very little consolation comes with the knowledge of their folly when they are being picked up in sections from out of the ruins.

Of course there are easier victims than these, such as would not recognize true inter-sexual love if they saw it through a magnifying glass; everything of the nature of a fancy or whim, of a sensation or emotion with them is love. Love-sick maidens are usually soft-brained, and their languorous swains, lascivious. The latter pose as "killers;" the former wear their heart on their sleeve, and are convinced that every second man they meet who treats them gallantly is smitten with their charms and is passionately in love with them.

Some go in for excitement and novelty, to break the monotony of virtuous restraint. They are anxious for a little adventure and romance. A good thing, too, to have these exploits to narrate to their friends. But they do not tell all to their friends; they would be ashamed to. If said friends are wise they can supply the deficiencies. And when it is all over, it is the same old story of the man that did not know the gun was loaded.

They therefore who would remain pure must of all necessity keep custody over their heart's affections, make right reason and faith their guide and make the will force obedience thereto. If wrong attachments are formed, then there is nothing to do but to eradicate them, to cut, tear and crush; they must be destroyed at any cost. A pennyweight of prudence might have prevented the evil; it will now take mortification in large and repeated doses to undo it. In this alone is there salvation.

CHAPTER 81

NOT GOOD TO BE ALONE

M an may come to discover that the state in which he finds himself placed, is not the one for which he was evidently intended by the Maker. We do not all receive the same gifts because our callings are different; each of us is endowed in accordance and in harmony with the ends of the Creator in making us. Some men should marry, others may not; but the state of celibacy is for the few, and not for the many, these few depending solely on an abundant grace of God.

Again, one may become alive to the fact that to remain in an abnormal position means to seriously jeopardize his soul's salvation; celibacy may, as for many it does, spell out for him, clearly and plainly, eternal damnation. It is to no purpose here to examine the causes of, and reasons for, such a condition of affairs. We take the fact as it stands, plain and evident, a stern, hard fact that will not be downed, because it is supported by the living proof of habit and conduct; living and continuing to live a celibate, taking him as he is and as there is every token of his remaining without any reasonable ground for expecting a change, this man is doomed to perdition. His passions have made him their slave; he cannot, it is morally impossible for him to do so, remain continent.

Suppose again that the Almighty has created the state of wedlock for just such emergencies, whereby a man may find a remedy for his weaknesses, an outlet for his passions, a regulator of his life here below and a security against damnation hereafter; and this is precisely the case, for the ends of marriage are not only to perpetuate the species, but also to furnish a remedy for natural concupiscence and to raise a barrier against the flood of impurity.

Now, the case being as stated, need a Catholic, young or —a no longer young—man look long or strive hard to find his path of duty already clearly traced? And in making this application we refer to man, not to woman, for reasons that are obvious; we refer, again, to those among men whose spiritual sense is not yet wholly dead, who have not entirely lost all respect for virtue in itself: who still claim to have an immortal soul and hope to save it; but who have been caught in the maelstrom of vice and whose passions and lusts have outgrown in strength the ordinary resisting powers of natural virtue and religion incomplete and half-hearted. These can appreciate their position; it would be well for them to do so; the faculty for so doing may not always be left with them.

The obligation to marry, to increase and multiply, was given to mankind in general, and applies to man as a whole, and not to the individual; that is, in the common and ordinary run of human things. But the circumstances with which we are dealing are outside the normal, sphere; they are extraordinary, that is say, they do not exist in accordance with the plan and order established by God; they constitute a disorder resulting from unlawful indulgence and wild impiety. It may therefore be, and it frequently is the case, that the general obligation to marry particularize itself and fall with its full weight on the individual, this one or that one, according to the circumstances of his life. Then it is that the voice of God's authority reaches the ear of the unit and says to him in no uncertain accents: thou shalt marry. And behind that decree of God stands divine justice to vindicate the divine right.

We do not deny but that, absolutely speaking, recourse to this remedy may not be imperiously demanded; but we do claim that the absolute has nothing whatever to do with the question which is one of relative facts. What a supposed man may do in this or that given circumstance does not in the least alter the position of another real, live man who will not do this or that thing in a given circumstance; he will not, because, morally speaking, he cannot; and he cannot, simply because through excesses he has forgotten how. And of other reasons to justify non-compliance with the law, there can be none; it is here a. question of saving one's soul; inconveniences and difficulties and obstacles have no meaning in such a contingency.

And, mind you, the effects of profligate celibacy are farther-reaching than many of us would suppose at first blush. The culprit bears the odium of it in his soul. But what about the state of those—or rather of her, whoever she may be, known or unknown—whom he, in the order of Providence, is destined to save from the precariousness of single life? If it is his duty to take a wife, whose salvation as well as his own, perhaps depends on the fulfilment of that duty, and if he shirks his duty, shall he not be held responsible for the results in her as well as in himself, since he could, and she could not, ward off the evil?

It has come to such a pass nowadays that celibacy, as a general thing, is a misnomer for profligacy. Making all due allowance for honorable exceptions, the unmarried male who is not well saturated with spirituality and faith is notoriously gallinaceous in his morals. In certain classes, he is expected to sow his wild oats before he is out of his teens; and by this is meant that he will begin young to tear into shreds the Sixth Commandment so as not to be bothered with it later in life. If he married he would be safe.

Finally what kind of an existence is it for any human being, with power to do otherwise, to pass through life a worthless, good-for-nothing nonentity, living for self, shirking the sacred duties of paternity, defrauding nature and God and sowing corruption where he might be laying the foundation of a race that may never die? There is no one to whom he has done good and no one owes him a tear when his barren carcass is being given over as food to the worms. He is a rotten link on the chain of life and the curse of oblivion will vindicate the claims of his unborn generations. Young man, marry, marry now, and be something in the world besides an eyesore of unproductiveness and worthlessness; do something that will make somebody happy besides yourself; show that you passed, and leave something behind that will remember you and bless your name.

CHAPTER 82

A HELPING HAND

The moralist is usually severe, and the quality of his censure is merciless, when he attempts to treat the unwholesome theme of moral deformity; and all his efforts are mere attempts, for no human language can do full justice to such a theme, or fully express the contempt such excesses deserve. It is just, then, that, when he stands in the presence of the moral leper who blushes not for his degradation, he flay with the whip of scorn and contempt, scourge with anathema and brand him with every stigma of infamy, in order that the load of opprobrium thus heaped upon his guilty head may at least deter the clean from such defilement.

But, if guilt is always guilt, the quality of guilt is varied. Just as all virtue is not equally meritorious, so to other sources than personal unworthiness may often be traced moral debility that strives against natural causes, necessary conditions of environment and an ever-present and ever-active influence for evil. A fall does not always betoken profound degradation nor a stain, acute perversity of the will. Those therefore who wrestle manfully with the effects of regretted lapses or weaknesses, who fight down, sometimes perhaps unsuccessfully, the strong tendencies of a too exuberant animal nature, who strive to neutralize an influence that unduly oppresses them,—against these, guilty though they may have been, is not directed the moralist's unmeasured censure. His reproaches in such cases tend less to condemn than to awake to a sense of moral responsibility; earnestness in pointing out remedy and safeguards takes the place of severity against wilfulness. For he knows that not a few sentences of condemnation Christ writes on the sands, as He did in a celebrated case, and many an over-zealous accuser he has confounded, like the villainous Pharisees whom He challenged to show a hand white enough to be worthy to cast the first stone.

Evidently such pity and commiseration should not serve to make vice less unlovely and thus undo the very work it is intended to perform. It should not have the characteristics of certain books and plays that pretend to teach morality by exposing vice in all its seductiveness. Over-sensitive and maudlin sympathy is as ridiculous as it is unhealthy; its tendency is principally to encourage and spoil. But a judicious, discreet and measured sympathy will lift up the fallen, strengthen the weak and help the timorous over many a difficulty. It will suggest, too, the means best calculated to insure freedom from slavery of the passions.

The first of these is self-denial, which is the inseparable companion of chastity; when they are not found together, seldom does either exist. And by self-denial is here meant the destruction of that eternal reference for self, that is at the bottom of all uncleanness, that makes all things, however sacred, subservient to one's own pleasures, that considers nothing unlawful but what goes against the grain of natural impulse and natural appetites. There may be other causes, but this self-love is a primary one. Say what you will, but one does not fall from his own level; the moral world is like the physical; if you are raised aloft in disregard for the laws of truth, you are going to come down with a thud. If you imagine all the pleasures of life made for you, and become lawful because your nature craves for them, you are taking a too high estimate of yourself; you are going before a fall He who takes a correct measure of himself, gets his bearings in relation to God, comes to realize his own weak points and several deficiencies, and acknowledges the obligations such a state of affairs places upon him, that one may sin, but he will not go far.

He may fall, because he is human, because strength sufficient to guard us against the assaults of impurity is not from us, but from God. The spirit of humility, therefore, which makes known to him his own insufficiency, must be fortified with the spirit of faith which makes him ask for support through prayer. It is faith that makes prayer possible, and living faith, the spirit of faith, that makes us pray aright. This kind of prayer need not express itself in words; it may be a habit, a long drawn out desire, an habitual longing for help coupled with firm confidence in God's mercy to grant our request. No state of soul however disordered can long resist such a power, and no habit of evil but in time will be annihilated by it.

The man or woman who undertakes to keep himself or herself pure, or to rise out of a habit of sin without the liberal use of divine supplication has in hand a very ungrateful task, and he or she will realize it before going far. And unless that prayer is sincere and heartfelt, a prayer full of faith that will not entertain the thought of failure, every effort will be barren of results. You must speak to God as to one near you, and remember that He is near you all the time.

Then there are the sacraments to repair every breach and to heal every wound. Penance will cleanse you, communion will adorn and equip you anew. Confession will give you a better knowledge of yourself every time you go; the Food of God will strengthen every fibre of your soul and steel you against the seductions that otherwise would make you a ready victim. Don't go once a year, go ten, twenty times and more, if necessary, go until you feel that you own yourself, that you can command and be obeyed. Then you will not have to be told to stop; you will be safe.

PART TWELVE

THEFT

CHAPTER 83

THOU SHALT NOT STEAL

The Seventh Commandment is protective of the right of property which is vested in every human being enjoying the use of reason. Property means that which belongs to one, that which is one's own, to have and to hold, or to dispose of, at one's pleasure, or to reclaim in the event of actual dispossession. The right of property embraces all things to which may be affixed the seal of ownership; and it holds good until the owner relinquishes his claim, or forfeits or loses his title without offense to justice. This natural faculty to possess excludes every alien right, and supposes in all others the duty and obligation to respect it. The respect that goes as far as not relieving the owner of his goods is not enough; it must safeguard him against all damage and injury to said goods; otherwise his right is non-existent.

All violations of this right come under the general head of stealing. People call it theft, when it is effected with secrecy and slyness; robbery, when there is a suggestion of force or violence. The swindler is he who appropriates another's goods by methods of gross deception or false pretenses while the embezzler transfers to himself the funds entrusted to his care. Petty thieving is called pilfering or filching; stealing on a large scale usually has less dishonorable qualificatives. Boodling and lobbying are called politics; watering stock, squeezing out legitimate competition, is called financiering; wholesale confiscation and unjust conquest is called statesmanship. Give it whatever name you like, it is all stealing; whether the culprit be liberally rewarded or liberally punished, he nevertheless stands amenable to God's justice which is outraged wherever human justice suffers.

Of course the sin of theft has its degrees of gravity, malice and guilt, to determine which, that is, to fix exactly the value of stolen goods sufficient to constitute a grievous fault, is not the simplest and easiest of moral problems. The extent of delinquency may be dependent upon various causes and complex conditions. On the one hand, the victim must be considered in himself, and the amount of injury sustained by him; on the other, justice is offended generally in all cases of theft, and because justice is the corner stone of society, it must be protected at all hazards. It is only by weighing judiciously all these different circumstances that we can come to enunciate an approximate general rule that will serve as a guide in the ordinary contingencies of life.

Thus, of two individuals deprived by theft of a same amount of worldly goods, the one may suffer thereby to a much greater extent than the other; he who suffers more is naturally more reluctant to part with his goods, and a greater injustice is done to him than to the other. The sin committed against him is therefore greater than that committed against the other. A rich man may not feel the loss of a dollar, whereas for another less prosperous the loss of less than that sum might be of the nature of a calamity. To take therefore unjustly from a person what to that person is a notable amount is a grievous sin. It is uniformly agreed that it is a notable loss for a man to be unduly deprived of what constitutes a day's sustenance. This is the minimum of grievous matter concerning theft.

But this rule will evidently not hold good applied on a rising scale to more and more extensive fortunes; for a time would come when it would be possible without serious guilt to appropriate good round sums from those abundantly blessed with this world's goods.

The disorders necessarily attendant on such a moral rule are only too evident; and it is plain that the law of God cannot countenance abuses of this nature. Justice therefore demands that there be a certain fixed sum beyond which one may not go without incurring serious guilt; and this, independent of the fortune of the person who suffers. Theologians have fixed that amount approximately, in this country, at five dollars. This means that when such a sum is taken, in all cases, the sin is mortal. It is not always necessary, it is seldom necessary, that one should steal this much in order to offend grievously; but when the thief reaches this amount, be his victim ever so wealthy, he is guilty of grave injustice.

This rule applies to all cases in which the neighbor is made to suffer unjustly in his lawful possessions; and it effects all wrongdoers whether they steal or destroy another's goods or co-operate efficaciously in such deeds of sin. It matters not whether the harm be wrought directly or indirectly, since in either case there may be moral fault; and it must be remembered that gross negligence may make one responsible as well as malice aforethought.

The following are said to co-operate in crime to the extent of becoming joint-partners with the principal agent in guilt: those in whose name the wrong is done, in obedience to their orders or as a result of any other means employed; those who influence the culprit by suggesting motives and reasons for his crime or by pointing out efficient means of arriving thereat; those who induce others to commit evil by playing on their weaknesses thereby subjecting them to what is known as moral force; those who harbor the thief and conceal his stolen property against their recovery; those whose silence is equivalent to approbation, permission or official consent; those finally who before, during or after the deed, abstain from performing a plain duty in preventing, deterring or bringing to justice the guilty party. Such persons as the foregoing participate as abettors in crime and share all the guilt of the actual criminals; sometimes the former are even more guilty than the latter.

The Tenth Commandment which forbids us to covet our neighbor's goods, bears the same relation to the Seventh as the Ninth does to the Sixth. It must, however, be borne in mind that all such coveting supposes injustice in desire, that is, in the means by which we desire to obtain what is not ours. To wish for, to long ardently for something that appeals to one's like and fancy is not sinful; the wrong consists in the desire to acquire it unjustly, to steal it, and thereby work damage unto the neighbor. It is a natural weakness in man to be dissatisfied with what he has and to sigh after what he has not; very few of us are free from this failing. But so long as our cravings and hankerings are not tainted with injustice, we are innocent of evil.

CHAPTER 84

PETTY THEFTS

A question may arise as to petty thefts, venial in themselves, but oft repeated and aggregating in the long run a sum of considerable value: how are we to deal with such cases? Should peculations of this sort be taken singly, and their individual malice determined, without reference to the sum total of injustice caused; or should no severe judgment be passed until such a time as sufficient matter be accumulated to make the fault grievous? In other words, is there nothing but venial sin in thefts of little values, or is there only one big sin at the end? The difficulty is a practical one.

If petty thefts are committed with a view to amass a notable sum, the simple fact of such an intention makes the offense a mortal one. For, as we have already remarked in treating of the human act, our deeds may be, and frequently are, vitiated by the intention we have in performing them. If we do something with evil intent and purpose, our action is evil whether the deed in itself be indifferent or even good.

Here the intention is to cause a grave injustice; the deed is only a petty theft, but it serves as a means to a more serious offense. The act therefore takes its malice from the purpose of the agent and becomes sinful in a high degree.

As to each repeated theft, that depends again on the intention of the culprit. If in the course of his pilferings he no longer adverts to his first purpose and has no intention in stealing beyond that of helping himself to a little of his neighbor's goods, he is guilty of nothing more than a venial sin. If, however, the initial purpose is present at every act, if at every fresh peculation the intention to accumulate is renewed explicitly or implicitly, then every theft is identical with the first in malice, and the offender commits mortal sin as often as he steals. Thus the state of soul of one who filches after this fashion is not sensibly affected by his arriving at a notable sum of injustice in the aggregate. The malice of his conduct has already been established; it is now completed in deed.

A person who thievishly appropriates small sums, but whose pilferings have no moral reference to each other, will find himself a mortal offender the moment his accumulated injustices reach the amount we have qualified as notable, provided he be at that moment aware of the fact, or even if he only have a doubt about the matter. And this is true whether the stolen sums be taken from one or from several persons. Even in the latter case, although no one person suffers serious damage or prejudice, justice however is seriously violated and the intention of the guilty party is really to perpetrate grave injustice.

However, such thefts as these which in the end become

accumulative, must of their nature be successive and joined together by some bond of moral union, otherwise they could never be considered a. whole. By this is meant that there must not exist between the different single thefts an interruption or space of time such as to make it impossible to consider reasonably the several deeds as forming one general action. The time generally looked upon as sufficient to prevent a moral union of this kind is two months. In the absence therefore of a specific intention to arrive at a large amount by successive thefts, it must be said that such thefts as are separated by an intervening space of two months can never be accounted as parts of one grave injustice, and a mortal sin can never be committed by one whose venial offenses are of this nature. Of course if there be an evil purpose, that alone is sufficient to establish a moral union between single acts of theft however considerable the interval that separates them.

Several persons may conspire to purloin each a limited amount. The circumstance of conspiracy, connivance or collusion makes each co-operator in the deed responsible for the whole damage done; and if the amount thus defrauded be notable, each is guilty of mortal sin.

We might here add in favor of children who take small things from their parents and of wives who sometimes relieve their husbands of small change, that it is natural that a man be less reluctant to being defrauded in small matters by his own than by total Strangers. It is only reasonable therefore that more latitude be allowed such delinquents when there is question of computing the amount to be considered notable; perhaps the amount might be doubled in their favor. The same might be said in favor of those whose petty thefts are directed against several victims instead of one, since the injury sustained individually is less.

The best plan is to leave what does not belong to one severely alone. In other sins there may be something gained in the long run, but here no such illusion can be entertained, for the spectre of restitution, as we shall see, follows every injustice as a shadow follows its object, and its business is to see that no man profit by his ill-gotten goods.

CHAPTER 85

AN OFT EXPLOITED, BUT SPECIOUS PLEA

It is not an infrequent occurrence for persons given to the habit of petty thefts and fraud, to seek to justify their irregular conduct by a pretense of justice which they call secret compensation. They stand arraigned before the bar of their conscience on the charge of niching small sums, usually from their employers; they have no will to desist; they therefore plead not guilty, and have nothing so much at heart as to convince themselves that they act within their rights. They elaborate a theory of justice after their ideas, or rather, according to their own desires; they bolster it up with facts that limp all the way from half-truths to downright falsities; and thus acquit themselves of sin, and go their way in peace. A judge is always lenient when he tries his own case.

Secret compensation is the taking surreptitiously from another of the equivalent of what is due to one, of what has been taken and is kept against all justice, in order to indemnify oneself for losses sustained. This sort of a thing, in

394 AN EXPLANATION OF CATHOLIC MORALS

theory at least, has a perfectly plausible look, nor, in fact, is it contrary to justice, when all the necessary conditions are fulfilled to the letter. But the cases in which these conditions are fulfilled are so few and rare that they may hardly be said to exist at all. It is extremely difficult to find such A case, and nearly always when this practice is resorted to, the order of justice is violated.

And if common sense in the case of any given individual fail to show him this truth, we here quote for his benefit an authority capable of putting all his doubts at rest. The following proposition was advanced: "Domestic servants who adjudge themselves underpaid for services rendered, may appropriate to themselves by stealth a compensation." This proposition has received the full weight of papal condemnation. It cannot be denied that it applies to all who engage their services for hire. To maintain the contrary is to revolt against the highest authority in the Church; to practise it is purely and simply to Sin.

A case is often made out on the grounds that wages are small, work very hard and the laborer therefore insufficiently remunerated. But to conclude therefrom the right to help oneself to the employer's goods, is a strange manner of reasoning, while it opens the door to all manner of injustice. Where is there a man, whatever his labor and pay, who could not come to the same conclusion? Who may not consider himself ill-paid? And who is there that really thinks he is not worth more than he gets? There is no limit to the value one may put on one's own services; and he who is justified to-day in taking a quarter of a dollar, would be equally justified to-morrow in appropriating the whole concern. And then what becomes of honesty, and the right of property? And what security can anyone have against the private judgment of his neighbor?

And what about the contract according to the terms of which you are to give your services and to receive in return a stipulated amount? Was there any clause therein by which you are entitled to change the terms of said contract without consulting the other party interested? You don't think he would mind it. You don't think anything of the kind; you know he will and does mind it. He may be generous, but he is not a fool.

"But I make up for it. I work overtime, work harder, am more attentive to my work; and thereby save more for my employer than I take." Here you contradict yourself. You are therefore not underpaid. And if you furnish a greater amount of labor than is expected of you, that is your business and your free choice. And the right you have to a compensation for such extra labor is entirely dependent on the free will of your employer. People usually pay for what they call for; services uncalled for are gratuitous services. To think otherwise betokens a befuddled state of mind.

"But I am forced to work harder and longer than we agreed." Then it is up to you to remonstrate with your employer, to state the case as it is and to ask for a raise. If he refuses, then his refusal is your cue to quit and go elsewhere. It means that your services are no longer required. It means, at any rate, that you have to stand the cut or seek to better your condition under other employers. It is hard! Of course it is hard, but no harder than a great many other things we have to put up with.

If my neighbor holds unjustly what belongs to me, or if he has failed to repair damages caused, to recover my losses by secret compensation has the same degree of malice and disorder. The law is instituted for just such purposes; you have recourse thereto. You may prosecute and get damages. If the courts fail to give you justice, then perhaps there may be occasion to discuss the merits of the secret compensation theory. But you had better get the advice of some competent person before you attempt to put it in practice; otherwise you are liable to get into a bigger hole than the one you are trying to get out of.

Sometimes the bold assertion is advanced that the employer knows perfectly that he is being systematically robbed and tolerates it. It is incumbent on this party to prove his assertion in a very simple way. Let him denounce himself to his employer and allow the truth or falsity thereof hang on the result. If he does not lose his job inside of twenty-four hours after the interview, he may continue his peculations in perfect tranquillity of conscience. If he escapes prosecution through the consideration of his former employer, he must take it for granted that the toleration he spoke of was of a very general nature, the natural stand for a man to take who is being robbed and cannot help it. To justify oneself on such a principle is to put a premium on shrewd dishonesty.

PART THIRTEEN

YOUR NEIGHBOR

CHAPTER 86

CONTUMELY

The Eighth Commandment concerns itself with the good name of the neighbor; in a general way, it reproves all sins of the tongue, apart from those already condemned by the Second and Sixth commandments, that is to say, blasphemous and impure speech. It is as a weapon against the neighbor and an instrument of untruth that the tongue is here considered.

By a good name is here intended the esteem in which a person is held by his fellow-men. Call it reputation, character, fame, renown, etc., a good name means that the bearer is generally considered above reproach in all matters of honesty, moral integrity and worth. It does not necessarily imply that such esteem is manifested exteriorly by what is technically known as honor, the natural concomitant of a good name; it simply stands for the knowledge entertained by others of our respectability and our title to honor. A good name is therefore one thing; honor is another. And honor consists precisely in that manifestation on the part of our fellows of the esteem and respect in which they hold us, the fruit of our good name, the homage rendered to virtue, dignity and merit. As it may therefore be easily seen, these two things—a good name and honor—differ as much as a sign differs from the thing signified.

The Eighth Commandment protects every man's honor; it condemns contumely which is an attack upon that honor. Contumely is a sign of contempt which shows itself by attempting to impair the honor one duly receives; it either strives to prevent that honor being paid to the good name that naturally deserves it, or it tries to nullify it by offering just the contrary, which is contumely, more commonly called affront, outrage, insult.

Now, contumely, as you will remark, does not seek primarily to deprive one of a good name; which it nearly always succeeds in doing, and this is called detraction; but its object is to prevent your good name from getting its desert of respect, your character supposedly remaining intact. The insult offered is intended to effect this purpose. Again, all contumely presupposes the presence of the party affronted; the affront is thrown in one's face, and therein consists the shocking indecency of the thing and its specific malice.

It must be remembered that anger, hatred, the spirit of vengeance or any other passion does not excuse one from the guilt of contumely. On the other hand, one's culpability is not lessened by the accidental fact of one's intended insults going wide of the mark and bearing no fruit of dishonor to the person assailed. To the malice of contumely may, and is often, added that of defamation, if apart from the dishonor received one's character is besmirched in the bargain. Contumely against parents offends at the same time filial piety; against God and His saints, it is sacrilegious; if provoked by the practice of religion and virtue, it is impious. If perpetrated in deed, it may offend justice properly so called; if it occasion sin in others, it is scandalous; if it drive the victim to excesses of any kind, the guilt thereof is shared by the contumelious agent.

Sometimes insult is offered gratuitously, as in the case of the weak, the old, the cripple and other unfortunates who deserve pity rather than mockery; the quality of contumely of this sort is brutal and fiendish. Others will say for justification: "But he said the same, he did the same to me. Can I not defend myself?" That depends on the sort of defense you resort to. All weapons of defense are not lawful. If a man uses evil means to wrong you, there is no justification, in Christian ethics, for you to employ the same means in order to get square, or even to shelter yourself from his abuse. The "eye-for-eye" principle is not recognized among civilized and Christian peoples.

This gross violation of personal respect may be perpetrated in many ways; any expression of contempt, offered to your face, or directed against you through a representative, is contumely. The usual way to do this is to fling vile epithets, to call opprobrious names, to make shameful charges. It is not always necessary that such names and epithets be inapplicable or such charges false, if, notwithstanding, the person in question has not thereby forfeited his right to respect. In certain circumstances, the epithet "fool" may hold all the opprobriousness of contumely: "thief" and "drunkard" and others of a fouler nature may be thus malicious for a better reason. An accusation of immorality in oneself or in one's parents is contumelious in a high degree. Our mothers are a favorite target for the shafts of contumely that through them reach us. Abuse is not the only vehicle of contumely; scorn, wanton ridicule, indecent mockery and caricature that cover the unfortunate victim with shame and confusion serve the purpose as well. To strike one, to spit on one and other ignoble attacks and assaults belong to the same category of crime.

The malice of contumely is not, of course, equal in all cases; circumstances have a great deal to do in determining the gravity of each offense. The more conspicuous a person is in dignity and the more worthy of respect, the more serious the affront offered him; and still more grave the offense, if through him many others are attainted. If again no dishonor is intended and no offense taken, or could reasonably be taken, there is no sin at all. There may be people very low on the scale of respectability as the world judges respectability; but it can never be said of a man or woman that he or she cannot be dishonored, that he or she is beneath contempt. Human nature never forfeits all respect; it always has some redeeming feature to commend it.

Chapter 87

Defamation

Defamation differs from contumely in that the one supposes the absence, the other, the presence, of the person vilified; and again, in that the former asperses the reputation of the victim while the latter attacks the honor due or paid to said reputation. A good name is, after the grace of God, mans most precious possession; wealth is mere trash compared with it. You may find people who think otherwise, but the universal sentiment of mankind stigmatizes such baseness and buries it under the weight of its opprobrium. Nor is it impossible that honor be paid where a good character no longer exists; but this is accidental. In the nature of things, reputation is the basis of all honor; if you destroy character, you destroy at the same time its fruit, which is honor. Thus will be seen the double malice of defamation.

To defame therefore is to lessen or to annul the estimation in which a person is held by his fellow-men. This crime may be perpetrated in two different manners: by making known his secret faults, and this is simple detraction; and by ascribing to him faults of which he is innocent, and this is calumny or slander. Thus it appears that a man's character may suffer from truth as well as from falsehood. Truth is an adorable thing, but it has its time and place; the fact of its being truth does not prevent it from being harmful. On the other hand, a lie, which is evil in itself, becomes abominable when used to malign a fellow-man.

There is one mitigating and two aggravating forms of defamation. Gossip is small talk, idle and sufficiently discolored to make its subject appear in an unfavorable light. It takes a morbid pleasure in speaking of the known and public faults of another. It picks at little things, and furnishes a steady occupation for people who have more time to mind other people's business than their own. It bespeaks smallness in intellectual make-up and general pusillanimity. That is about all the harm there is in it, and that is enough.

Libel supposes a wide diffusion of defamatory matter, written or spoken. Its malice is great because of its power for evil and harm. Tale-bearing or backbiting is what the name implies. Its object is principally to spread discord, to cause enmity, to break up friendships; it may have an ulterior purpose, and these are the means it employs. No limit can be set to its capacity for evil, its malice is especially infernal.

It is not necessary that what we do or say of a defamatory nature result, as a matter of fact, in bringing one's name into disfavor or disrepute; it is sufficient that it be of such a nature and have such a tendency. If by accident the venomous shaft spend itself before attaining the intended mark, no credit is due therefore to him who shot it; his guilt remains what it was when he sped it on its way. Nor is there justification in the plea that no harm was meant, that the deed was done in a moment of anger, jealousy, etc., that it was the result of loquacity, indulged in for the simple pleasure of talking. These are excuses that excuse not.

There are those who, speaking in disparagement of the neighbor, speak to the point, directly and plainly; others, no less guilty, do it in a covert manner, have recourse to subterfuge and insinuation. They exaggerate faults and make them appear more odious, they put an evil interpretation on the deed or intention; they keep back facts that would improve the situation; they remain silent when silence is condemnatory; they praise with a malignant praise. A mean, sarcastic smile or a significant reticence often does the work better than many words and phrases. And all this, as we have said, independently of the truth or falsehood of the impression conveyed.

Listeners share the guilt of the defamers on the principle that the receiver is as bad as the thief. This supposes of course that you listen, not merely hear; that you enjoy this sort of a thing and are willing and ready to receive the impression derogatory to the neighbor's esteem and good name. Of course, if mere curiosity makes us listen and our pleasure and amusement are less at the expense of the neighbor's good name than excited by the style of the narrator or the singularity of the facts alleged, the fault is less; but fault there nevertheless is, since such an attitude serves to encourage the traducer and helps him drive his points home. Many sin who could and should prevent excesses of this kind, but refrain from doing so; their sin is greater if, by reason of their position, they are under greater obligations of correction.

Although reputation is a priceless boon to all men, there are cases wherein it has an especial value on account of the peculiar circumstances of a man's position. It not infrequently happens that the whole success of a man's life depends on his good name. Men in public life, in the professions, religious and others similarly placed, suffer from defamation far more than those in the ordinary walks of life; and naturally those who injure them are guilty of more grievous wrong. And it goes without saying that a man can stand an immoral aspersion better than a woman. In all cases the malice is measured by the injury done or intended.

CHAPTER 88

DETRACTION

To absolve oneself of the sin of detraction on the ground that nothing but the truth was spoken is, as we have seen, one way of getting around a difficulty that is no way at all. Some excuses are better than none, others are not. It is precisely the truth of such talk that makes it detraction; if it were not true, it would not be detraction but calumny—another and a very different fault. It would be well for such people to reflect for a moment, and ask themselves if their own character would stand the strain of having their secret sins and failings subjected to public criticism and censure, their private shortcomings heralded from every housetop. Would they, or would they not, consider themselves injured by such revelations? Then it would be in order for them to use the same rule and measure in dealing with others.

He who does moral evil offends in the sight of God and forfeits God's esteem and friendship. But it does not follow that he should also forfeit the esteem of his fellow-men. The latter evil is nothing compared with the first; but it is a great misfortune nevertheless. If a man's private iniquity is something that concerns himself and his God, to the exclusion of all others, then whosoever presumes to judge and condemn him trespasses on forbidden ground, and is open to judgment and condemnation himself before his Maker.

All do not live in stone mansions who throw stones. If there is a mote in the neighbor's eye, perhaps there is a very large piece of timber in your own. Great zeal in belaboring the neighbor for his faults will not lessen your own, nor make you appear an angel of light before God when you are something very different. If you employed this same zeal towards yourself, you would obtain more consoling results, for charity begins at home. One learns more examining one's own conscience than dissecting and flaying others alive.

It may be objected that since detraction deals with secret sins, if the facts related are of public notoriety, there is no wrong in speaking of them, for you cannot vilify one who is already vilified. This is true; and then, again, it depends. First, these faults must be of public notoriety. A judicial sentence may make them such, but the fact that some, many, or a great many know and speak of them will not do it. The public is everybody, or nearly everybody. Do not take your friends for the public, when they are only a fraction thereof. If you do you will find out oftener than it is pleasant that your sins of detraction are sins of slander; for rumors are very frequently based on nothing more substantial than lies or distorted and exaggerated facts set afloat by a calumniator.

Even when a person has justly forfeited, and publicly, the consideration of his fellowmen, and it is not, therefore, injurious to his character to speak of his evil ways, justice may not be offended, but charity may be, and grievously. It is a sin, an uncharity, to harp on one's faults in a spirit of spite, or with the cruel desire to maintain his dishonor; to leave no stone unturned in order to thoroughly blacken his name. In doing this you sin against charity, because you do something you would not wish to have done unto you. Justice itself would be violated if, even in the event of the facts related being notorious, you speak of them to people who ignore them and are not likely ever to come to a knowledge of them.

If you add, after telling all you know about a poor devil, that he did penance and repaired his sin, you must not imagine that such atonement will rehabilitate him in the minds of all. Men are more severe and unforgiving than God. Grace may be recovered, but reputation is a thing which, once lost, is usually lost for good. Something of the infamy sticks; tears and good works will not, cannot wash it away. He, therefore, who banks too much on human magnanimity is apt to err; and his erring constitutes a fault.

"But I confided the secret to but one person; and that one a dear friend, who promised to keep it." Yes, but the injured party has a right to the estimation of that one person, and his injury consists precisely in being deprived of it. Besides, you accuse yourself openly. Either what you said was void of all harm, or it was not. In the one case, why impose silence! In the other, why not begin yourself by observing the silence you impose upon others! Your friend will do what you did, and the ball you set rolling will not stop until there is nothing left of your victim's character.

Of course there are times when to speak of another's

faults is derogatory neither to justice nor to charity; both may demand that the evil be revealed. A man to defend himself may expose his accuser's crookedness; in court his lawyer may do it for him, for here again charity begins at home. In the interests of the delinquent, to effect his correction, one may reveal his shortcomings to those who have authority to correct. And it is even admitted that a person in trouble of any kind may without sin, for the purpose of obtaining advice or consolation, speak to a judicious friend of another's evil ways.

Zeal for the public good may not only excuse, but even require that the true character of a bad man be shown up and publicly censured. Its object is to prevent or undo evil, to protect the innocent; it is intended to destroy an evil influence and to make hypocrisy fly under his own colors. Immoral writers, living or dead, corrupt politicians and demagogues, unconscionable wretches who prey on public ignorance, may and should be, made known to the people, to shield them is to share their guilt. This should not be done in a spirit of vengeance, but for the sole purpose of guarding the unwary against vultures who know no law, and who thrive on the simplicity of their hearers.

CHAPTER 89

CALUMNY

To the malice of detraction calumny adds that of falsehood. It is a lie, which is bad; it is a report prejudicial to the character of another, which is worse; it is both combined, out of which combination springs a third malice, which is abominable. All the more so, since there can exist no excuse or reason in the light of which this sin may appear as a human weakness. Because slander is the fruit of deliberate criminal spite, jealousy and revenge, it has a character of diabolism. The calumniator is not only a moral assassin, but he is the most accomplished type of the coward known to man. If the devil loves a cheerful liar, he has one here to satisfy his affections.

This crime is one that can never be tolerated, no matter what the circumstances; it can never be justified on any grounds whatsoever; it is intrinsically evil, a sin of injustice that admits no mitigation. When slander is sworn to before the courts, it acquires a fourth malice, that of irreligion, and is called false testimony. It is not alone perjury, for perjury does not necessarily attack the neighbor's good name; it is perjured calumny, a crime that deserves all the reprobation it receives in this world—and in the next.

To lie outright, deliberately and with malice afore-thought, in traducing a fellow-man, is slander in its direct form; but such conditions are not required to constitute a real fault of calumny. It is not necessary to be certain that what you allege against your neighbor be false; it is sufficient that you be uncertain if it be true. An unsubstantiated charge or accusation, a mere rumor given out as worthy of belief, a suspicion or doubt clothed so as to appear a certainty, these contain all the malice and all the elements of slander clearly characterized. Charity, justice and truth alike are violated, guilt is there in unquestioned evidence. Whatever subterfuge, equivocation or other crooked proceeding be resorted to, if mendacity in any form is a feature of the asper-sions we cast upon the neighbor, we sin by calumny, purely and simply.

Some excuse themselves on the plea that what they say, they give out for what it is worth; they heard it from others, and take no responsibility as to its truth or falsehood. But here we must consider the credulity of the hearers. Will they believe it, whether you do or not? Are they likely to receive it as truth, either because they are looking for just such reports, or because they know no better? And whether they believe it or not, will they, on your authority, have suffi-cient reason for giving credence to your words? May it not happen that the very fact of your mentioning what you did is a sufficient mark of credibility for others? And by so doing, you contribute to their knowledge of what is false, or what is not proven true, concerning the reputation of a neighbor.

For it must be remembered that all imprudence is not guiltless, all thoughtlessness is not innocent of wrong. It is easy to calumniate a person by qualifying him in an off-hand way as a thief, a blackleg, a fast-liver, etc. It is easy, by adding an invented detail to a statement, to give it an altogether different color and turn truth into falsehood. But the easiest way is to interpret a man's intentions according to a dislike, and, by stringing in such fancies with a lot of facts, pass them on unsuspecting credulity that takes all or none. If you do not think well of another, and the occasion demand it, speak it out; but make it known that it is your individual judgment and give your reasons for thus opining.

The desperate character of calumny is that, while it must be repaired, as we shall see later, the thing is difficult, often impossible; frequently the reparation increases the evil instead of diminishing it. The slogan of unrighteousness is: "Calumniate, calumniate, some of it will stick!" He who slanders, lies; he who lies once may lie again, a liar is never worthy of belief, whether he tells the truth or not, for there is no knowing when he is telling the truth. One has the right to disbelieve the calumniator when he does wrong or when he tries to undo it. And human nature is so constructed that it prefers to believe in the first instance and to disbelieve in the second.

You may slander a community, a class as well as an individual. It is not necessary to charge all with crime; it is sufficient so to manipulate your words that suspicion may fall on any one of said class or community. If the charge be particu-

larly heinous, or if the body of men be such that all its usefulness depends on its reputation, as is the case especially with
religious bodies, the malice of such slander acquires a dignity
far above the ordinary.

The Church of God has suffered more in the long
centuries of her existence from the tongue of slander than
from sword and flame and chains combined. In the mind of
her enemies, any weapon is lawful with which to smite her,
and the climax of infamy is reached when they affirm, to
justify their dishonesty, that they turn Rome's weapons
against her. There is only one answer to this, and that is the
silence of contempt. Slander and dollars are the wheels on
which moves the propaganda that would substitute Gospel
Christianity for the superstitions of Rome. It is slander that
vilifies in convention and synod the friars who did more for
pure Christianity in the Philippines in a hundred years than
the whole nest of their revilers will do in ten thousand. It is
slander that holds up to public ridicule the congregations
that suffer persecution and exile in France in the name of
liberty, fraternity, etc. It is slander that the long-tailed
missionary with the sanctimonious face brings back from the
countries of the South with which to regale the minds of
those who furnish the Bibles and shekels. And who will
measure the slander that grows out of the dunghill of Protestant ignorance of what Catholics really believe!

CHAPTER 90

RASH JUDGMENT

The Eighth Commandment is based on the natural right every fellow-man has to our good opinion, unless he forfeits it justly and publicly. It forbids all injury to his reputation, first, in the estimation of others, which is done by calumny and detraction; secondly, in our own estimation, and this is done by rash judgment, by hastily and without sufficient grounds thinking evil of him, forming a bad opinion of him. He may be, as he has a right to be, anxious to stand well in our esteem as well as in the esteem of others.

A judgment, rash or otherwise, is not a. doubt, neither is it a suspicion. Everybody knows what a doubt is. When I doubt if another is doing or has done wrong, the idea of his or her guilt simply enters my mind, occurs to me and I turn it over and around, from one side to another, without being satisfied to accept or reject it. I do not say: yes, it is true; neither do I say: no, it is not true. I say nothing, I pass no judgment; I suspend for the moment all judgment, I doubt.

A doubt is not evil unless there be absolutely no reason for doubting, and then the doubt is born of passion and malice. And the evil, whatever there is of it, is not in the doubt's entering our mind— something beyond our control; but in our entertaining the doubt, in our making the doubt personal, which supposes an act of the will.

Stronger than doubt is suspicion. When I suspect one, I do not keep the balance perfectly even between yes and no, as in the case of doubt; I lean mentally to one side, but do not go so far as to assent one way or the other. Having before me a person who excites my suspicion, I am inclined to think him guilty on certain evidence, but I fear to judge lest I should be in error, because there is evidence also of innocence. If my suspicion is based on good grounds, it is natural and lawful; otherwise it is rash and sinful; it is uncharitable and unjust to the person suspected. A suspicion often hurts more than an accusation.

Doubt and suspicion, when rash, are sinful; but the malice thereof is not grave unless they are so utterly unfounded as to betoken deep-seated antipathy and aversion and a perverse will; or unless in peculiar circumstances the position of the person is such as to make the suspicion gravely injurious and not easily condoned. There is guilt in keeping that suspicion to oneself; to give it out in words is calumny, whether it be true or not, simply because it is unfounded.

In a judgment there is neither doubt nor suspicion; I make my own the idea presented to my mind. The balance of assent, in which is weighed, the evidence for and against, is not kept even, nor is it partially inclined; It goes down with its full weight, and the party under consideration stands convicted before the tribunal of my judgment. I do not say, I wonder if he is guilty; nor he most likely is guilty; but: he is guilty—here is a deliberate judgment. Henceforth my esteem ceases for such a person. Translated in words such a judgment is not calumny because it is supposedly founded in reason; but it is detraction, because it is injurious.

Such a judgment, without any exterior expression, is sinful if it is rash. And what makes it rash? The insufficiency of motive on which it is based. And whence comes the knowledge of such sufficiency or insufficiency of motive? From the intelligence, but mostly from the conscience. That is why many unintelligent people judge rashly and sin not, because they know no better. But conscience nearly always supplies intelligence in such matters and ignorance does not always save us from guilt. An instinct, the wee voice of God in the soul, tells us to withhold our judgment even when the intelligence fails to weigh the motives aright. To contemn this voice is to sin and be guilty of rash judgment.

In the language of ordinary folks, not always precise and exact in their terms, an opinion is frequently a judgment, to think this or that of another is often to judge him accordingly. The suspicions of suspicious people are at times more than suspicions and are clearly characterized judgments. To render a verdict on the neighbor's character is a judgment, by whatever other name it is called; all that is necessary is to come to a definite conclusion and to give the assent of the will to that conclusion.

When the conduct of the neighbor is plainly open to interpretation, if we may not judge immediately against him, neither are we bound to give him the benefit of the doubt; we may simply suspend all judgment and await further evidence. In our exterior dealings this suspicion should not affect our conduct, for every man has a right to be treated as an honest man and does not forfeit that right on the ground of a mere probability. This, however, does not prevent us from taking a cue from our suspicion and acting guardedly towards him. This does not mean that we adjudge him dishonest, but that we deem him capable of being dishonest, which is true and in accordance with the laws of prudence.

Neither are we bound to overlook all evidence that points to a man's guilt through fear of judging him unfavorably. It is not wrong to judge a man according to his merits, to have a right opinion of him, even when that opinion is not to his credit. All that is necessary is that we have good reason on Which to base that opinion. If a neighbor does evil in our presence or to our knowledge he forfeits, and justly, our good opinion; he is to blame, and not we. We are not obliged to close our eyes to the truth of facts, and it is on facts that our judgments are formed.

CHAPTER 91

MENDACITY

To lie is to utter an untruth, with full knowledge that it is an untruth. The untruth may be expressed by any conventional sign, by word, deed, gesture, or even by silence. Its malice and disorder consists in the opposition that exists between our idea and the expression we give to it; our words convey a meaning contrary to what is in our mind; we say one thing and mean another. If we unwittingly utter what is contrary to fact, that is error; if we so clumsily translate our thoughts as to give a false impression of what we mean, and we do the best we can, that is a blunder; if in a moment of listlessness and inattention we speak in a manner that conflicts with our state of mind, that is temporary mental aberration. But if we knowingly give out as truth what we know is not the truth, we lie purely and simply.

In misrepresentations of this kind it is not required that there be a plainly formulated purpose of deceiving another; an implicit intention, a disposition to allow our words to run their natural course, is sufficient to give such utterances a character of mendacity. For, independently of our mental attitude, it is in the nature of a lie to deceive; an intention, or rather a pretense to the contrary, does not affect that nature. The fact of lying presupposes that we intend in some manner to practise deception; if we did not have such a purpose we would not resort to lying. If you stick a knife into a man, you may pretend what you like, but you did certainly intend to hurt him and make him feel badly.

Nor has any ulterior motive we may have in telling an untruth the power to change its nature; a lie is a lie, no matter what prompted it. Whether it serves the purpose of amusement, as a jocose lie; or helps to gain us an advantage or get us out of trouble, as an officious lie; or injures another in any way, as a pernicious lie: mendacity is the character of our utterances, the guilt of willful falsehood is on our soul. A restriction should, however, be made in favor of the jocose lie; it ceases to be a lie when the mind of the speaker is open to all who listen and his narration or statement may be likened to those fables and myths and fairy tales in which is exemplified the charm of figurative language. When a person says what is false and is convinced that all who hear him know it is false, the contradiction between his mind and its expression is said to be material, and not formal; and in this the essence of a lie does not consist.

A lie is always a sin; it is what is called an intrinsic evil and is therefore always wrong. And why is this? Because speech was given us to express our thoughts; to use this faculty therefore for a contrary purpose is against its nature, against a law of our being, and this is evil. The obnoxious consequences of falsehood, as it is patent to all, constitute an evil for which falsehood is responsible. But deception, one of those consequences, is not in itself and essentially, a moral fault. Deception, if not practised by lying and therefore not intended but simply suffered to occur, and if there be grave reason for resorting to this means of defense, cannot be put down as a thing offensive to God or unjustly prejudicial to the neighbor. But when deception is the effect of mendacity, it assumes a character of malice that deserves the reprobation of man as it is condemned by God. And this is another reason why lying is essentially an evil thing, and can never, under any circumstances be allowed or justified.

This does not mean that lying is always a mortal sin. In fact, it is oftener venial than mortal. It becomes a serious fault only in the event of another malice being added to it. Thus, if I lie to one who has a right to know the truth and for grave reasons; if the mendacious information I impart is of a nature to mislead one into injury or loss, and this thing I do maliciously; or if my lying is directly disparaging to another; in these cases there is grave malice and serious guilt. But if there is no injustice resulting from a lie, I prevaricate against right in lying, but my sin is not a serious offense.

This is a vice that certainly deserves to be fought against and punished always and in all places, especially in the young who are so prone thereto, first because it is a sin; and again, because of the social evils that it gives rise to. There is no gainsaying the fact that in the code of purely human morals, lying is considered a very heinous offense that ostracizes a man when robbery on a large scale, adultery and other first-degree misdemeanors leave him perfectly honorable.

This recalls an instance of a recent courtroom. A young miscreant thoroughly imbued with pharisaic morals met with a bold face, without a blush or a flinch, accusations of misconduct, robbery and murder; but when charged with being a liar, he sprang at his accuser in open court and tried to throttle him. His fine indignation got the best of him; he could not stand that.

Among pious-minded people two extreme errors are not infrequently met with. The one is that a lie is not wrong unless the neighbor suffers thereby; the falsity of this we have already shown. According to the other, a lie is such an evil that it should not be tolerated, not one lie, even if all the souls in hell were thereby to be liberated. To this we answer that we would like to get such a chance once; we fear we would tell a whopper. It would be wicked, of course; but we might expect leniency from the just Judge under the circumstances.

CHAPTER 92

CONCEALING THE TRUTH

The duty always to tell the truth does not imply the obligation always to tell all you know; and falsehood does not always follow as a result of not revealing your mind to the first inquisitive person that chooses to put embarrassing questions. Alongside, but not contrary to, the duty of veracity is the right every man has to personal and professional secrets. For a man's mind is not public property; there may arise at times circumstances in which he not only may, but is in duty bound to withhold information that concerns himself intimately or touches a third person; and there must be a means to protect the sacredness of such secrets against undue curiosity and inquisitiveness, without recourse to the unlawful method of lying. Silence is not an effective resource, for it not infrequently gives consent one or the other way; the question may be put in such a manner that affirmation or negation will betray the truth. To what then shall one have recourse?

Let us remark in the first place that God has endowed

human intelligence with a native wit, sharpness and cunning that has its legitimate uses, the exercise of this faculty is evil only when its methods and ends are evil. Used along the lines of moral rectitude strategy and tact for profiting by circumstances are perfectly in order, especially when one acts in the defense of his natural rights. And if this talent is employed without injustice to the neighbor or violence to the law of God, it is no more immoral than the plain telling of truth; in fact it is sometimes better than telling the truth.

But it must be understood that such practices must be justified by the circumstances. They suppose in him who resorts thereto a right to withhold information that overrides the right of his interrogator. If the right of the latter to know is superior, then the hiding of truth would constitute an injustice, which is sinful, and this is considered tantamount to lying. And if the means to which we resort is not lying, as we have defined it, that is, does not show a contradiction between what we say and what we mean, then there can be no fear of evil on any side.

Now, suppose that instead of using a term whose signification is contrary to what my mind conceives, which would be falsehood, I employ a word that has a natural double meaning, one of which is conform to my mind, the other at variance. In the first place, I do not speak against my mind; I say what I think; the word I use means what I mean. But the other fellow! that is another matter. He may take his choice of the two meanings. If he guesses aright, my artifice has failed; if he is deceived, that is his loss. I do him no injustice, for he had no right to question me. If my answer embarrasses him, that is just what I intended, and I am guilty of no evil for that; if it deceives him, that I did not intend but willingly suffer; I am not obliged to enter into explanations when I am not even bound to answer him. Of the deception, he alone is the cause; I am the occasion, if you will, but the circumstances of his inquisitiveness made that occasion necessary, and I am not responsible.

This artifice is called equivocation or amphibology; it consists in the use of words that have a natural double meaning; it supposes in him who resorts to it the right to conceal the truth, a right superior to that of the tormentor who questions him. When these conditions are fulfilled, recourse to this method is perfectly legitimate, but the conditions must be fulfilled. This is not a weapon for convenience, but for necessity. It is easy to deceive oneself when it is painful to tell the truth. Therefore it should be used sparingly: it is not for every-day use, only emergencies of a serious nature can justify its employ. Another artifice, still more delicate and dangerous, but just as legitimate when certain conditions are fulfilled, is what is known as mental restriction. This too consists in the employ of words of double meaning; but whereas in the former case, both meanings are naturally contained in the word, here the term employed has but one natural signification, the other being furnished by circumstances. Its legitimate use supposes that he to whom the term is directed should either in fact know the circumstances of the case that have this peculiar significance, or that he could and should know them. If the information drawn from the answer received is insufficient, so much the better; if he is misinformed, the fault is his own, since neither genuine falsehood nor evident injustice can be attributed to the other.

An example will illustrate this better than anything else. Take a physician or lawyer, the custodian of a professional secret, or a priest with knowledge safeguarded by the seal of the confessional. These men either may not or should not reveal to others unconcerned in the matter the knowledge they, possess. There is no one but should be aware of this, but should know that when they are questioned, they will answer as laymen, and not as professionals. They will answer according to outside information, yes or no, whether on not such conclusion agree with the facts they obtained under promise of secrecy. They simply put out of their mind as unserviceable all professional knowledge, and respond as a man to a man. Their standing as professional men puts every questioner on his guard and admonishes him that no private information need be expected, that he must take the answer given as the conclusion of outside evidence, then if he is deceived he has no one to blame but himself, since he was warned and took no heed of the warning

Again we repeat, the margin between mental restriction and falsehood is a safe, but narrow one, the least bungling may merge one into the other. It requires tact and judgment to know when it is permissible to have recourse to this artifice and how to practise it safely. It is not a thing to be trifled with. In only rare circumstances can it be employed, and only few persons have the right to employ it.

CHAPTER 93

RESTITUTION

A peculiar feature attaches to the sins we have recently treated, against the Fifth, Sixth, Seventh, and Eighth commandments. These offenses differ from others in that they involve an injury, an injustice to our fellow-man. Now, the condition of pardon for sin is contrition; this contrition contains essentially a firm purpose that looks to the future, and removes in a measure, the liability to fall again. But with the sins here in question that firm purpose not only looks forward, but backward as well, not only guarantees against future ill-doing, but also repairs the wrong criminally effected in the past. This is called restitution, the undoing of wrong suffered by our neighbor through our own fault. The firm purpose to make restitution is just as essential to contrition as the firm purpose to sin no more; in fact, the former is only a form of the latter. It means that we will not sin any more by prolonging a culpable injustice. And the person who overlooks this feature when he seeks pardon has a moral constitution and make-up that is sadly in need of repairs; and of such persons there are not a few.

Justice that has failed to protect a man's right becomes restitution when the deed of wrong is done. Restitution therefore that is based on the natural right every man has to have and to hold what is his, to recover it, its value or equivalent, when unduly dispossessed, supposes an act of injustice, that is, the violation of a strict right. This injustice, in turn, implies a moral fault, a moral responsibility, direct or indirect; and the fault must be grievous in order to induce a grave obligation. Now, it matters not in the least what we do, or how we do it, if the neighbor suffer through a fault of ours. If any human creature sustains a loss to life or limb, damage to his or her social or financial standing, and such injury can be traced to a moral delinquency on our part, we are in conscience bound to make good the loss and repair the damage done. To do evil is bad; to perpetuate it is immeasurably worse. To refuse to remove the evil is to refuse to remove one's guilt; and as long as one persists in such a refusal, that one remains under the wrath of God.

Restitution concerns itself with things done or left undone, things said or left unsaid; it does not enter the domain of thought. Consequently, just as an accident does not entail the necessity of repairing the injury that another sustains, neither does the deliberate thought or desire to perpetrate an injustice entail such a consequence. Even if a person does all in his power to effect an evil purpose, and fails, he is not held to reparation, for there is nothing to repair. As we have said more than once, the will is the source of all malice in the sight of God; but injustice to man requires material as well as formal malice; sin must have its complement of exterior deed before it can be called human injustice.

We deem it unnecessary to dwell upon the gravity of the obligation to make restitution. The balance of justice must be maintained exact and impartial in this world, or the Almighty will see that it is done in the next. The idea that God does not stand for justice destroys the idea that God exists. And if the precept not to commit injustice leaves the guilty one free to repair or not to repair, that precept is self-contradictory and has no meaning at all. If a right is a right, it is not extinguished by being violated and if justice, is something more than a mere sound, it must protect all rights whether sinned against or not.

It might be convenient for some people to force upon their conscience the lie that restitution is of counsel rather than of precept, under the plea that it is enough to shoulder the responsibility of sin without being burdened with the obligation of repairing it, but it is only a soul well steeped in malice that will take seriously such a contention. Neither is restitution a penance imposed upon us in order to atone for our faults; it is no more penitential in its nature than are the efforts we make to avoid the faults we have fallen into in the past. It atones for nothing; it is simply a desisting from evil. When this is done and forgiveness obtained, then, and not till then, is it time to think of satisfying for the temporal punishment due to sin.

Naturally it is much more easy to abstain from committing injustice than to repair it after it is done. It is often very difficult and very painful to face the consequences of our evil ways, especially when all satisfaction is gone and nothing remains but the hard exigencies of duty. And duty is a thing that it costs very little to shirk when one is already hardened by a habit of injustice. That is why restitution is so little heard of in the world. It is a fact to be noted that the Catholic Church is the only religious body that dares to enforce strictly the law of reparation. Others vaguely hold it, but rarely teach it, and then only in flagrant cases of fraud. But she allows none of her children to approach the sacraments who has not already repaired, or who does not promise in all sincerity to repair, whatever wrong he may have done to the neighbor. Employers of Catholic help sometimes feel the effects of this uncompromising attitude of the Church; they are astonished, edified and grateful.

We recall with pleasure an incident of an apostate going about warning people against the turpitudes of Rome and especially against the extortions of her priests through the confessional. He explained how the benighted papist was obliged under pain of eternal damnation to confess his sins to the priest, and then was charged so much for each fault he had been guilty of. An incredulous listener wanted to know if he, the speaker, while in the toils of Rome had ever been obliged thus to disgorge in the confessional, and was answered with a triumphant affirmation. At which the wag hinted that it would be a good thing not to be too outspoken in announcing the fact as his reputation for honesty would be likely to suffer thereby, for he knew, and all Catholics knew, who were those whose purse the confessor pries open.

CHAPTER 94

UNDOING THE EVIL

Whenever a person, through a spirit of Police or grossly culpable negligence, becomes responsible for serious bodily injury sustained by another, he is bound, as far as in him lies, to undo the wrong and repair the injustice committed. The law of personal rights that forbade him to lay violent hands on another, now commands that the evil be removed by him who placed it. True, physical pain and tortures cannot be repaired in kind; physical injury and disability are not always susceptible of adequate reparation. But there is the loss incurred as a result of such disability, and this loss may affect, not one alone, but many.

Death, too, is of course absolutely irreparable. But the killing of the victim in nowise extinguishes the obligation of reparation. The principal object is removed; but there remain the loss of wages, the expenses necessitated by illness and death; there may be a family dependent on the daily toil of the unfortunate and made destitute by his removal. One must be blind indeed not to see that all these losses are laid at the door of the criminal, a direct result of his crime, foreseen, too, at least confusedly, since there is a moral fault; and these must be made good, as far as the thing is possible, otherwise the sin will not be forgiven.

Slander must be retracted. If you have lied about another and thereby done him an injury, you are bound in conscience to correct your false statement, to correct it in such a manner as to undeceive all whom you may have misled. This retraction must really retract, and not do just the contrary, make the last state of things worse than the first, which is sometimes the case. Prudence and tact should suggest means to do this effectively: when, how and to what extent it should be done, in order that the best results of reparation may be obtained. But in one way or another, justice demands that the slanderer contradict his lying imputations and remove by so doing the stain that besmirches the character of his victim.

Of course, if it was by truth and not falsehood, by detraction and not calumny, that you assailed and injured the reputation of another, there is no gainsaying the truth; you are not justified in lying in order to make truth less damaging. The harm done here is well nigh irreparable. But there is such a thing as trying to counteract the influence of evil speech by good words, by mentioning qualities that offset defects, by setting merit against demerit; by attenuating as far as truth will allow the circumstances of the case, etc. This will place your victim in the least unfavorable light, and will, in some measure, repair the evil of detraction.

Scandal must be repaired, a mightily difficult task; to reclaim a soul lost to evil through fatal inducements to sin is paramount, almost, to raising from the dead. It is hard, desperately hard, to have yourself accepted as an angel of light by those for whom you have long been a demon of iniquity. Good example! Yes, that is about the only argument you have. You are handicapped, but if you wield that argument for good with as much strength and intensity as you did for evil, you will have done all that can be expected of you, and something may come of it.

The wrong of bodily contamination is a deep one. It is a wrong, and therefore unjust, when it is effected through undue influence that either annuls consent, or wrings it from the victim by cajolery, threat, or false promise. It becomes immeasurably aggravated when the victim is abandoned to bear alone the shame and burdensome consequences of such injustice.

Matrimony is the ordinary remedy; the civil law will force it; conscience may make it an obligation, and does make it, unless, in rare cases, there be such absolute incompatibility as to make such a contract an ineffective and ridiculous one, an inefficient remedy, or none at all. When such is the case, a pecuniary compensation is the only alternative. A career has been blasted, a future black with despair stares the victim in the face, if she must face it unaided; a burden forced upon her that must be borne for years, entailing considerable expense. The man responsible for such a state of affairs, if he expects pardon for his crime, must shoulder the responsibility in a manner that will repair at least in part the grave injustice under which his victim labors.

If both share the guilt, then both must share the burden. If one shirks, the other must assume the whole. The great victim is the child. That child must get a Christian bringing-up, or some one will suffer for it; its faith must be safe-guarded. If this cannot be done at home, then it must be placed where this can be done. If it is advantageous for the parent or parents that their offspring be raised in ignorance of its origin, it is far more advantageous for the child itself. Let it be confided to good hands, but let the money necessary for its support be forthcoming, since this is the only way to make reparation for the evil of its birth.

I would add a word in regard to the injustice, frequent enough, of too long deferring the fulfilment of marriage promises. For one party, especially, this period of waiting is precarious, fraught with danger and dangerous possibilities. Her fidelity makes her sacrifice all other opportunities, and makes her future happiness depend on the fulfilment of the promise given. Charms do not last forever; attractions fade with the years. If affection cools, she is helpless to stir up the embers without unmentionable sacrifice. There is the peril. The man who is responsible for it, is responsible for a good deal. He is committing an injustice; there is danger of his not being willing to repair it, danger that he may not be able to repair it. His line of duty is clear. Unless for reasons of the gravest importance, he cannot in surety of conscience continue in a line of conduct that is repugnant alike to natural reason and common decency, and that smacks of moral make-up that would not bear the scrutiny of close investigation.

CHAPTER 95

PAYING BACK

A man who has stolen, has nothing more urgent and imperative to perform, on this side of eternity, than the duty of refunding the money or goods unjustly acquired, or the value thereof. He may possibly consider something else more important; but if he does, that man has somehow unlearned the first principles of natural honesty, ignores the fundamental law that governs the universe, and he will have a difficult time convincing the Almighty that this ignorance of his is not wholly culpable. The best and only thing for him to do is to make up his mind to pay up, to disgorge his ill-gotten goods, to make good the losses sustained by his neighbor through his fault.

He may, or may not, have profited to any great extent by his criminal proceedings; but there is no doubt that his victim suffered injustice; and that precisely is the root of his obligation. The stolen goods may have perished in his hands and he have nothing to show; the same must be said of the victim the moment his possessions disappeared; with this difference, however, that justice was not violated in one case, and in the other, it was. The lawful owner may be dead, or unfindable among the living; but wherever he may be, he never intended that the thief should enjoy the fruit of his crime. The latter's title, vitiated in its source, cannot be improved by any circumstance of the owner's whereabouts. No one may thrive on one's own dishonesty.

You say this is hard; and in so saying, you lend testimony to the truth of the axiom that honesty is the best policy. There is no one but will agree with you; but such a statement, true though it be, helps matters very little. It is always hard to do right; blame Adam and Eve for it, and think of something more practicable. But must I impoverish myself? Not to the extent of depriving yourself of the necessaries of life. But you must deprive yourself to the extent of settling your little account, even if you suffer something thereby. But how shall I be able to refund it all! You may never be able to refund it all; but you may start in immediately and do the best you can; resolve to keep at it; never revoke your purpose to cancel the debt. In case your lease of life expires before full justice is done, the Almighty may take into consideration your motives and opportunities. They do say that hell is paved with good intentions; but these intentions are of the sort that are satisfied with never coming to a state of realization.

But I shall lose my position, be disgraced, prosecuted and imprisoned. This might happen if you were to write out a brief of your crime and send the same, signed and sworn to, to your employer. But this is superfluous. You might omit the details and signature, enclose the sum and trust luck for the rest. Or you might consult your spiritual adviser; he might have had some experience in this line of business. The essential is not that you be found out, but that you refund.

It may happen that several are concerned in a theft. In this case, each and every participant, in the measure of his guilt, is bound to make restitution. Guilt is the object, restitution is the shadow; the following is fatal. To order or advise the thing done; to influence efficaciously its doing; to assist in the deed or to profit knowingly thereby, to shield criminally the culprit, etc., this sort of co-operation adds to the guilt of sin the burden of restitution. Silence or inaction, when plain duty would call for words and deeds to prevent crime, incriminates as well as active participation, and creates an obligation to repair.

There is more. Conspiracy in committing an injustice adds an especial feature to the burden of restitution. If the parties to the crime had formed a preconcerted plan and worked together as a whole in its accomplishment, every individual that furnished efficient energy to the success of the undertaking is liable, in conscience, not for a share of the loss, but for the sum total. This is what is called solidarity; solidarity in crime begets solidarity in reparation. It means that the injured party has a just claim for damages, for all damages sustained, against any one of the culprits, each one of whom, in the event of his making good the whole loss, has recourse against the others for their share of the obligation. It may happen, and does, that one or several abscond, and thus shirk their part of the obligation; the burden of restitution may thus be unevenly distributed. But this is one of the risks that conspirators in sin must take; the injured party must be protected first and in preference to all others.

No Catholic can validly receive the sacrament of penance who refuses to assume the responsibility of restitution for injustices committed, and who does not at least promise sincerely to acquit himself at the first favorable opportunity and to the extent of his capacity. This means that only on these conditions can the sin be forgiven by God. That man is not disposed sufficiently to receive absolution who continually neglects opportunities to keep his promise; who refuses to pay any, because he cannot pay all; who decides to leave the burden of restitution to his heirs, even with the wherewith to do so. It is better not to go to confession at all than to go with these dispositions; it is better to wait until you can make up your mind.

Chapter 96

Getting Rid of Ill-Gotten Goods

I t may happen that a person discover among his legitimately acquired possessions something that does not in reality belong to him. He may have come by it through purchase, donation, etc.; he kept it in good faith, thinking that he had a clear title to it. He now finds that there was an error somewhere, and that it is the property of some one else. Of course, he is not the lawful owner, and does not become such by virtue of his good faith; although, in certain given circumstances, if the good faith, or ignorance of error, last long enough, a title may be acquired by prescription, and the possessor become the lawful owner. But we are not considering the question of prescription.

It is evident, then, that our friend must dispossess himself in favor of the real owner, as soon as the latter comes upon the scene and proves his claim. But the possessor may in all innocence have alienated the goods, destroyed or consumed them; or they may have perished through accident or fatality. In the latter case, nothing remains to refund, no one is to blame, and the owner must bear the loss. Even in the former case, if the holder can say in conscience that he in nowise became richer by the possession and use of the goods in question, he is not bound to make restitution. If, however, there be considerable profits, they rightly belong to the owner, and the possessor must refund the same.

But the question arises as to how the holder is to be compensated for the expenditure made in the beginning and in good faith when he purchased the goods which he is now obliged to hand over to another. Impartial justice demands that when the rightful owner claims his goods, the holder relinquish them, and he may take what he gets, even if it be nothing. He might claim a compensation if he purchased what he knew to be another's property, acting in the interests of that other and with the intention of returning the same to its owner. Otherwise, his claim is against the one from whom he obtained the article, and not against him to whom he is obliged to turn it over.

He may, if he be shrewd enough, anticipate the serving of the owner's claim and secure himself against a possible loss by selling back for a consideration the goods in question to the one from whom he bought them. But this cannot be done after the claim is presented; besides, this proceeding must not render it impossible for the owner to recover his property; and he must be notified as to the whereabouts of said property. This manoeuvre works injustice unto no one. The owner stands in the same relation to his property as formerly; the subsequent holder assumes an obligation that was always his, to refund the goods or their value, with recourse against the antecedent seller.

The moment a person shirks the responsibility of refunding the possessions, by him legitimately acquired, but belonging rightfully to another, that person becomes a possessor in bad faith and stands towards the rightful owner in the position of a thief. Not in a thousand years will he be able to prescribe a just title to the goods. The burden of restitution will forever remain on him; if the goods perish, no matter how, he must make good the loss to the owner. He must also disburse the sum total of profits gathered from the illegal use of said goods. If values fluctuate during the interval of criminal possession, he must compute the amount of his debt according to the values that prevailed at the time the lawful owner would have disposed of his goods, had he retained possession.

Finally, there may be a doubt as to whether the object I possess is rightfully mine or not. I must do my best to solve that doubt and clear the title to ownership. If I fail, I may consider the object mine and may use it as such. If the owner turn up after the prescribed time, so much the worse for the owner. An uncertainty may exist, not as to my proprietorship, but as to whom the thing does belong. If my possession began in good faith and I am unable to determine the ownership, I may consider myself the owner until further developments shed more light on the matter.

It is different when the object was originally acquired in bad faith. In such a case, first, the ill-gotten goods can never be mine; then, there is no sanction in reason, conscience or law for the conduct of those who run immediately to the first charitable institution and leave there their conscience money; or who have masses said for the repose of the souls of those who have been defrauded, before they are dead at all perhaps. My first care must be to locate the victim; or, if he be certainly deceased or evidently beyond reach, the heirs of the victim of my fraud. When all means fail and I am unable to find either the owner or his heirs, then, and not till then, may I dispose of the goods in question. I must assume in such a contingency as this, that the will of the owner would be to expend the sum on the most worthy cause; and that is charity. The only choice then that remains with me is, what hospital, asylum or other enterprise of charity is to profit by my sins, since I myself cannot be a gainer in the premises.

It might be well to remark here that one is not obliged to make restitution for more than the damages call for. Earnestness is a good sign, but it should not blind us or drive us to an excess of zeal detrimental to our own lawful interests. When there is a reasonable and insolvable doubt as to the amount of reparation to be made, it is just that such a doubt favor us. If we are not sure if it be a little more or a little less, the value we are to refund, we may benefit by the uncertainty and make the burden we assume as light as in all reason it can be made. And even if we should happen to err on the side of mercy to ourselves, without our fault, justice is satisfied, being fallible like all things human.

CHAPTER 97

WHAT EXCUSES FROM
RESTITUTION

Those who do not obtain full justice from man in this world will obtain it in the next from God. If we do not meet our obligations this side of the tribunal of the just Judge, He will see to it that our accounts are equitably balanced when the time for the final reckoning comes. This supposes, naturally, that non-fulfilment of obligations is due on our part to unwillingness—a positive refusal, or its equivalent, wilful neglect, to undo the wrongs committed. For right reason and God's mercy must recognize the existence of a state of unfeigned and hopeless disability, when it is impossible for the delinquent to furnish the wherewithal to repair the evils of which he has been guilty. When this condition is permanent, and is beyond all remedy, all claims are extinguished against the culprit, and all losses incurred must be ascribed to "an act of God," as the coroner says. For no mart can be held to what is impossible.

Chief among these moral, as well as legal, bankrupts is

the good-for-nothing fellow who is sorry too late, who has nothing, has no hopes of ever having anything, and who therefore can give nothing. You cannot extract blood from a beet, nor shekels from an empty purse. Then a man may lose all his belongings in a catastrophe, and after striving by labor and economy to pay off his debts, may see himself obliged to give up the task through sickness, misfortune or other good causes. He has given all he has, he cannot give more. Even though liabilities were stacked up mountain-high against him, he cannot be held morally responsible, and his creditors must attribute their losses to the misfortune of life—a rather unsubstantial consolation, but as good a one as the poor debtor has.

There are other cases where the obligations of restitution are not annulled, but only cancelled for the time being, until such a time as circumstances permit their being met without grave disaster to the debtor. The latter may be in such a position that extreme, or great, want would stare him in the face, if he parted with what he possesses to make restitution. The difficulty here is out of all proportion with the injustice committed for, after all, one must live, and charity begins at home, our first duty is toward ourselves. The creditors of this man have no just claim against him until he improves his circumstances; in the meantime, the burden of responsibility is lifted from his shoulders.

The same must be said when the paying off of a debt at any particular time, be it long or short, would cripple a man's finances, wipe out his earnings to such an extent as to make him fall considerably below his present position in life. We might take a case during the late coal famine, of a man who, in order to fill his contracts of coal at six dollars a ton, would be obliged to buy it at fifteen and twenty dollars a ton; and thereby sacrifice his fortune. The thing could not be expected, it is preposterous. His obligee must wait and hope for better times.

A man's family is a part of himself. Therefore the payment of a just debt may be deferred In order to shield from want parents, wife, children, brothers or sisters. Life, limb and reputation are greater possessions than riches; consequently, rather than jeopardize these, one may, for the time, put aside his obligations to make restitution.

All this supposes, of course, that during the interval of delay the creditor does not suffer inconveniences greater than, or as great as, those the debtor seeks to avoid. The latter's right to defer payment ceases to exist the moment it comes into conflict with an equal right of the former to said payment. It is against reason to expect that, after suffering a first injustice, the victim should suffer a second in order to spare the guilty party a lesser or an equal injury. Preference therefore must be given to the creditor over the debtor when the necessity for sacrifice is equal, and leniency must be refused when it becomes cruelty to the former.

Outside these circumstances, which are rare indeed, it will be seen at once that the creditor may act an unjust part in pressing claims that accidentally and temporarily become invalid. He has a right to his own, but he is not justified in vindicating that right, if in so doing, he inflicts more damage than equity calls for. The culprit has a right not to suffer more than he deserves, and it is mock justice that does not respect that right. If the creditor does suffer some loss by the delay, this might be a circumstance to remember at the final settlement but for the present, there is an impediment to the working of justice, placed by the fatal order of things and it is beyond power to remove it.

CHAPTER 98

DEBTS

Before closing our remarks, necessarily brief and incomplete, on this subject, so vast and comprehensive, we desire in a few words to pay our respects to that particular form of injustice, more common perhaps than all others combined, which is known as criminal debt, likewise, to its agent, the most brazen impostor and unconscionable fraud that afflicts society, the man who owes and will not pay. More people suffer from bad debts than from stealing and destruction of property. It is easier to contract a debt, or to borrow a trifle, than to steal it outright; it is safer, too. Imprudence is one of the chief characteristics of this genus of iniquity. "I would sooner owe you this than cheat you out of it:" this, in word or deed, is the highly spiritual consolation they offer those whom they fleece and then laugh at.

The wilful debtor is, first of all, a thief and a robber, because he retains unjustly the lawful possessions of another. There is no difference between taking and keeping what belongs to the neighbor. The loss is the same to a man whether he is robbed of a certain amount or sells goods for which he gets nothing in return. The injustice is the same in both cases, the malice identical. He therefore who can pay his debts, and will not, must be branded as a thief and an enemy to the rights of property.

The debtor is guilty of a second crime, of dishonesty and fraud against his fellow-man, by reason of his breaking a contract, entered upon with a party in good faith, and binding in conscience until cancelled by fulfilment. When a man borrows or buys or runs an account on credit, he agrees to return a quid pro quo, an equivalent for value received. When he fails to do so, he violates his contract, breaks his pledge of honor, obtains goods under false pretense. Even if he is sincere at the time of the making of the contract, the crime is perpetrated the moment he becomes a guilty debtor by repudiating, in one way or another, his just debts. Now, to injure a person is wrong; to break faith with him at one and the same time is to incur guilt of a double dye.

There is likewise an element of contumely and outrage in such dishonest operations; the affront offered the victim is contemptible. Men have often been heard to say, after being victimized by imposture of this sort: "I do not mind the loss so much, but I do object to being treated like a fool and a monkey." One's feelings suffer more than one's purse. Especially is this the case when the credit is given or a loan made as a favor or service, intended or requested, only to be requited by the blackest kind of ingratitude.

And let us not forget the extent of damage wrought unto worthy people in hard circumstances who are shut out from the advantages of borrowing and buying on credit by the nefarious practices of dishonest borrowers and buyers. A burnt child keeps away from the fire. A man, after being defrauded palpably a few times, acquires the habit of refusing all credit; and he turns down many who deserve better, because of the persecution to which he is subjected by rogues and scoundrels. Every criminal debtor contributes to that state of affairs and shares the responsibility of causing honest people to suffer want through inability to get credit.

And who are the persons thus guilty of a manifold guilt? They are those who borrow and buy knowing full well they will not pay, pile debt upon debt knowing full well they cannot pay. Others, who do not repudiate openly their oblig- ations, put off paying indefinitely for futile reasons: hard times, that last forever; ships coming in, whose fate is yet unlearned; windfalls from rich relatives that are not yet born, etc.; and from delay to delay they become not only less able, but less willing, to settle their accounts. Sometimes you meet a fellow anxious to square himself for the total amount; half his assets is negotiable, the other half is gall. He threatens you with the alternative of half or none; he wants you to accept his impudence at the same figures at which he himself values it. And this schemer usually succeeds in his endeavor.

Others there are who protest their determination to pay up, even to the last cent; their dun-bills are always kept in sight, lest they forget their obligations; they treasure these bills, as one treasures a thing of immense value. But they live beyond their means and income, purchase pleasure and luxury, refuse to curtail frivolous expenses and extravagant outlay. And in the meantime their debts remain in status quo, unredeemed and less and less redeemable, their determination holds good, apparently; and the creditor breaks commandments looking on and hoping.

Some do violence to their thinking faculty by trying to find justification, somehow, for not paying their debts. The creditor is dead, they say; or he has plenty and can well afford to be generous. An attempt is often made at establishing a case of occult compensation, its only merit being its ingenuity, worthy of a better cause. All such lame excuses argue a deeper perversity of will, a malice well-nigh incurable; but they do not satisfy justice, because they are not founded on truth.

A debt has a character of sacredness, like all moral obligations; more sacred than many other moral obligations, because this quality is taken directly from the eternal prototype of justice, which is God. You cannot wilfully repudiate it therefore without repudiating God. You must respect it as you respect Him. Your sins and your debts will follow you before the throne of God. God alone is concerned with your sins; but with your debts a third party is concerned. And if God may easily waive His claims against you as a sinner, a sterner necessity may influence His judgment of you as a debtor, through respect for the inviolable rights of that third party who does not forgive so readily.

www.ingramcontent.com/pod-product-compliance
Lightning Source LLC
Chambersburg PA
CBHW021209130626
46554CB00004B/1145

* 9 7 9 8 9 9 9 7 5 6 0 8 4 *